Fine
WoodWorking
on Making Period
Furniture

Fine WoodWorking *on* Making Period Furniture

37 articles selected by the editors of *Fine Woodworking* magazine

The Taunton Press

Cover photo by Gary Bogue

BOOKS & VIDEOS

for fellow enthusiasts

First printing: January 1985
Second printing: October 1986
Third printing: October 1987
Fourth printing: June 1990
Fifth printing: June 1994
International Standard Book Number: 0-918804-30-2
Library of Congress Catalog Card Number: 84-52101
Printed in the United States of America

A FINE WOODWORKING Book

FINE WOODWORKING® is a trademark of The Taunton Press, Inc.,
registered in the U.S. Patent and Trademark Office.

The Taunton Press
63 South Main Street
Box 5506
Newtown, Connecticut 06470-5506

Contents

Introduction

In eighteenth-century America, colonial times, the usual state of things was rough. Water and horse power might help the woodworker wring timber out of logs, but everything else was done by hand. To make a smoothly polished surface, one had to throw his back, and considerable skill, into the task. Thus a refined and artificial object, such as a mahogany bureau or walnut chair, was a rare, valuable, and almost magical thing. Despite (or because of) the difficulties, the eighteenth century became a golden age in American design.

We still look to eighteenth-century furniture for inspiration, and many people will have nothing else in their homes. In this collection of 37 articles reprinted from the first nine years of *Fine Woodworking* magazine, expert woodworkers explore their relationships to that pre-industrial golden age. You'll find precise plans for favorite old pieces, technical explanations of how to reproduce the details that characterize fine antiques, and practical design discussions for those who would capture the taste of the eighteenth century in their own creations.

John Kelsey, editor

In Search of Period Furniture Makers
What they do about what the 'old guys' did

by Rick Mastelli

About a year ago we received a letter from a reader, Grover W. Floyd II of Knoxville, Tenn., telling about the cabinetmaker with whom he had been studying, whom he believed to be "among the nation's finest." The letter included a newspaper clipping about Robert G. Emmett, 77, quoting him as having promised himself, "If I ever got to touch a piece of Goddard furniture, I never would wash my hands. But now I have seen the back of a genuine Goddard piece and its drawers. And I wash my hands. My construction is better."

It wasn't long before I had arranged a trip to Knoxville to meet Emmett and to see his furniture. The visit turned out to be the start of an odyssey—to the back rooms of museums, to historic sites and to the shops of reproduction cabinetmakers, all to gain a perspective on what Emmett was to show me. Here he was declaring his furniture construction to be better than that of 18th-century master craftsmen, to be "second to none in the world."

I met Floyd first, a 29-year-old Scotsman who works out of a 500-sq. ft. shop, modestly equipped with the basic machines, all kept in faultless tune. When I arrived he was at the table saw, stacking and slicing arrowhead inlay banding ⅒ in. thick, practicing a technique he had learned from Emmett. He showed me a number of simple blanket chests, identical in design but of different sizes—experiments in proportion. Floyd is a professional cabinetmaker who earns his living restoring and building traditional furniture. But since

he met Emmett, he's considered himself a student. He brought me to meet the teacher.

Even at 77 Emmett retains a full head of white hair, neatly parted and laid down. Along with his mustache, it frames a face styled in the 1920s, aged, but well kept. He talked of his future, for which he was "hoping to put a little something away," and of his desire to share what he'd learned, to help revive the making of American furniture. And he talked of his past: "The main thing is the construction. I've gone into that deeper than any man ever has. I've lived furniture. I've dreamed it. My poor wife: a widow all these years."

The furniture he showed me did not belie the devotion he claimed. There's a Pembroke table, among ten he made in the early 1940s in a number of different woods, most of them inlaid, some simply banded, others with shells or bleeding hearts. The construction, Emmett points out, is exceptional. The width of the tabletop is marginally oversized for the skirt, so shrinkage across the grain, between the rule joints, will not stop the leaves from dropping free. The rule joints themselves are cut over an arc slightly greater than 90°, to ensure that there is no space when the leaves are down through which to see the hinges. The knuckle joint for the leaf support stops its swing at two points instead of one. This prevents the support from acting as a lever and breaking out the pivot pin. Also the joint is cut and the pin is driven not quite plumb, but canted, so the leaf support swings slightly up. This ensures, in

Emmett's Pembroke table is solid satinwood with maple and pine secondary wood and vermilion, holly and ebony inlay. The rule joint, right, is cut over an arc greater than 90° to keep the hinges concealed when the leaf is down. The leaf rests ¼ in. away from the skirt on a wooden button, which can be shaved down as the top shrinks to ensure that the leaf will rest always perpendicular. The knuckle joint of the leaf support, center, is not rounded, as is traditional, but square-sectioned, so in swinging open, the knuckles are stopped at two points. One is at the far side of the support, against the outside of the skirt; the other is in mortises cut in the skirt. These two stops keep the leaf support from acting as a lever to break out the pivot pin.

spite of seasonal dimensional changes, that the leaf can always be supported exactly level with the center section of the tabletop.

Such careful attention to details characterizes all the work he shows me. He learned, he says, by repairing older pieces in his father's antique shop, correcting the consequences of flaws in construction. "I got so tired of repairing cracked knuckle joints and having to leave drop-leaf tables with their leaves up because they wouldn't set down straight—there ain't nothing you can do about that once the top shrinks, except rebuild the whole bottom or the whole top—that I resolved never to build anything that won't last right. I don't care if nobody built things this way before. Those old guys give me a lot in the way of design and styling, I can't beat that. But their construction, I take what they give me and go on from there." He details his experience with American antiques: the sides of highboys and lowboys, cracked because they were glued crossgrain to the leg posts; bracket feet cracked or missing because they were glued crossgrain to support blocking; drawers protruding or stuck shut because carcases have twisted; drawers broken apart because stylishly thin dovetail pins didn't hold.

For 21 years, Emmett was the salaried cabinetmaker of a wealthy Knoxville family. His patron provided almost unlimited facilities, choice woods, and put minimal constraints on time or cost. "They would come to me with a picture of a Philadelphia highboy or a Goddard-Townsend kneehole and say, 'Robert, make me one of these.' And I'd study up on it and figure out how to make it, and sometimes a year or so later I'd have the piece done."

I left Emmett's shop with photos of his work and a list of preoccupying questions. How could 18th-century cabinetmakers have conceived such sophisticated designs and not have figured that wood moves, or not have known that if glued crossgrain it will crack? Did they know and not care? Or was Emmett wrong: were only the shoddy pieces built this way? Is it true that most 18th-century pieces have structural problems? And if so, what about craftsmen reproducing those pieces today? In pursuit of stylistic authenticity, do they imitate faulty constructions? Or do other reproduction cabinetmakers share Emmett's devotion to improving construction?

*   *   *

Emmett's reproduction of the Townsend-Goddard kneehole bureau (shown on the next page) posed the most intriguing questions. Built on an independent, full-blind dovetailed bracket-foot frame, with half sliding-dovetailed dustboards, the blocking and shells carved from solid curly cherry, the reproduction begged comparison with its source. Could the original be anything like this tour-de-force? I arranged to meet with Pat Kane, curator of American decorative arts at the Yale University Art Gallery in New Haven, Conn., where a Newport kneehole resides. Yale's Garvan collection includes some of the best American 18th-century furniture and indeed, as we walk past them, I notice many of the highboys, lowboys and secretaries have split sides and cracked feet.

The kneehole bureau, dated 1755-1785, is of Honduras mahogany, dark with stain and patina. Thus the first impression it makes is quite different from Emmett's curly cherry reproduction, which seems fairly on fire with color and figure. The Newport blockfront sits dark and quiet on its pedestal, its kneehole like a cave. Its age is evident from the way it has worn and settled into itself. It has dignity. The drawer insides

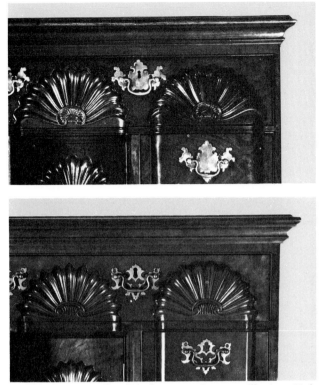

Details, Newport kneehole bureaus: Garvan collection, Yale University Art Gallery (top); Emmett's reproduction (bottom).

are a greyed, mild-grained tulip poplar, in striking contrast to Emmett's shimmering blistered poplar. But it isn't just the materials or their newness that makes Emmett's blockfront the more assertive. Comparing the original closely with the photos I have brought from Knoxville, I see that Emmett's carving is simpler, his shaping bolder, his reliefs sharper. At the periphery of the concave shell, Emmett's carved line approaches a zigzag, punctuated with V-grooves not present in the Newport shell, which curves more gently in and out. Emmett's ogee foot bulges emphatically, and his moldings are heavier. The effect is surreal. Emmett's piece seems to take the original design and say "THIS is what I am."

I ask Kane what she thinks of Emmett's work. It is masterful, she says, but overdone. She prefers the original blockfront. I ask if she knows of any 18th-century blockfronts with carved shells and elaborate molding in such a highly figured, difficult wood as curly cherry. Maybe some Connecticut piece, she says, but probably not: 18th-century craftsmen did not usually model highly figured wood, they rather displayed it in flat surfaces, as in highboy drawers.

I point out the construction of Emmett's piece. She's never seen a full-blind-dovetailed bracket foot, sometimes a splined miter, but generally the bracket pieces are simply mitered together with a glue block behind. The direction of the glue block's grain? Vertical, perpendicular to the grain of the bracket pieces. Does she encounter many cracked and broken bracket feet? Yes, it's quite common. How about drawer dividers, are they full dustboards, half-dovetailed into the carcase side? Hardly; it's usually only Philadelphia pieces (later I find out it's Williamsburg pieces too) that include full dustboards, usually dadoed into the sides. The blocking—is it applied or carved from the solid? The blocking is usually solid,

My Construction of a Newport Kneehole Bureau

The first Goddard-Townsend kneehole bureau I saw was in *The Magazine Antiques* in May, 1922. I fell in love with this wonderful design but did not get to build it until 1963—good thing, for in the twenties I would have made a mess of it. In 1938, on a trip to the lumberyard, I came across a pile of curly cherry boards, aged and rich, 12 in. or 14 in. wide by 16 ft. long. I was so excited, I carried 100 ft. of that wood out of there myself; honestly I don't think I could have lifted it if it hadn't been curly. It was that wood I eventually used for my kneehole bureau. By

1963 I had seen a few other photos of kneeholes, but I never managed to get more than three dimensions: 34 in. high by 20 in. deep by 37 in. wide. I didn't know if that last measurement was to the edge of the top or to the edge of the carcase, and I'd never seen anything but the front of one of these pieces. I know what I built isn't exactly like the original, but I spent enough years trying to imitate the construction and workmanship of the old masters to know of their shortcomings. I hope what I've done can be seen as continuing where they left off. —*Robert Emmett*

The half-blind dovetails between the pine subtop and the carcase side could as well be through dovetails, because the molding would cover the joint; except I find it easier to make a good, square case if the opposite boards are the same size. I clamp them together and run them over the jointer, end grain first, then edge grain to clean up any tear-out.

I make my dovetails and pins equal size because I got tired of repairing drawerfronts with those thin pins that break out. I cut the sides of my tails on the table saw set at 22°; then I chisel the waste and the pins. All of these drawer fronts and the kneehole door are solid curly cherry; the top drawer front is carved from 12/4 stock. Most carvers prefer to use straight-grained woods, but I love figured wood too much to avoid it just because it's difficult to work.

I use full, thin dustboards, half-dovetailed to the sides all the way to the back of the case to help hold it together. I make this joint shallower than the full dovetails of the drawer dividers so the amount of wood taken out of the sides does not weaken them.

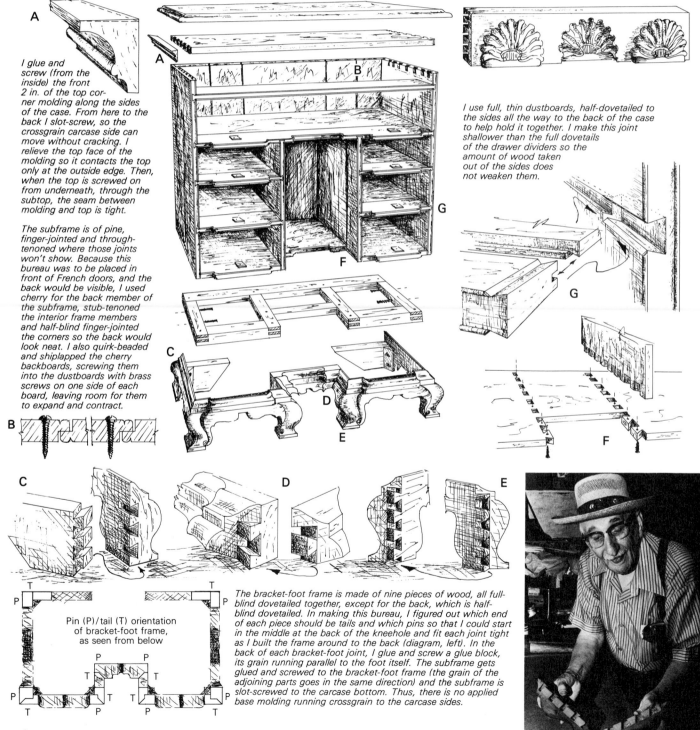

I glue and screw (from the inside) the front 2 in. of the top corner molding along the sides of the case. From here to the back I slot-screw, so the crossgrain carcase side can move without cracking. I relieve the top face of the molding so it contacts the top only at the outside edge. Then, when the top is screwed on from underneath, through the subtop, the seam between molding and top is tight.

The subframe is of pine, finger-jointed and through-tenoned where those joints won't show. Because this bureau was to be placed in front of French doors, and the back would be visible, I used cherry for the back member of the subframe, stub-tenoned the interior frame members and half-blind finger-jointed the corners so the back would look neat. I also quirk-beaded and shiplapped the cherry backboards, screwing them into the dustboards with brass screws on one side of each board, leaving room for them to expand and contract.

Pin (P)/tail (T) orientation of bracket-foot frame, as seen from below

The bracket-foot frame is made of nine pieces of wood, all full-blind dovetailed together, except for the back, which is half-blind dovetailed. In making this bureau, I figured out which end of each piece should be tails and which pins so that I could start in the middle at the back of the kneehole and fit each joint tight as I built the frame around to the back (diagram, left). In the back of each bracket-foot joint, I glue and screw a glue block, its grain running parallel to the foot itself. The subframe gets glued and screwed to the bracket-foot frame (the grain of the adjoining parts goes in the same direction) and the subframe is slot-screwed to the carcase bottom. Thus, there is no applied base molding running crossgrain to the carcase sides.

but the convex shells are applied. Kane says yes, these particular shells have held up well; she has seen some cracked.

Visiting a museum with the curator at your side is a wonderful opportunity. It's my first chance to see the inside, back and bottom of a famous piece of furniture, and, naively, I am taken with how mundane it is. The boards are roughsawn, unfinished; the numbered drawers and the word "upper" scrawled on the upper drawer divider attest to the piece's real-shop origin. Galleries today display contemporary furniture, whose undersides are finished with the same preciousness as their faces. (Emmett's, in that sense, is contemporary furniture.) It's good to know a great piece of furniture can have its back nailed on. But it's not so good to know that beneath the finely worked face are some unquestionably troublesome constructions. Not only are the glue blocks running crossgrain to the bracket-foot members, but the bracket feet themselves aren't even attached to the carcase. They're attached to the moldings, outside the line of gravity of the carcase. And the molding is merely nailed (on the side, crossgrain) to the carcase. I can't understand how the thing is standing there, until I realize it's resting on its glue blocks. No wonder the feet are so vulnerable, they're only molding.

I leave Yale understanding better why Emmett got absorbed in redesigning traditional construction, and I sense too how the inner strength of his pieces came to be reflected in their faces. Nonetheless, I need to know about 18th-century furniture makers: What did these inconsistencies in construction mean to them? I arrange to meet with Robert Trent, research associate, and Robert Walker, furniture restorer, both at the Boston Museum of Fine Arts.

*   *   *

The kneehole bureau at the Museum of Fine Arts is by Edmund Townsend (1736-1811), a grandson of Solomon, the progenitor of 13 Townsend cabinetmakers. With the seven Goddard cabinetmakers, related to the Townsends by marriage, they produced the remarkably consistent, well-developed Newport style. This kneehole is mahogany, like the one at Yale, though the grain is more rowed. The curves, however, are less pronounced, and there is almost as much difference in composure between this blockfront and the one at Yale as there is between the Yale blockfront and Emmett's. These convex shells are almost perfect domes, with only the barest undulation at the periphery. The beading is softer. The ogee foot is straighter. The brasses are more sedate. The construction is virtually the same as in the Yale blockfront.

When I show my photographs and drawings of Emmett's blockfront to Trent and Walker, they hear me out. Finally, Trent says, "Well that's fine, but it looks like he's building a suspension bridge.... There's no question that it's possible to improve upon the designs, but what people appreciate about the old stuff is the fact that it was produced under pressure and with a commitment to making a profit. It's the deftness of it—getting an effect with a reasonable input of time and money. I know there were wealthy people supporting the Townsend-Goddard shops, but it was still a business."

What about the structural weaknesses in the design, I ask. "I don't think those are structural problems," says Walker, "I think those are atmospheric problems. People say to me, 'I've got this foot that keeps dropping off my chair. What can I do about it?' They're asking the wrong question. They should be asking, 'What should I do about the *environment* that my chair is in? What do I do to control it?'"

Bracket feet and highboy side cracked because of crossgrain construction. Courtesy Yale University Art Gallery, Garvan collection.

I was to hear this argument again from other curators and furniture restorers. Wallace Gusler (see page 16) at Colonial Williamsburg in Virginia told me most problems with 18th-century furniture are 20th-century problems. Insulated homes with central heating have created a significantly drier winter environment for furniture than was so for the first 150 years of its existence. Cabinetmakers 200 years ago did not have to deal with today's extremes of wood movement. But this only points the question: If you were reproducing an 18th-century piece today, would it make any sense to duplicate constructions that have become inadequate? "Not at all," answered Trent, "but Emmett isn't simply eliminating weaknesses here, he's souping this thing up; it's become a showpiece, a jewel. It's modern furniture, and I don't see how it's economically realistic."

Are structural shortcomings compromises, then, with economic reality? Trent continues, "People talk as if 18th-century cabinetmakers were building pieces of architecture that were going to last forever, and that's not what they were trying to do. I don't think they had any interest beyond the gen-

Newport kneehole bureau, circa 1770, by Edmund Townsend. Courtesy Museum of Fine Arts, Boston; Karolik collection.

Left, Gerald Curry's reproduction of a Queen Anne highboy in walnut. Right, Douglas Campbell at his tenoner made from a Sears table saw. The extension table is hinged at the far end of the main table and is raised and lowered by a threaded rod. On this swinging table is mounted a 1-HP motor belted to a saw arbor. Both this arbor and the saw's regular one are fitted with plywood blades (to cut the tenon shoulders) and a Sears molding head with straight knives (to waste the wood and produce the cheeks). With a miter gauge and an angle block, Campbell's tenoner can quickly make the double-angled tenons on traditional chair stretchers.

eration it was owned in, and, of course, most of the pieces didn't last more than a couple of generations."

I leave Boston beginning to realize the variety of attitudes possible toward making period furniture. But if Emmett's work is unrealistic, what, according to cabinetmakers who earn their livings building reproductions, is realistic?

*   *   *

For four years, Gerald Curry has run a one-man reproduction shop in Auburn, Maine. He's built a stable business in part by paying attention to promotion. He advertises, and answers inquiries with a 20-page catalog of Queen Anne and Chippendale furniture. In it Curry writes about the authenticity of working mainly with hand tools, and about the concentration and harmony afforded by working alone on one piece at a time. It is an attractive and—to people contemplating parting with $3,000 for a reproduction—a reassuring presentation.

I am a little surprised, then, when I drive up to his shop, which has neither sign nor showroom. It is a barn with gate doors and a noisy gas heater. The machines are few and simple: a 6-in. jointer, a Sears shaper, no thickness planer. Curry began woodworking as a finish carpenter in Boston; then he did commercial and domestic installations. Wanting to do "something nicer" than kitchen cabinets, he haunted the Museum of Fine Arts to learn about proportion and what makes a good piece good. "At first," he says, "I went to furniture stores. That's where a lot of people go wrong. They look at pieces two or three times removed from the originals. Many reproductions are composites. Proportions, detailing, construction don't have much to do with what they originally were. When I do a reproduction I try to make it as authentic and exact as possible, but I know 1980 slips in."

We look at a Queen Anne highboy in walnut (above), almost finished. The molding, upon close inspection, retains the uniformity of the router and shaper. The flat surfaces, though hand-planed, are sanded fine and sealed with a contemporary oil/varnish mix. How does this compare with his usual work? "Usually I talk to people for quite a while before beginning a piece. Different people want different things. The guy I'm making this highboy for is used to 20th-century perfection—smooth, machined surfaces, no rough edges. I'm talk-

ing with another fellow about a similar piece and he's very concerned that the drawer bottoms and inside be left rough-planed. He likes the idea of its being obviously handmade." I ask why people buy reproductions. "I get people sending me photographs of museum pieces or advertisements from antique dealers. This Queen Anne highboy, for instance: The original is priced at $30,000. I'm doing this reproduction for $3,500. And it's a more usable piece. The one in the advertisement has problems. The side is cracked, it's missing a brass, it needs restoration work that may cost as much as this piece new. And how can you feel comfortable using a piece of furniture that costs $30,000? I know I wouldn't."

I show Curry my talisman, the pictures and construction drawings of Emmett's curly cherry kneehole bureau. Curry nods; he is well aware that many of the pieces he copies have construction problems. Emmett's improvements make sense, but Curry can't expect his customers to pay for full-blind dovetailed bracket feet.

*   *   *

In search of reproduction cabinetmakers the name Douglas Campbell kept coming up. Campbell recently moved to Newport, R.I., having turned to cabinetmaking 20 years ago at age 30, when, for health, he had to quit salvage diving. Three years ago he was in Denmark, Maine, employing eight men, drying wood in his own kiln and turning out a dozen pieces a week. ("I've got nothing against Grand Rapids," he told me. "If it weren't for Grand Rapids, you and I wouldn't have anything to sit on.") His business was doing well, except that Maine is far away from most potential customers. An accessible shop and showroom were in order.

Campbell found that Newport, with a history of 18th-century prosperity and turn-of-this-century affluence, still attracts people with money. Now he makes $1,000 worth of furniture a week, working by himself. With a year's work on order, he's looking to open a larger shop, and wishing business might ease up a little in the meantime.

Campbell is the sort of fellow who can grin at you and say, "I don't fool around." He's learned to work fast, he tells me, out of desperation. "It's making things work that buys the groceries. No matter how cute some people want to be, it doesn't mean anything until you sell the piece. That's how you get the opportunity to make another. . . . When I started out I knew nothing about woodworking. I bought a hundred dollars worth of old hand tools, and it was ridiculous. I worked so hard—hand-planing sugar maple boards four sides—it was pathetic. I still don't have a decent hand plane. But that's all right. I don't use them anymore."

Campbell's work, though built fast, is not unsound. His joints are mortise and tenon ("I have dowels I bought 20 years ago; I don't use dowels"). He stabs out his mortises with a hollow-chisel mortiser ("I hope I never have to cut them any other way"), and he cuts tenons on a tenoner homebuilt from a Sears table saw. I ask Campbell how he feels about working in fabled Newport, just three blocks from where the building that housed John Townsend's shop still stands and eight blocks from John Goddard's. "I don't mind a bit," he says. "Oh, I read up on them some, but it was a business. Most of what you learn isn't anything to dream on. I was reading how John Goddard was finishing a piece—it was on order—and someone walked in off the street *with cash*, and he sold it to him, right there. Now that makes sense to me; I'd do that if I needed the money."

I debate whether there is any point in showing Campbell my pictures of Emmett's work. There is a reproduction of a Newport blockfront in his showroom. Its construction follows the original, though the joinery and detailing are coarser. The top drawer is that of a butler's desk: the front unlatches and hinges down, revealing a writing surface and pigeonhole gallery—a lucrative idea, Campbell points out. "You could do well converting chests of drawers to butler's desks. All you'd have to do is have your customer send you the top drawer of

his chest, and you could copy the materials, dimensions and finish." I ask if he's built any kneehole bureaus. He has. Does he like them? "Actually," he says, "I hate the looks of the damn things." I decide not to show him the photos of Emmett's work.

*   *   *

Harold Ionson ushered me into his shop in Westwood, Mass., settled back against a bench and nodded the brim of his blue baseball cap at the surroundings. "This," he said, "is where I play." Do you make a living here too, I ask? "Oh no," he says, "there isn't any money in this business, never has been. That's why all the fine custom shops died. Even when I got out of trade school in 1938, they were dying then. You can't count on people's taste. All my life I made things for other people, 90% of whom didn't appreciate what kind of work it was. I arrived at a point in my life, at age 55, when I decided I was going to play the rest of my life and build a few things for myself. I wanted a couple of banjo clocks. It's too much setting up for just one. So I built 24. If people want to buy the ones I don't want, fine, but that isn't why I built them."

A museum curator in Boston had recommended Ionson to me as one who makes careful reproductions of the furniture of John and Thomas Seymour. The Seymours came from England in 1785 and excelled here in making double-tambour desks of mahogany and satinwood, inlaid with rosewood, ebony and ivory. They worked not in the familiar Queen Anne or Chippendale style, but in those of the Federal period. Their adaptations of Hepplewhite and Sheraton were distinctly American. They alternated tambours of curly and bird's-eye maple, for instance, with mahogany, and painted case interiors an American robin's-egg blue. They are rich

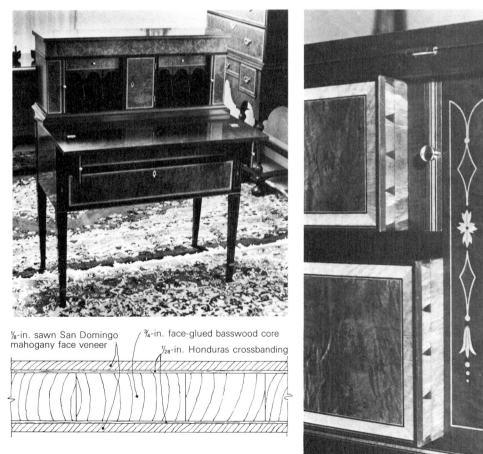

Harold Ionson, above, and one of his 11 Seymour-style, double-tambour desks, right. This one is in San Domingo mahogany and maple burl with satinwood and ebony inlay. The keyholes are bordered in ivory; enamel pulls have yet to be mounted on the bottom drawers. Ionson deals with the problem of wood movement in his cabinet sides by making his own thick-veneered plywood. Face-gluing the core (as shown in the drawing) orients the grain so that maximum expansion and contraction take place in the thickness rather than in the width of the plywood.

⅛-in. sawn San Domingo mahogany face veneer

¾-in. face-glued basswood core

¹⁄₂₈-in. Honduras crossbanding

and colorful pieces, little known to most people simply because they are now out of fashion.

What attracted Ionson to Seymour? "The beauty. You put a bunch of pieces in a room and the Seymour piece will stand out, even from 50 feet away—*that's* a Seymour piece. And the workmanship is good, even inside. Most of the old pieces, you probably know, are rather rough inside: glue blocks, wedges, they really hacked them together. Before the Federal period, furniture depended on carving for its beauty. I'm not much of a carver. They were massive pieces, too. Not badly proportioned, just large. In the Federal period, furniture became delicate and feminine. It got its beauty from figured veneers, inlays and exotic woods. Now a lot of people say, 'Oh, this is a veneered piece, it's cheap.' And they have good reason to think that way. Furniture manufacturers brought that on, veneering everything, burlap bags almost, which gave veneered furniture a bad name. But originally, only the finest pieces were veneered—because it's ten times more work."

Ionson is working on one of a run of eleven folding-leaf, double-tambour desks. They are like Seymour's desks, though not copies of any particular one. Ionson's construction is more sophisticated. He makes his lumber-core plywood from ⅛-in. sawn San Domingo mahogany, laminated over Honduras mahogany crossbanding and a basswood core. The core is face-joined rather than edge-joined (diagram, page 7) so that the maximum expansion and contraction takes place in the thickness of the stock rather than across its width. In spite of the dimensional stability this provides, Ionson does not glue these panels solidly to the legs. For added insurance against cracks that have occurred even in veneered panels, he mortises the legs, fixing the panel at the top and allowing it to float in oversize mortises at the bottom. All the tenons are pinned, the ones toward the bottom through elongated holes. Veneer conceals the pins. The drawer faces are veneered, too, and rabbeted out to receive satinwood and ebony banding, then cockbeaded. Even the end-grain edges of the drawer fronts are veneered so that when the dovetail pins are cut, they contrast well with the pine drawer sides. In short, practically the whole piece is veneered and inlaid, yet because the veneer is thick, the surface is remarkably substantial. It doesn't look ready to delaminate, it doesn't even look like veneer. "I couldn't work this way before I retired," he remarks. "I had a living to make."

David Salisbury explaining 18th-century woodworking at the reconstructed Anthony Hay shop at Colonial Williamsburg.

I am anxious to get Ionson's reaction to Emmett's work: The technical attention each has given the original designs seems something they have in common. Right away Ionson is taken with the full-blind dovetailed bracket feet. "Now that's not bad, that's good, that's nice." So is the rest of the piece, he decides. The dovetails on the drawers look too uniform for his taste, "but I won't disagree with him. I've seen those thin pins fail." Ionson wants to know how much time Emmett spent. I tell him 1,200 hours. Says Ionson, "That's 30 weeks. There wasn't any grass growing under his feet while he was doing this." I play devil's advocate and point out how economically unrealistic the work is. Ionson replies, "Oh, that's all right. Nothing's too good for me."

* * *

Colonial Williamsburg in Virginia is the premier restoration site of 18th-century life in America. At least 17 cabinetmakers worked at Williamsburg between 1720 and 1776, making furniture widely known for its refined construction and restrained styling (see page 16). At the Anthony Hay shop, rebuilt on its original foundation, I met David Salisbury, who came to Williamsburg to learn 18th-century woodworking. He was reproducing four bookcases for an 18th-century interior. Not only were their style and construction authentic, but he was using only authentic tools and techniques. This shop does not sustain itself by the pieces it produces. Its main purpose is to be a living museum, and much of the craftsmen's workday is spent explaining to visitors how Anthony

Mack Headley, Jr., left, removes the clamps from one of a set of twelve side chairs he is reproducing for Colonial Williamsburg. Below, the work of three Headley generations: Grandfather Boyd, Sr.'s, lowboy (right), his son Mack Headley, Sr.'s, Chippendale slipper chair (left) and Mack Jr.'s, Philadelphia Chippendale armchair (center).

Hay and his contemporaries made furniture.

Mack Headley, Jr., was master cabinetmaker here for three years; Salisbury had been his apprentice. When I went to see Headley at his shop in Winchester, Va., I learned why he had left. At Williamsburg he'd been able to study many fine original pieces of furniture, and had come to understand them. Now it was time to apply what he had learned.

Headley, 29, is a third-generation cabinetmaker. The family shop produces several hundred pieces of period furniture a year, including custom work and restorations. At its largest, when run by grandfather Boyd Headley, Sr., the shop employed 14 people. Now it's seven people, producing sound furniture in factory volumes and at factory prices—in the shop outside the house. "We used to build everything," says Boyd's son, Mack, Sr. "We're a little more specialized now than my father was. I draw the line at Victorian stuff, he didn't draw the line anywhere." Mack, Sr., tells of the transformation of Empire chests: "We used to take Empire chests—my father would get a truckload for $10 apiece—and we'd cut off the bonnet drawer and get rid of the panel sides and replace those turned feet with bracket feet and carve in a couple of quarter-columns and we'd have a Chippendale chest. 'Add a hundred years to the piece and a hundred dollars to the price,' my father used to say. Once a man got the hang of it, he could do one in 24 hours."

Mack, Jr., did not return to the family business upon leaving Williamsburg. "Dad and I just have different ideas about furniture," Mack says. "It takes me ten days to make a chair; it takes him two. We're both happier in separate shops." Mack, like his father, was brought up using machines to make furniture. It wasn't until he went to Williamsburg that he did much handwork. "In joinery and in carving especially, when you make an exact reproduction, you commit yourself to learning how the maker used his tools. The better you understand that, the better the reproduction you can make. A lot of people getting started are anxious to declare their independence, not willing to put themselves aside for awhile to study how early craftsmen worked. If you try to be too creative when you do a reproduction, you're going to miss a lot of what it has to teach you; it's very much a learning experience."

Headley's reproductions are each true to an individual style (see box, below). Variety is a matter for customer relations: "What do you enjoy in your furniture?" he asks. "If a customer hasn't come to me with a particular piece in mind, or with a photograph, I ask if it's high-style or country that appeals to him, if he wants the piece to depend on its sculptural qualities or on its carving. You have to decide when you start a piece what you intend to be its graces. Period furniture forms are well established. Variations within them, therefore, allow for subtle effects. One chair will stand out because of a slightly more forward cant to its legs, and this calls attention to the splat, which can be shaped to direct the eye to a particularly delicate crest rail. You don't appreciate a lot of these things until you put two chairs next to one another. Then the overall similarities make the differences more pronounced."

I show Emmett's work to Headley. He has seen full-blind

Two reproductions

The sidechair (right) that I reproduced from a piece by Peter Scott (1694-1775) shows how strongly he was influenced by early Georgian design, even after he'd lived thirty years in this country. The emphasis is sculptural; the carving flat and subordinated to gently rounded, reflective surfaces. The cabriole leg satisfies a restrained and sober taste, ending in a flattened ball and claw that suggests weight.

The armchair (left) is my interpretation of a pattern popular with high-style Philadelphia chairmakers in the early 1770s. The curves are freer and defined by elaborate carving that plays a larger role in the design. The leg is curvier and stands higher and lighter on its ball. The claw itself is tense with sinews and bones, yet because the transition to the ankle is more gradual and the final shape closer to the original blank, this foot is easier to carve than a Scott foot.

In construction, the Scott chair has the rail running behind the kneeblock rather than above it, which allows an extra ¾ in. for the mortise-and-tenon joint between the leg and rail. The Scott kneeblock is also supported by glueblocks absent from the later Philadelphia-style piece.
—*Mack Headley, Jr.*

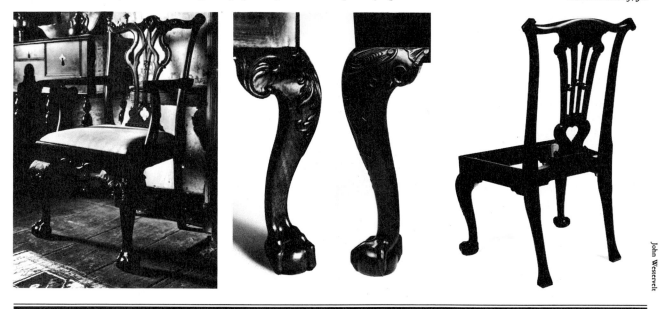

John Westervelt

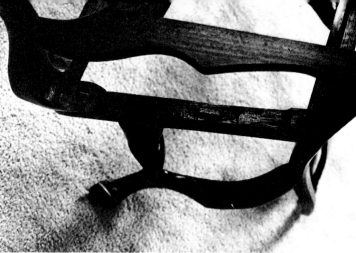

Eugene Landon, left, among some of his 500 molding planes and other 18th-century tools. The underside of one of his reproductions, a Chippendale armchair, above, reveals how closely he copies the original textures.

dovetailed bracket feet among the more demanding constructions at Williamsburg. He does not disagree with Emmett's technology, but raises the issue of context: "For extra work and extra time, you have to have a patron who is willing to pay. Here in Virginia there was an old moneyed aristocracy, very conscious of what was currently fashionable in England and expecting the more elaborate English constructions. So that's what cabinetmakers here were paid to produce. In New England, they had to use less time-consuming constructions because the newly moneyed merchants there wouldn't pay otherwise. There are records of English cabinetmakers who tried to establish themselves in Boston and just couldn't do it. The important thing is to understand that there were reasons for pieces to have been produced the way they were."

Later that day Mack's father put it this way: "A lot of people would dearly love to be artists for a living. But I haven't found enough people who'll pay for pure art."

*   *   *

Almost a year after receiving the letter from Grover Floyd I drove up to Eugene Landon's place in Montoursville, Pa. It was raining. The driveway was mud, and piled in the mud, uncovered to the rain, were flitches of walnut and cherry. A few of the walnut pieces were crotches with curly sections more than 15 in. wide. The cherry boards were 12 ft. long. All were dripping with rain, thoroughly wet. Most of the sapwood had deteriorated and was crumbling off. One cherry flitch had a check 3 ft. long, right up the middle.

I'd first seen Landon's work in 1980 in photos of the inaugural exhibition of the Appalachian Center for Crafts. His Queen Anne side chair looked intriguingly old. The surface texture, the joint lines, its presence seemed not typical of a reproduction, certainly not a recent one. Yet it was.

After I wipe the mud off my feet, I learn that Landon had been for 20 years a paint and varnish chemist, though he'd built and restored furniture as a hobby and part-time business since he was in high school. Six years ago he left his job to do it full time. Now, never having advertised, relying solely on referrals for business, he does 40 to 50 pieces a year, about half of which are restorations. "People from all over bring me their basket cases," he says. "But I've been very fortunate to work on some of the greatest pieces of furniture in this country. That's how I've learned. Old pieces have a soul—they'll talk to you, if you listen. It's amazing how consistent the old guys were once they found the right way to do something. I find it creative to figure out how a piece was

done, retracing the steps the maker must have gone through." He points out scribe marks on an old chair. They show how the marking-gauge fence was placed on the outside surfaces to ensure visual balance despite irregular stock size. "I used to work from photographs," he says, "but no photograph is going to show you the little things, the mark of the hand that gives a piece its character. So the pieces I get in for restoration, they're what I copy and learn from, though if I copied all I wanted to, I wouldn't have time to do the work they're in here for. Actually I'd like to cut back on my restorations, so I can build more. But I can't, they're my source of learning."

So I am talking to yet another student of 18th-century design and construction whose textbook is the doing of it. Emmett, unable to directly contact the furniture he was reproducing, idealized its construction. Ionson's improvements are more modest, though no less technically modern or sophisticated. Mack Headley Jr.'s craftsman-scholarship is most sensitive to the historic and aesthetic identity of the pieces he copies. Landon's attentions take him close to anachronism. He doesn't use sandpaper. He owns and uses more than 500 wooden planes, having sold his shaper long ago because "you don't get the little tear-out or imperfections the old guys did." His other power tools he expects similarly to get rid of; he uses them rarely and always obliterates their markings with traditional hand tools. If the glue blocks in an original were split or hewn out with an ax, Landon gets out his 18th-century hatchet. The result is a piece that, as Ionson might say, is rather rough inside. I ask Landon about the constructional shortcomings that initiated my search. Does he glue panels crossgrain to leg posts as they originally were? Of course. Does he not expect them to crack? "It delights me when they crack," he says. "It makes them more authentic."

I realize I have come full circle since I met Emmett. As we look out the window of Landon's shop at the dripping flitches, I ask if that's where he dries his wood. "Well," he says, "I've got to move that down to the cellar. I've got 10,000 feet of wood down there and a half-dozen walnut logs in the backyard. I saw all my own wood. What I do is throw it in a pile and leave it there for four or five years. The outside rots and you can just kick the sapwood off with your foot. It gives the walnut that good brown color. They used to bury wood in the barnyard, you know. That's how the old guys did it."   □

Rick Mastelli is director of video productions for The Taunton Press. Robert G. Emmett died in 1983 at the age of 81.

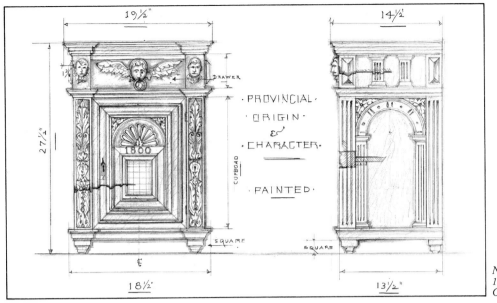

Inside the drawing:

·PROVINCIAL·

·ORIGIN·
&
·CHARACTER·

·PAINTED·

(dimensions: 19½", 14½", 27½", 18½", 13½", DRAWER, CUPBOARD, SQUARE)

Norwegian cupboard, 17th century, Sandwig Collection, Lillehammer.

Lester Margon's Measured Drawings

The late Lester Margon left an invaluable legacy for furniture designers and craftsmen in his five books of measured drawings of museum pieces (see page 26). As a young man, he studied interior design and decorating at Cooper Union Art School in New York. Margon worked for Schmieg-Kotzian and W. & J. Sloane in New York City and many furniture manufacturers in Grand Rapids, Sheboygan and Chicago. He traveled all over Europe and made 400 measured drawings of furniture masterpieces. Much of this furniture was bombed during World War II, and Margon's drawings remain the only authentic records. The Norwegian cupboard and the Austrian commode shown here are the last two to be published; many of the others may be found in his books.

Margon's books include *Construction of American Furniture Treasures* (1949), reprinted by Dover Publications, Inc., 180 Varick St., New York, N.Y. 10014; *World Furniture Treasures* (1954), Reinhold Publishing Corp. (out of print); *Masterpieces of American Furniture* (1965), *Masterpieces of European Furniture* (1967), and *More American Furniture Treasures* (1975), all distributed by Hastings House Publishers, Inc., 10 E. 40th St., New York, N.Y. 10016. □

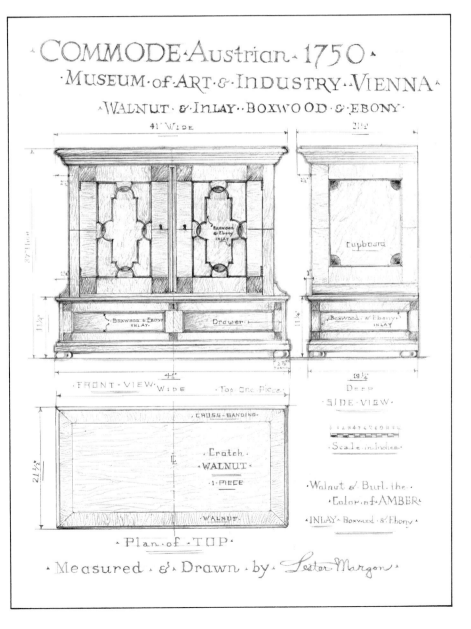

·COMMODE·Austrian·1750·
·MUSEUM·of·ART·&·INDUSTRY·VIENNA·
·WALNUT·&·INLAY·BOXWOOD·&·EBONY·

·FRONT·VIEW· Wide   ·Top One Piece·

·SIDE·VIEW·

·Plan·of·TOP·

·Scale·in·Inches·

·Walnut·&·Burl·the·
·Color·of·AMBER·
·INLAY·Boxwood·&·Ebony·

·Measured·&·Drawn·by· Lester Margon·

Wallace Nutting
Advocate of the Pilgrim Century

by Bill Dulaney

• Woodworking by artificial light is unsatisfactory • Prefer a fine reproduction to a cheap antique • Mahogany is better than maple or cherry • Highboys and lowboys are structurally unsound • Beeswax mixed with turpentine is as good a finish as can be found • No furniture built after 1830 is worth reproducing •

Such Olympian pronouncements might be expected from a dogmatic master cabinetmaker. They were, in fact, delivered with finality by Wallace Nutting, a man who couldn't plane a board. Nonetheless, Nutting's eye for line and proportion, and his pursuit of perfection (although tempered at times by commercial reality), gained for him the continuing interest of both connoisseur and craftsman, and established him as a major figure in stimulating interest in early American decorative arts.

Nutting was born in 1861 near Marlboro, Mass. Educated at Harvard and at Hartford and Union Theological Seminaries, he won acclaim as a dynamic Congregational minister before leaving the pulpit at age 44 to pursue his interest in American antiques. Although Nutting cited ill-health and nervous exhaustion as reasons for leaving the ministry (he enjoyed preaching but wearied of counseling), he exhibited enormous energy in pursuing his more worldly interests. He pronounced upon, photographed, collected, reproduced, bought and sold, and lectured and wrote about American antiques with a sweep unmatched before or since. He even tasted antiques, a procedure he recommended for detecting shoe polish used to hide end grain in new wood.

Today, Nutting is best known to the public for his hand-tinted photographs of landscapes and colonial interiors, and his prodigious output of books on early American furniture. These volumes remain landmark references, and though considered incomplete by many, they are ubiquitous elements of many a collector's library. Yet his role in the world of American antiques was more colorful and lively than his stilted photographs. Nutting's activities between the World Wars gained for him the reputation of authoritative writer on antiques (super-collectors such as Henry Francis du Pont and Henry Ford referred to his three-volume *Furniture Treasury* when buying, while the masses were told how to furnish their homes by Nutting's articles in popular magazines). A discriminating collector—Nutting's ownership of an item was calculated to increase its price as much as tenfold—he was overseer of a workshop whose reproductions were bought by collectors, curators, and a public desiring to furnish their homes and offices tastefully.

Nutting, impressive and imperious.

In 1917, with his picture business thriving, Nutting turned to reproducing American antique furniture and ironware. At a 17th-century ironworks site in Saugus, Mass., he set up shop and declared that his reproductions would be "in the best form, put together in the finest manner." He placed above each workman's bench a copy of his Ten Construction Commandments (facing page), "to encourage individuality and to make men while making furniture."

Nutting picked the brains of museum directors, antique dealers and major collectors. He took photographs, borrowed pictures (which were often unreturned), measured furniture, and had detailed drawings made. He spent endless hours on the road chasing what he judged to be the finest furniture styles. By the mid-1930s, Nutting estimated that he had authorized the reproduction of some 1,000 different items of furniture. He asserted in a 1924 catalog: "There is no article of furniture known to have been used before 1720 which my reproductions fail to duplicate in style." Most of the reproductions were intended for the public (whose taste Nutting doubted), and were marketed through gift shops as well as department and furniture stores. His reproductions were sold throughout the United States, and also in Canada, England, Australia, Mexico and China.

At the peak of production, 25 craftsmen labored in Nutting's shop. Many, if not most, were foreign-born or were first-generation Americans. In a 1938 letter, Nutting said he preferred foreign workers because they were better trained than Americans. Wishing to romanticize the activities of his shop, however, he stated in one of his reproduction catalogs: "The force consists of fine American mechanics, men of character, whom it is a privilege to know. Many live on their own little farms . . ." And, he might have added, cared little for beauty of line or furniture of the Pilgrim Century. With few exceptions, they were skilled craftsmen living in and around Boston who were interested in making a living and who regarded Nutting as something of an oddity.

"Whatever is new is bad..."—Attempts have been made to link Nutting with the Arts and Crafts Movement and the philosophy of its leading American exponent, Gustav Stickley, who preached plain lines and the importance of function for furniture. Such efforts appear to have been based largely on Nutting's early promotional material, which appealed to the simple virtues of home and hearth. It is true that Nutting and Stickley both appreciated handcrafted furniture and opposed the fussiness of Victorian styles. But Nutting was also a traditionalist who scorned efforts such as Stickley's to develop new furniture forms. He asserted: "It may absolutely be affirmed, so far as the forms of domestic art and architecture are concerned, that whatever is new is bad....New furniture is either a reproduction or it is not. If not, it lacks style and character and merit, because no new style has been evolved that can bear comparison, side by side, for a moment with the old styles." So steadfast was Nutting in his reverence for the old that he initially found little merit in furniture styles and woods used after the early 18th century.

Apparently fascinated with Windsor chairs, in 1917 Nutting wrote his first book on that subject, A *Windsor Handbook,* and he amassed over 100 different styles of the chair. Other early Nutting favorites were the substantial cabinet pieces in maple, oak, pine and walnut, which, to Nutting, characterized the Pilgrim life and American development up to 1720. He cautioned that persons "looking for 'mahoganized' imitations" need not stop at his shop.

Eventually, Nutting found it necessary to adapt his taste to changing market demands. He began to see the virtue of a cabriole leg and the beauty of mahogany, and he began to appreciate Queen Anne and Chippendale furniture. He recalls in his autobiography: "My first attempt at mahogany was to copy the most beautiful and elaborate piece of American furniture—a secretary in Providence which had been bought from Goddard. I took six of my craftsmen to study it by the hour and to make all measurements and sketches....I knew if I made that piece as well as the old, I could make anything." He was apparently satisfied with his craftsmen's efforts, for he regarded the block-front secretary (shown on page 14) with its nine shell carvings as the gem of his reproductions. It was his most expensive piece, wholesaling for $1,800 in 1930. A Nutting employee recalls that only six were produced.

Perfection vs. profit—While Nutting-the-romantic could wax rhapsodic about block-fronts, court cupboards and Windsor chairs, Nutting-the-businessman was by 1930 producing 17th-century versions of an oak radiator cover, a stenographer's swivel chair, an oak typewriter chest and a check-writing desk intended for bank use. Such items were but a nod by Nutting toward commercial realities, for, while the country was heading deeper into economic depression, he continued reproducing furniture "of all good periods including mahogany." As economic conditions worsened, he cut his work force and asked remaining employees to accept furniture reproductions in lieu of pay, which some reluctantly did. Nutting estimated in 1936 that he had lost $100,000 in the furniture business. While some of his losses may be attributed to the Depression, his employees recall that Nutting's quest for perfection often proved costly.

A cabinetmaker remembers: "Nutting would approve a pattern for a bureau or chair and the men would turn out a dozen or so, and they would all get sold. Nutting would then call in his foreman and say we were to make more. But he would say to change this and change that. We'd have to recut patterns and reshape templates, and it would cost half again

to make the new chair. He said he didn't care if it cost him $1,000 if he was right, and he always thought he was right."

Doctrinaire in judgment and possessed of a monumental ego (he once gave a studio portrait of himself as a birthday present to a 17-year-old great nephew), Nutting never doubted the merit of his work. He asserted in a 1930 catalog: "My furniture, when homes are broken up, is never sold as second-hand. In all instances that have come to my attention, it has brought more than was paid for it! Wide-awake persons now know that my name branded on furniture means style and quality." He predicted that his reproductions would be "the antiques of tomorrow," and he was right in the sense that some of them, found in both private and museum study collections, today do command prices close to those of their antique counterparts. His Windsor chairs sell for between $300 and $700, depending on style. A Nutting reproduction of a Brewster chair that retailed for $50 in 1937 sold for $850 at auction forty years later. A Connecticut sunflower chest originally offered by Nutting for $275 brought $1,285 at the same auction. An oval Windsor stool produced in Nutting's shop could have been bought for $7.25 in 1928; the asking price today is over $200.

While Nutting would have been pleased by this confirmation of the value of his reproductions some 40 years after his death, he would hardly have been surprised. Their quality was recognized during his lifetime by such important students and collectors of American antiques as Luke Vincent Lockwood and Francis P. Garvan. Garvan, whose collection is housed in the Yale University Art Gallery, bought one of each of Nutting's finest reproductions, according to Nutting's bookkeeper, Ernest John Donnelly.

For Nutting, the most gratifying recognition of his work must have come from Colonial Williamsburg. That relation-

WALLACE NUTTING FURNITURE CONSTRUCTION

1. All work to be of the best quality.

2. If the old method is best, use it.

3. If the work can be done better by hand, do it that way.

4. Use long and large mortises, and large square white oak pins.

5. Make all joined work to fit perfectly, using draw bore where it is better.

6. Match the color where two pieces come together.

7. Follow the sample strictly. Take no liberties.

8. The hand and the mouth do not work effectively at the same time.

9. Keep busy, do your best, and no fault will be found.

10. Let nothing leave your hands until you are proud of the work.

TEN   CONSTRUCTION   COMMANDMENTS

To Insure Individuality and Make Men While Making Furniture.

Christmas 1925   *Wallace Nutting*

Nutting signed this copy of his Ten Construction Commandments, which was apparently used as a promotional Christmas greeting in 1925. A copy of the Commandments was placed above the bench of each of his workmen.

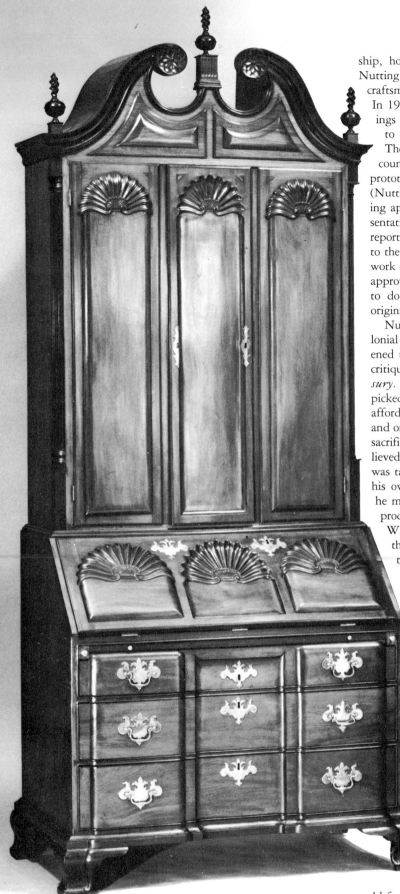

ship, however, illustrated the conflict sometimes posed for Nutting when he was forced to balance commerce against craftsmanship and to choose between perfection and profit. In 1932, representatives of Williamsburg, seeking furnishings for restored and reconstructed buildings and unable to secure enough period furniture, turned to Nutting. They ordered 12 Flemish armchairs to be used in the council chambers of Colonial Williamsburg's capitol. The prototype chair, reproduced under Nutting's direction (Nutting himself, as previously noted, had no woodworking aptitude), was rejected. Colonial Williamsburg's representative made a critical sketch (shown on facing page), reporting that the arms, posts and carving were not faithful to the original. Unfortunately, Nutting had proceeded with work on the remaining 11 chairs before having the first one approved. He resisted efforts to rework the chairs, agreeing to do so only after viewing the prototype alongside the original at the Wadsworth Atheneum in Hartford, Conn.

Nutting eventually produced 12 chairs acceptable to Colonial Williamsburg and was paid $112.50 each. He softened the blow to his vanity by offering a largely negative critique of the original chair in his book, *Furniture Treasury*. He disposed of the chair's merits in two sentences, picked it apart for a page, and then concluded, "This chair affords a rich opportunity for the study of the old methods, and one is bound to say that in this example everything was sacrificed to appearances." Nutting may have honestly believed that the antique chair from which the reproduction was taken should have been constructed along the lines of his own unacceptable prototype. His workmen recall that he more than once tried to improve upon originals by reproducing them with bolder turnings and deeper carvings. When others sought to alter the work of the masters, he thought it akin to barbarism. But for Nutting himself to do so was to confer perfection.

Two grades of furniture—That Nutting's shop could reproduce furniture acceptable to Colonial Williamsburg and major collectors of the day as well as to the public at large adds support to speculation that Nutting might have manufactured two grades of furniture: one for collectors and others interested in superior products, unmarked and indistinguishable from the original; the second for the general public, clearly marked and clearly reproductions. There is no solid evidence of such a practice by Nutting, and an explanation may be that he sold his furniture reproduction and picture businesses in 1922. Unhappy with the new owner's products, however, he repurchased both businesses a year later. In any case, in the eyes of both amateur collector and connoisseur, there are clear differences in quality among comparable items supposedly coming from Nutting's shop.

Nutting himself once noted that some of his products were being bought and sold as antiques: "A child's high chair made by me, and sold for nineteen dollars, was artificially aged and resold for a cool thousand. Nobody but the maker could have discovered the imposition.... Thus even museums have been hoaxed, and the public is buying new furniture and paying ten prices for it." Museums continue to be fooled by his reproductions:

This block-front secretary of the 'Goddard School' was Nutting's favorite reproduction. He kept one beside his desk in his office. A cabinetmaker who worked for Nutting recalls that only six of the 9-ft.-tall pieces were reproduced.

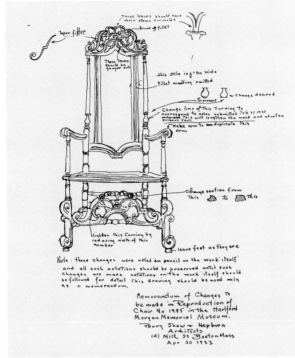

This sketch with corrections was made by a representative of Colonial Williamsburg to guide Nutting in reproducing 12 Flemish armchairs for the capitol's council chambers. The sketch is of Nutting's prototype chair, which was judged unacceptable by Colonial Williamsburg.

Winterthur Museum a few years ago removed from exhibition a supposedly 18th-century Windsor high chair after it was suspected of having originated in Nutting's shop.

Three different markings were used on Nutting reproductions: paper label, Wallace Nutting's signature carved in script, and WALLACE NUTTING burned into the wood in block letters (chair bottom or drawer side). The paper labels appear to have been used on the first reproductions in 1917 and until at least 1927. Nutting noted in a 1920s catalog, however, that henceforth he would acknowledge only those items with his name burned into them in block letters. He added: "I will not be responsible for a script letter formerly used as such a mark." The script letter was possibly used during the 1922-23 period when he had temporarily retired from his business. To further confuse identification of Nutting reproductions, there are pieces of furniture with a Nutting catalog number burned into them but not the Nutting name. And, finally, some unfinished items left Nutting's shop without mark or label. Promotional material stated that Nutting's name would not be stamped on furniture sold without finish "because of danger of swelling and unsatisfactory finish." Ironically, while Nutting railed against fakery, his efforts to protect his name by disassociating himself from his own unfinished furniture may have contributed to some reproductions finding their way into antique collections.

Photographer and writer—Nutting appears to have consistently lost money in his furniture reproduction business, a situation he attributed to the public's inability to estimate good

Bill Dulaney is a professor of journalism at The Pennsylvania State University, and a Nutting collector.

work properly—"It never did, even in the ages of better taste," he said. His picture business kept the whole enterprise afloat. His black-and-white photographs were hand-tinted by up to 100 colorists known as "Nutting girls," and signed by Nutting (or more usually by an employee who could copy his signature). An office catalog listed 10,620 different photographs, and Nutting once estimated that his prints hung in ten million American homes. Consigned to attics by the World War II generation, Nutting's prints are today collected enthusiastically. A print that sold for $3 or $4 in Nutting's time today brings as much as $40.

Although pictures and furniture are no longer being produced with the Nutting name, Nutting's writings have run through numerous editions. He wrote 18 books (plus revised editions), and his mammoth *Furniture Treasury* (volumes one and two), published in 1928, is now in its twelfth printing. As critics have noted, Nutting misidentified provenance and maker for more than a few of the 5,000 items pictured in *Furniture Treasury*. Yet he corrected many of these errors in volume three (1933), and volumes one and two still remain an indispensable reference work. Nutting's collection of furniture of the Pilgrim Century (1620-1720) is also an invaluable resource. Nutting sold the collection—in order to repurchase his businesses in 1923—to J.P. Morgan, who gave it to the Wadsworth Atheneum.

While Nutting continued to buy and sell antiques and to reproduce them until shortly before his death in 1941, his waning years were not happy. Beset by financial problems, trying to make a few dollars on antiques with which he would rather not have been publicly associated (bucket benches and strap hinges), lashing out in shrill prose at the New Deal, and bitter over what he regarded as the public's failure to appreciate his reproductions, Nutting, in 1938, wrote to a friend and former employee: "Business is worse here. We cannot sell anything because so few people are earning, and when the people have to leave us, then we are taxed to support them and then we have nothing to pay the terrible taxes with. . . . It is age that really compels me to quit. But the fad for different styles would also be enough. We make some very fine pieces, several each, and the public is stuck in another tack. Another thing, they want a different color anyway."

Few, if any, art historians regard Nutting as a scholar; his interest in furniture was style and proportion, not social history. Nutting did, however, with his boundless energy and eye for style and line, manage to leave in his reproductions, in his writings and in his collection of furniture of the Pilgrim Century a legacy that continues to interest, inform and occasionally awe students of American decorative arts. □

Further reading

The following books by Wallace Nutting are of interest to woodworkers and are still in print:

The Clock Book (revised edition, reprint of 1924 edition), Associated Book, 147 McKinley Ave., Bridgeport, Conn. 06606, 1975. Hardcover.

Furniture of the Pilgrim Century (two volumes), Peter Smith Publ. Co., 6 Lexington Ave., Magnolia, Mass. 01930, 1965. Harcover set.

Furniture Treasury, Macmillan Publ. Co., 866 Third Ave., New York, N.Y. 10022. Vols. 1, 2, and 3.

Wallace Nutting Supreme Edition General Catalog, Schiffer Publ., Ltd., Box E, Exton, Pa. 19341, 1978. Paperback.

A Windsor Handbook, Charles E. Tuttle Co., Inc. 28 S. Main St., Drawer F, Rutland, Vt. 05701, 1973. Paperback.

Variations in 18th-Century Casework
Some 'old masters' built better than others

by Wallace B. Gusler

Some people, in their reverence for the "old masters," believe the 18th-century furniture makers knew all and could do no wrong. Others claim that traditional excellence is a myth. The truth is that furniture construction in the 18th century varied almost as much as style—both construction techniques and style can be spread on a spectrum ranging from London high-style to English and American urban and provincial, to rural, and to non-professional folk art. The style and construction of a particular piece of furniture was affected by the economic and commercial conditions prevailing at the time and place it was made, as well as by the professional and ethnic background of the maker. Patronage was extremely important—provincial furniture was supported by provincial patrons, who were either ignorant of more sophisticated production, or else unable or unwilling to pay what it would have cost. Generalized statements praising or criticizing 18th-century furniture construction do not consider the varieties of context, and are not very useful.

In the English-speaking portion of the 18th-century world, London was the center for both stylistic and technological developments in cabinetmaking as in most other fields. Though Continental developments did shape London cabinetwork, in considering American furniture, it is London's leading role that is most important. Proclaiming American furniture superior to English examples, as patriotic curators, dealers and students have done, represents an inversion of values. The most highly developed construction in chairs and case furniture known from Colonial America was produced in Williamsburg, Va.—not because of any American technological developments, but because cabinetmakers there followed the highest levels of London style and technology. And what fostered this extraordinary production was the advanced economic, political and social status of Colonial Virginia. Wealthy patrons there were attuned to London's cultural life and demanded the latest London styles and technology.

Casepieces attributed to the shop of Peter Scott (1694-1775) of Williamsburg are of outstanding construction, and possess features not found in pieces from other

A: *Desk-and-bookcase, attributed to the Peter Scott shop in Williamsburg, Va., circa 1760. Walnut, poplar, yellow pine and beech; 90¾ in. by 44½ in. by 23½ in.* B: *Carcase construction of the Scott desk-and-bookcase is modeled after English techniques, using full, thin dustboards with kicker strips below.* C: *Lower portion of a Boston chest on chest, circa 1760, has drawer runners nailed directly to sides and one full dustboard. A crack is visible at the bottom of the carcase side, and the dovetail of the middle drawer blade has been forced out from the carcase edge; both defects are the result of troublesome crossgrain construction.*

A

B

C

Photos: Delmore A. Wenzel; Courtesy Colonial Williamsburg

American cabinetmaking centers. Examining the case furniture of this shop and comparing it with English developments and with other American production reveals things useful to contemporary and reproduction cabinetmakers alike.

The main case construction of Scott's desk-and-bookcase, shown in photo *A,* is of the board and dovetail type. Dovetail case construction was introduced into England from the Continent in the second half of the 17th century. Early examples with dustboards have "full bottoms," i.e., dustboards as thick as the drawer blades that continue to the back of the case. (The English cabinetmaker's term "drawer blade" may be unfamiliar, but it avoids the ambiguity of the term "divider," which is also used for partitions *within* a drawer, and of the term "rail," which is used for just about any narrow piece of wood that happens to be horizontal.)

The English (apparently in the George I period, 1714-1727) developed a dustboard thinner than the drawer blade, which makes the case lighter in weight, and this is the type Scott used here (photo *B*). The drawer blades are about 3 in. wide and ⅞ in. thick and made of solid walnut. They are dovetailed into the carcase sides and the joints covered at the front by a glued strip ³⁄₁₆ in. thick. (Leaving the dovetail joints exposed, as in some Boston casepieces and in much rural American and English furniture, is a provincial detail not in line with the finished approach of London furniture.) Rabbeted into the back of the drawer blades are ½-in. thick dustboards that extend all the way to the back of the case. The sides of the case have dadoes cut the full thickness of the drawer blades to receive these dustboards. Narrow strips of

wood inserted below the dustboard keep the dustboard at the top of the dado. These strips, which are sometimes called kickers, have two other functions: They keep the drawer beneath from tipping down when it is opened, and they also provide solid support under the dustboard where the drawer above runs.

This dustboard construction avoids several problems seen in cheaper constructions of the period. Because the grain of the dustboards runs in the same direction as the grain of the top, bottom and sides of the case, they can expand and contract compatibly as they respond to humidity changes. Full dustboards also hold the case square, preventing the sides from cupping or twisting out of plane. The kickers that wedge the dustboards in the dado are slightly shorter than the depth of the case, leaving a gap between their ends and the backboards. This prevents them from pushing out the backboards or drawer blades when the sides of the case shrink. These strips are not nailed but are glued only on the end that butts against the drawer blade. This allows the sides to expand and contract without restriction.

The cheaper alternatives to this full-dustboard construction are of two general types. The one seen most often is simply a drawer blade dovetailed into the carcase side, the joint left uncovered (photo *C*). The drawer support is inserted into the dadoed sides and nailed, or is nailed to the plain sides of the case. This solution is obviously simpler, faster and cheaper than dustboard construction but it has serious drawbacks. The grain of these nailed-in drawer supports runs across the grain of the case sides; thus the supports become battens impeding the movement of the sides. The nails further complicate the situation, causing compression shrinkage between them. Split sides often result, and sometimes split tops and bottoms as well. These drawer supports can also force the drawer blades out of their housings and push the backboards from their rabbets. Additionally, cases built this way lack the stability that full dustboards provide. In the Boston bombe example (photo *C*), the single full dustboard in the center of the case shows that the maker understood the problem and its proper solution. His compromise was probably a result of economic necessity.

The other major type of construction used instead of dustboards consists of a joined frame. The front of the frame is the drawer blade, the back element fits against the backboards, and the two side elements form the drawer supports. These two sides are usually mortised into the front and back elements of the frame; therefore, although dadoed into the carcase sides, they need not be glued or nailed there. The top drawer cavity on the Massachusetts desk (photo *D*) is constructed this way. Frames do not usually split the case sides, but can push the drawer blades out of their housings, or push the backboards off, when the sides of the case shrink. This frame method was very popular in the back country of Pennsylvania, Maryland, Virginia and North Carolina, and perhaps it derives from a Germanic approach. Unlike the Massachusetts example shown here, examples from these areas usually have frames at every drawer blade.

Typical of Philadelphia, the thin dustboard in a high chest of drawers (photo *E*) appears to be the product of a loss or misunderstanding of the London construction seen in the Scott case. Instead of the dado being cut the full thickness of the drawer blade, it is thin, receiving the thin dustboard snugly and omitting the kicker. This construction was usual in Colo-

D: *Massachusetts slant-top desk, circa 1770, has a full frame, but no dustboard behind the drawer blade of the top-drawer cavity. Usually the side member of this frame is not glued to the sides; often it forces the drawer blade or the back boards out as the case side shrinks.* **E:** *Philadelphia high chest, made by Henry Cliffton in 1753, has a thin dustboard, but no kicker to keep the drawer from tipping down when opened. (The two square glue blocks on the side of the chest are a recent repair.)*

D   E

nial Philadelphia and to some extent in other areas. During the Federal period it became common in American production.

The range of construction techniques in 18th-century furniture can also be seen in carcase base-moldings and bracket feet. Scott of Williamsburg followed advanced London practice. He glued base moldings to a series of secondary wood blocks, which were in turn glued to the bottom of the case (photo *F*). The base molding is not attached directly to the carcase, but overlaps it by ¹⁄₁₆ in. to ⅛ in.—just enough to prevent a visible gap. This arrangement allows the case to expand and contract without great stress developing between the sides and the molding. The gaps between the blocks add some flexibility, and since the blocks are smaller than the sides and bottom and made of a weaker secondary wood (pine or poplar, usually), they give way first.

Scott's base construction is rarely found in other areas of Colonial America. The most common systems are of two types, both of which present shrinkage problems. In one system, the base molding is glued and nailed directly to the sides of the carcase. In the other a wide frame is glued and nailed to the case bottom, the nails often driven through and clenched. These batten frames are sometimes made entirely of primary wood whose edge is molded, but more commonly the primary-wood molding is nailed and glued to a frame of secondary wood. Both of these systems restrict the movement of the crossgrain sides, causing them to crack.

Bracket-foot construction in Scott's shop has two sophisticated features unknown in cabinetwork from other American cities. Both features can be found in production from major London establishments. The ogee bracket feet are formed from two-ply laminated boards, the outer portion of primary wood (walnut or mahogany) and the inner of yellow pine. This two-ply composition provides two grain patterns at the weakest point, where the ogee curve swings inward, therefore

F: *Bottom of the Scott desk-and-bookcase in photo A shows the English method of applying molding to segmented glue blocks instead of directly to the carcase side and front. This system allows the carcase sides and bottom to expand and contract without cracking.*

G: *Typical bracket-foot construction, as in this view of the Massachusetts slant-top desk (see photo D), employs a corner glue block with the grain running perpendicular to the grain of the bracket members. Cracked bracket feet are common. Note that the base-molding glue blocks run all the way into the corner, unlike the glue block construction shown in photo F.*

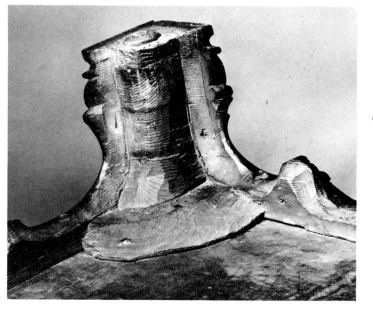

H: *Bracket foot of a Scott bookcase, above, and of a London-made china cabinet, right, both show composite glue-blocking and laminated bracket members: primary wood on the outside and secondary on the inside. These two features, unknown in combination in American shops other than Scott's, have ensured exceptionally good survival of his bracket feet.*

helping to prevent fracturing at this critical location. Additionally, the softer secondary ply provides a resilient core that enables the foot to withstand greater shocks without breaking than if it were constructed entirely of hardwood.

The essential strength of the 18th-century bracket foot is the glue-blocking inside its corner. In the better pieces, the weight of the case is on these glue blocks and not on the brackets. The blocks are directly below the corners of the case, while the brackets are directly below the base molding. In pieces where the weight is taken by the brackets, the base molding is often broken loose, allowing the case corner to slide downward. The typical glue-blocking in bracket feet is made up of a square, vertical piece glued into the corner formed by the two brackets (photo *G*). The grain is perpendicular to the horizontal grain of the brackets. Excessive or sudden changes in relative humidity can cause the brackets to shrink, often breaking the glue joint since the block does not shrink in like amount. In some cases the glue-block joint holds and the brackets split at their weak point where the ogee swings inward. After splitting, each segment shrinks unto itself, leaving a gap at the fracture point.

Another defect of this construction shows up when the case is moved. If slid along the floor, the foot glue block is liable to catch on an uneven area and snap off.

By the mid-18th century, a composite glue-blocking technique that solved these problems had evolved in some London shops. Composite glue-blocking consists of several layers of secondary wood blocks stacked one on the other to build up a vertical foot block. All the grain in the glue blocking runs horizontally, parallel to the grain of the bracket itself. In addition, the blocks are stacked crossgrain, which alternates the grain orientation at the joint between glue-block and bracket-foot member to provide long-grain gluing surfaces to each side of the bracket. The layers are also face-glued together, producing an extremely strong foot (photo *H*). Scott's pieces combine this feature of foot construction with the laminated bracket, and his is the only American shop known to do so. Several other Williamsburg shops used composite-blocked feet, as did some in Norfolk, Va., and Annapolis, Md., but to my knowledge, this construction does not make a single appearance in the furniture of Boston, Newport, New York, Philadelphia or Charleston.

In summary, if it is to 18th-century American furniture that the craftsman and designer look for instruction, it is wise to realize that there were various construction methods as well as levels of sophistication. All American production is an off-shoot of the English techniques that were most highly developed in London. The transition to America involved some loss or distortion of the original systems. Cabinet shops producing furniture closest to London in style and construction centered in Williamsburg. According to the degree of sophistication in typical case constructions, the other centers range, from high-style to provincial, as follows: Charleston, Philadelphia, New York, Newport, and Boston/Salem. Other cities should be in this list, but their production has been too little studied to reach definitive conclusions. □

Wallace Gusler is curator of furniture at Colonial Williamsburg. His book, Furniture of Williamsburg and Eastern Virginia, 1710-1790 *(Virginia Museum of Fine Arts, Box 7260, Richmond, Va. 23221), covers in detail the production of the Scott and other Virginia shops.*

Post-and-Panel Chests
A 19th-century design

by Jim Richey

Experts on antique furniture usually advise, "Buy it and leave it alone." They didn't see the 140-year-old chest of drawers we brought home. Once sturdy and clear-finished, it was wobbly and covered with ugly paint. A previous owner had cured its loosened joints by driving nails through the cheeks of the mortises. Proper restoration had to start with complete disassembly.

While rebuilding, I realized that the post-and-panel construction of this unadorned country antique is really quite sophisticated and deserves to be better known. It is strong and handsome, and not likely to crack apart over the years. Hundreds of these chests survive: They were made throughout the Ohio River Valley states, of local hardwoods by village cabinetmakers who cared more for function than for fashion.

The post-and-panel chest is designed to cope with seasonal humidity changes and long-term panel shrinkage without damage. All the critical dimensions of the chest are determined by long-grain members—posts and rails. Built like a post-and-beam barn, the chest is strong enough to handle the strains of cross-country moving. Yet, there are disadvantages. The joinery is difficult, the material list calls for more and thicker wood than slab-sided construction and the finished chest seems to weigh a ton.

The old chest shown on the next page is 44 in. high, 44½ in. wide and 20½ in. deep. The top, front and sides are solid cherry. The back, drawer sides and drawer bottoms are poplar. The side panels are 16 in. wide, cut from a single board. Nowadays, unless you have access to unusually wide, clear stock, you would have to glue up two boards for the side panels. It is also perfectly acceptable to construct two (or more) panels per side with a stile between that's mortised into the top and bottom rails. Authentic 1830 panels are flat on the outside, beveled on the inside. The bevels can be turned to the outside for an attractive, if not authentic, effect. As with all frame-and-panel construction, the panel is left unglued in its groove, free to move as humidity changes.

If you decide to adapt the post-and-panel design to a chest project, carefully cut and dry-fit all the joints first. The mortise-and-tenon joints where rail meets post are crucial to a strong chest. Single tenons on the ends of the rails will work, but divided tenons mated with divided mortises are stronger and not much harder to make. Drawbore and peg the mortise-and-tenon joints, if desired, to gain extra strength and to reduce the number of clamps needed for assembly. Don't substitute one horizontal tenon for the two vertical tenons shown in the sketch at the ends of the drawer dividers; a horizontal tenon here won't hold, and it will weaken the posts.

Don't try to glue up the carcase all at once. First glue up the more complex side assemblies. The drawer-guide supports (with the drawer guides yet to be screwed on) need not be glued in; the post-and-rail frame will hold them in. With the side assemblies done, you can glue up the back or leave it

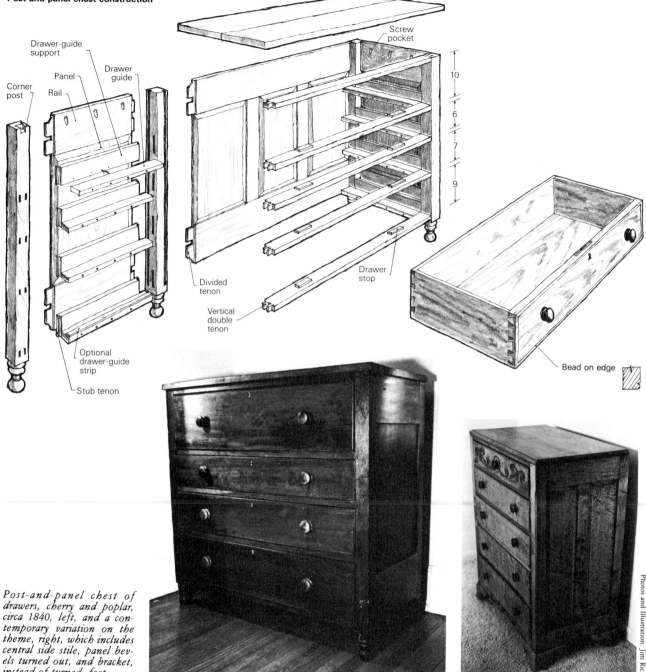

Post-and-panel chest construction

Drawer-guide support

Panel

Drawer guide

Corner post

Rail

Screw pocket

10

6

7

9

Divided tenon

Vertical double tenon

Drawer stop

Optional drawer-guide strip

Stub tenon

Bead on edge

Post-and-panel chest of drawers, cherry and poplar, circa 1840, left, and a contemporary variation on the theme, right, which includes central side stile, panel bevels turned out, and bracket, instead of turned, feet.

unglued and fit it into the side assemblies piece by piece. The best way to assemble the whole carcase is to lay one of the sides on the floor and fit the back rails, panel, and front drawer dividers into the posts. Then fit the other side onto the other end. Turn the carcase upright, clamp it together and glue in the top drawer divider, which is dovetailed into the posts. With the carcase completed, the drawer guides can be screwed in flush with the drawer dividers. The guides will wear in time and so should not be glued, making their replacement easier.

Fasten the top to the frame with screws through screw-pockets cut in the top side rails. The screw holes should be large enough to allow for some movement of the top. If the top is warped, put the concave side down to reduce gapping at the front. After the frame is together, cut the drawer parts to fit the drawer openings. Use traditional drawer construction with dovetailed corners and solid, beveled-panel bottoms.

Most antique chests have a turned foot at the bottom of the legs ending at the floor with a ball. If you prefer molded bracket feet to turned posts, just rabbet out a portion of the face and side at the bottom of the front posts equal to the height of the foot. Fasten the bracket foot below the resulting shoulder with screws from the back. Since part of the post touches the floor and backs up the feet, the arrangement is quite strong. □

Jim Richey, of Ponca City, Okla., is Methods of Work editor of Fine Woodworking *magazine.*

Queen Anne

Styling elements in table designs

by Franklin H. Gottshall

The Queen Anne style is generally the most popular of all the good English styles of the 18th century and is a good choice for craftsmen wishing to put together their own period design. The style's popularity is due to the fact that in the beginning it was distinguished for its clean lines, beautiful curved elements and restraint in the use of ornament.

Queen Anne's short reign (1702-1714) was not distinguished for any personal influence she gave to the progress of fashion in her day, and so it must be assumed that the craftsmen themselves were largely responsible for the changes and improvements in furniture design during her reign. The happy result was that craftsmen, who understood both the practical possibilities as well as the limitations of their craft, were largely free of the domination by patrons whose wealth and position did not necessarily reflect good taste. Thus, at least in its early stages, the style was relatively free of the excesses in form, embellishment and elaboration so prevalent immediately preceding this style, and in those which followed.

Cupboards, cabinets, chairs and tables became less elaborate and fussy, and were designed with a view to their function rather than to ostentation and display. Technical improvements in both design and construction were made with pleasing results. The changes brought about by these factors, as well as an improvement of the economy in England during this period, made it possible for more people to share in the amenities which had previously been largely reserved for the privileged few.

While the Queen Anne style came into being during the very beginning of the 18th century, its influence, once it was well established, continued well into the latter part of the century. Artists like William Hogarth greatly influenced design at this time, especially the employment of the reverse curve, both structurally and decoratively. Also sometimes called the cyma curve, it is used consistently and with good effect in Queen Anne style.

On a portrait of himself, which now hangs in the National Gallery of London, Hogarth painted a palette on which appears a reverse curve with the caption "The line of beauty and grace." This aroused so much discussion that an explanation was demanded of him. He explained it by saying that "a beautiful curve by its serpentine, flamelike waving and winding simultaneously in different directions leads the eye in a pleasing manner from one end to the other." He sought to explain it further by saying that the principles involved were "fitness, variety, uniformity, simplicity, intricacy, and quantity — all of which cooperate in the production of beauty, mutually correcting and restraining each other occasionally."

In addition to this, he portrayed Queen Anne furniture in many of his paintings, which enjoyed wide distribution during the first half of the 18th century.

The American colonies not only imported a great deal of furniture, once trade was well established, but they also made reproductions and adapted the styles to their own requirements. Fortunately, in the majority of cases, their adaptions reflected the simple, clean-cut lines and attributes by which we identify the style in America today.

Some styles of legs and feet found on Queen Anne furniture. Among the most widely used were the trifid (three-toed) webbed foot (second from left, also shown in cross section) and the pad foot (third from left). The ball-and-claw (second from right, below) later became a Chippendale hallmark. The Spanish foot is shown at right (above.).

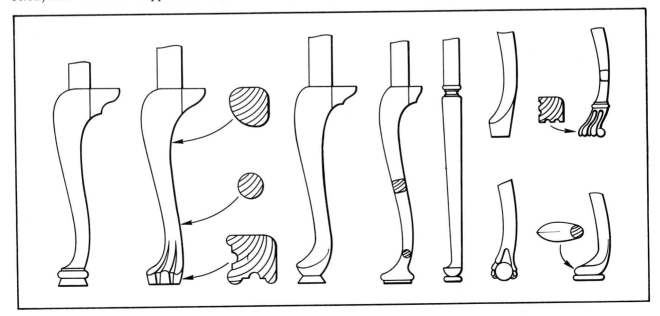

Some Queen Anne Styling Elements

Shell carvings for knees of legs.
Also used for aprons of tables and lowboys.

Queen Anne lowboy.

Sunburst carving on drawer.

Brass drawer pulls (good ones always
have carefully beveled outlines).

Molding around top of lowboy.

Square or
roughly
octagonal
hardwood
pin.

No offset where
leg and rail come
together.

Aprons which may be adapted
to lowboys, tables, etc.

At present, good American Queen Anne furniture is more highly prized by American collectors of antiques than its English counterparts. Among the reasons for this are that skillful cabinetmakers like William Savery and others did notable work in the style, basing their work on the early, simple, clean-cut patterns imported from Europe. They used walnut rather consistently because it was available and plentiful in the areas where they worked. Maple, a wood not native to the mother country, was also used; so was poplar as a secondary wood for drawer sides and like members.

About 1720 and thereafter there was a gradual substitution from walnut to mahogany in England, but this change did not take place in America to any great extent until a long time later, because mahogany was more expensive and no great improvement over the native walnut.

One of the most appealing developments of the Queen Anne style was the small dressing table or "lowboy," so-named to distinguish it from the "highboy," a similar piece with a chest of drawers on top. Lowboys are about table height, rarely exceeding 30 inches. (An antique purporting to be a lowboy which is much taller, or wider than the example shown, is probably a converted highboy and worth a lot less.)

As the Queen Anne style metamorphosed into Chippendale, ornament became more and more elaborate, often featuring quarter columns and other refinements. But the best (and most highly prized) furniture of the Queen Anne style is characterized by the minimal decoration, simple outlines, beautifully formed curves and sound, sturdy construction of the early period. The modern craftsman would do well to adhere to these principles. □

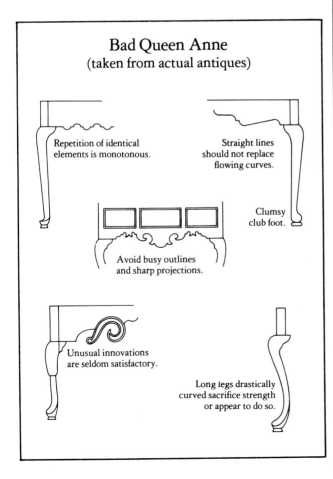

Bad Queen Anne
(taken from actual antiques)

Repetition of identical elements is monotonous.

Straight lines should not replace flowing curves.

Clumsy club foot.

Avoid busy outlines and sharp projections.

Unusual innovations are seldom satisfactory.

Long legs drastically curved sacrifice strength or appear to do so.

Design Sources
Conventions stand in for genius

by Cary Hall

The amateur cabinetmaker usually stumbles into the fascinating world of wood by trying to make something his or her spouse sketched on a shopping list. Hooked, he buys some tools, maybe a book, and learns about the voluptuous delights of successfully mating two pieces of recalcitrant wood. Further seduced by the beauty of freshly worked wood, he finally approaches a level of competence that enables him, with some trepidation, to take on a real woodworking project. He makes the joints tight and the finish smooth only to find, once it's complete, that it's a well-made mess, offensive to the eye, destined for those distant reaches of the house reserved for furniture-to-be-ashamed-of. There are also some professionals who lavish their skill on atrocities. The reason is obvious—being an expert cabinetmaker doesn't automatically make one a skilled and expert furniture designer.

So you love wood and beautiful joinery. But you lack that rare muse whispering in your ear, "Another 1/32 off and it'll be just right." Small changes in furniture dimensions, changes so small as to be imperceptible on a drawing, make astonishing differences in appearance. The compromises between appearance, strength and ease of construction require something more than training and experience. Truly original design requires inborn talent, and such talent is extremely rare.

We amateurs need some guidance. I get it from the past, in particular from the golden age of furniture design, the Chippendale era (about 1750 to 1800). During this period the Queen Anne leg blossomed, together with the ogee foot, the ball and claw foot, fluted columns, cyma curve molding and other design conventions that simplify the problem of laying out good-looking furniture. In effect, the furniture designers of this period established a large number of design choices that could be combined to make a tasteful piece. Drawers could be lipped, or the discontinuity graced by beading. Quarter-columns made corners elegant. Molding provided easy transition to curving legs. Shell carvings fitted well into furniture ornamentation.

Furniture-makers in our time, equipped with modern tools, have progressed beyond the conventions that made things easier for the Chippendale-era designers. The delightful flowing creations of today are, by all odds, the best-looking furniture the world has so far seen. But modern furniture can't easily be copied. The lines are so fine and critical that a very small deviation from the original can spoil the piece entirely. And there's just no way to combine and alter modern furniture designs to arrive at a different piece in the same style. Modern furniture is for artists and trained designers, not for cabinetmakers.

We can, however, follow in the footsteps of the Colonial cabinetmakers who took the basic designs of Chippendale, Hepplewhite and Sheraton and built pieces that still make the eyes sparkle and the hands tremble. Generally, our Colonial furniture makers were inspired copyists, and by combining the standard features—the square tapered legs, the shell carvings, the ogee legs—the amateur can also come up with furniture that from a decent distance stands some chance of comparison with the stuff in museums. Most of us, however, need some idea of sizes and actual shapes—we just aren't good enough to look at a photograph and be able to sketch up a piece that will come out of the shop looking good.

Fortunately, some authors have turned out books with dimensioned plans. Few of us will follow these plans exactly, and more to the point, shouldn't try. Many have a dimension wrong somewhere, and blindly following the plan may lead to parts that won't fit. Many books offer detailed dimensioned plans or carefully executed drawings such as those by Lester Margon (see list, page 11). My favorites are two of Franklin Gottshall's books, *Heirloom Furniture* and *Reproducing Antique Furniture*, which give a library of attractive designs. They are not exact copies, as in Lester Margon's books, and each has some usually helpful construction tips.

As a practical example, let's take a design out of Gottshall's *Reproducing Antique Furniture* and see what happens. On page 138 is a lovely block-front chest-on-chest, a piece that Goddard would have been pleased to claim as his own. The problem is, this chest-on-chest is too big for most bedrooms, the upper drawers are too high for daily use, and the pediment is mighty ambitious without adding too much to the basic furniture need, a chest of drawers. The lower section is just perfect for a chest of drawers, provided you adjust the overall dimensions while keeping the block fronts proportional. The need was, in my own case, for several chests, each wandering well away from Gottshall's dimensions.

Now it's time to be careful. We go over Gottshall's fine drawings. We discover that the legs cannot be made as shown on the side view in fig. 3. We puzzle over fig. 21, where the leg curves have been reversed, further confusing the issue. We note his instructions for laying out the shell carving and find that making each shell flute identical just won't work.

Because we are changing all the dimensions anyway, we don't really delve into the accuracy of the printed dimensions. We do bear in mind that the plans for the corner cabinet (p. 154) have a half-dozen inaccuracies, so we check every layout of our modified plan to make sure it can be assembled. It takes concentration to fathom the relationships of the block-front recessions and projections and of the base moldings. We are particularly impressed by the thickness of the mahogany needed for the drawer fronts and the catastrophic loss of expensive wood if a gross mistake is made.

All of us have preferences concerning the way a piece is put together. My own stubbornly held choice is to dovetail upper and lower carcase corners of a chest of drawers, to make something the professionals call a "true chest." This sturdy four-sided box then carries the drawers and sits on a removable base. This construction method is quite different from the interior design of the Gottshall piece used as a model.

The corner dovetails of the chest could perhaps be made by machine, but making them by hand is a delightful way to spend time, and the splendid feeling one gets when a corner is fitted and everything just matches and you tap the wood a bit to make it go—well, it's indecently sensual.

I mortise the drawer runners into the sides (no glue here) and tenon the rails into the sides. With my preferred construction method, the basic four-sided box, the rails, the runners, the stiles (if any) and the drawer partitions must all be assembled in one gluing session. Realization that a few minutes of delay can ruin a couple of weeks of work is a marvelous stimulant to one's attention. The stack of parts in less than an hour's time becomes a recognizable object, so put together that it can never again be taken apart. I pin all tenons and the end dovetails.

The top drawer needs carving into the Goddard shell design. Gottshall lays out the design, essential for someone not adept at interpreting a murky picture and detailing the carving barely shown. This sort of carving doesn't require the artistic sense that allows one to call oneself a woodcarver, but it is a most pleasant occupation, shaving away slices of mahogany to arrive at the stylized shell.

The block fronts and the rails have to be fitted vertically so that everything is aligned when the drawers are closed. No matter how carefully I cut the drawers to make the block fronts, and the rails to fit the upper lips of the drawers, there will be misalignment. I have become reconciled to my own inability to measure and cut several parts and then bring them together for an acceptable fit. Consequently, I allow a little excess wood and plane and carve the drawer fronts and rails into proper alignment after the drawers are assembled.

After lining up the block fronts, dovetailing and assembling the drawers, and fitting the molding (which covers the top dovetails) I make the base assembly—frame, legs and molding. I go overboard on making my bases strong with a good deal more wood than shown in the book plans, and pins where they can't be seen. I don't use dowel joints, but I do use dowels to pin tenons and to pin pieces where the strain is perpendicular to the dowel, not parallel to it. Carving the legs is pleasant; it's a joy to see the complex curves emerge. The molding can't be completed with a router or shaper because of the changes in direction, and it too must be hand-carved at the interior corners.

Close fits are essential throughout. If you trial-assemble a piece, without glue or pins, and shake it, there can be no movement—it must be steady as a rock. Any looseness in furniture means that it has a limited life, since looseness will always increase until the thing disintegrates. One test I use is to check that one leg of a completed piece is a little clear of the floor. Few floors are as accurately level as the furniture legs of closely made projects, and one leg clear means that the piece is rigid enough to resist sagging to fit a slightly uneven floor.

I made two block-front chests from the one Gottshall drawing, one close to the original proportions of the base of the chest-on-chest, and one somewhat taller. I also got a third chest out of the same basic design. It has quarter-column corners like the upper section of the Gottshall design, but with the same legs as the first two chests.

One of the problems with this sort of work is that the dimensions of the legs should really be changed a bit to match the revised dimensions of the chests. I am just not good enough to figure out how much and where. Probably few cabinetmakers are talented enough to make such small changes during construction to gain maximum proportional appeal. I find it difficult to worry about this lack, although it may, 300 years from now, keep my work out of somebody's museum of 20th-century homecraft. □

Cary Hall, of Hampton, Ga., is a semi-retired civil engineer and a dedicated amateur woodworker.

FIG. 2

FIG. 4

FIG. 3

Block-front chest-on-chest, taken from Reproducing Antique Furniture *by Franklin H. Gottshall,* © *1971 by Franklin H. Gottshall. Used by permission of Crown Publishers, Inc., New York.*

Cary Hall's variations on a theme: This chest, adapted from Gottshall's design, measures 20 in. deep, 35⅛ in. wide and 47½ in. high. Material is mahogany outside and Southern pine inside.

This chest has quarter-column corners, but the same feet as the other two. It measures 18½ in. deep, 36¼ in. wide and 49¾ in. high. The outside is mahogany, inside is Southern pine.

Block-front chest at left closely resembles the base of Gottshall's large chest-on-chest. It measures 20 in. deep, 43½ in. wide and 37⅜ in. high. Material is mahogany outside and Southern pine inside.

Photos: J. O. Strickland

Making Period Furniture **25**

Restoring an old desk—*I've salvaged an old, walnut roll-top desk from the basement of a great aunt. It's in many pieces, some rotted and waterstained, and the wood is coated with coal dust from a nearby furnace. How can I clean up the desk and restore it? I've tried using a mixture of linseed oil, turpentine, and vinegar as a cleaning agent. The desk has an inlaid leather top and I'd like to restore that too.* —Sam Stafford, Louisville, Ky.

GREG LANDREY REPLIES: First, vacuum all of the desk parts to remove any loose dirt. Stubborn dirt and stains can be removed with a soft cloth dampened with a weak detergent and water solution. A 1% (1 gm to 100 ml of water) solution of Soilax 3 works well. This product can be bought at the grocery store or a janitorial supply house. Odorless mineral spirits is another solvent for this cleanup job, but I advise against using any kind of linseed oil solution, because if it isn't entirely removed, it can remain on the surface and leave a tacky film that will attract dust and turn dark.

Glue disassembled parts with liquid hide glue, an adhesive similar to the one originally used on the desk. If you need a stronger bond, try white glue, but remember that white-glued joints are more difficult to take apart later. Rot, if not too far gone, can sometimes be hardened with several coats of a surface finish. Use a consolidant called Xylamon LX (which is available from Conservation Materials Ltd., Box 2884, Sparks, Nev. 89431) if you want your repair to be stronger. As a last resort, you can inject a two-part resin epoxy into any rotted areas. If the old wood is beyond repair, splice in new wood and match its color later with stains.

If the old finish remains in good condition after cleanup, protect it with a coat of carnauba wax applied with 0000 steel wool or a soft cloth. Don't apply wax to bare wood, however, because it will penetrate and be difficult to remove later if you want to apply another kind of finish. If the old finish can't be saved, try removing it with denatured alcohol or a non-flammable paint remover. Rubbing water stains with denatured alcohol may tone them down; stains can be used to match colors where patches or repairs have taken place. Shellac is probably the appropriate finish for a desk of this era, though it has limited resistance to heat and water. Harder finishes such as lacquer or varnish could also be used. If the leather top is in good shape, a cleanup with saddle soap may be enough to restore it to serviceable condition. If you can't save the old leather, consider replacing it.

Clock acoustics—*I have a commission to build a mantle-type wooden clock case. I've listened to several chime clocks and they sound like an orchestra playing with jackets over their instruments. What can I do to make my clock produce a resonant, delightful sound?*
—*Roger G. Joshua Sherman, Baltimore, Md.*

ANDY MARLOW REPLIES: If you are working to a fixed clock design, you can't change the shape of the clock's sound chamber much, and you would have to change it quite a bit to make much difference anyway. Rods or gongs mounted on hardwood will produce more volume but a harsher sound; softwood, a softer and more pleasing note. I'd experiment with the material on the striking surface of the hammers. They are usually faced with a hard leather button. You'll get a surprising variation in sound quality by using a softer leather such as chamois or a piece of kid glove. Don't forget to drill holes in the clock back to let the sound out.

Measured Drawings
How I make them

by Lester Margon

I was one of the lucky fellows to secure admission to the old Cooper Union Art School in New York City. It was a three-year evening course in various aspects of architectural design, interior decoration and related arts. The course was free except for the purchase of the necessary materials.

First-year students in the interior decoration class were required to make an original color sketch of a room of their choice. I selected a Louis XVI foyer in tones of gray with highlights of gold. The exhibition attracted considerable attention. Mr. Wilson Hungate, director of the drafting room of W & J Sloane, liked my sketch and invited me to join his staff of designers as an apprentice. I was glad of this opportunity and worked there on Fifth Avenue for seven years, advancing from apprentice to full-fledged interior designer.

As time went on, conditions changed: W & J Sloane no longer required 17 men in the drafting room. Formerly, all the work had been done to special order, but then mass production showed its ugly head and there was less work.

Several Sloane designers found good jobs at tremendous salaries in Chicago, Sheboygan and Grand Rapids. I heard of an opening at Stickley Brothers of Grand Rapids, and after some negotiations, they suggested that I submit an original sketch for a bedroom group. I made a colored rendering with stencil decorations, a new note which they liked. It was not long before I was on my way to Michigan.

The work proved rather difficult, not only doing the drafting but supervising the work in the factory. By the end of the year I was ready to resign and try my hand at freelancing for smaller factories. This proved fairly successful. I joined the Grand Rapids Designers Association and thereby met many of the leaders in the industry.

In 1924 the Exposition of Decorative Arts was planned in Paris. The club was invited to send a representative to the inaugural services, and I was selected. I was amazed. My dream of Paris was to become a reality. It entailed a three-month vacation with all expenses paid. What an opportunity!

After ceremonies consisting of many introductions and long speeches in French, which I did not appreciate, we spent days visiting the exposition and the many exhibits, led by a member of the academy who spoke English. Much of this proved mighty interesting and instructive. But being in Paris for the first time, my next objective was to visit the Louvre.

This is such a huge and sprawling establishment that it

The late Lester Margon was a long-time interior designer, widely known for his books of measured drawings of the finest museum pieces. See page 11 for more of his drawings.

·A·DUNCAN·PHYFE·CHAIR·

·1810·

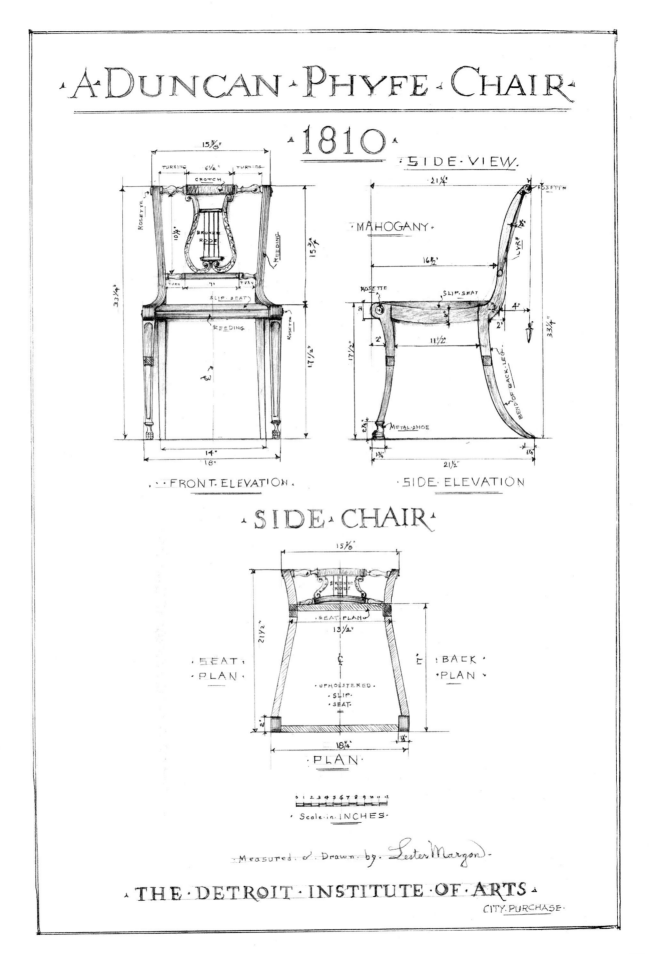

·SIDE·VIEW·

·MAHOGANY·

·FRONT·ELEVATION·

·SIDE·ELEVATION·

·SIDE·CHAIR·

·SEAT·
·PLAN·

·BACK·
·PLAN·

·UPHOLSTERED·
·SLIP·
·SEAT·

·PLAN·

0 1 2 3 4 5 6 7 8 9 10 11 12
·Scale·in·INCHES·

·Measured·&·Drawn·by· Lester Margon·

·THE·DETROIT·INSTITUTE·OF·ARTS·

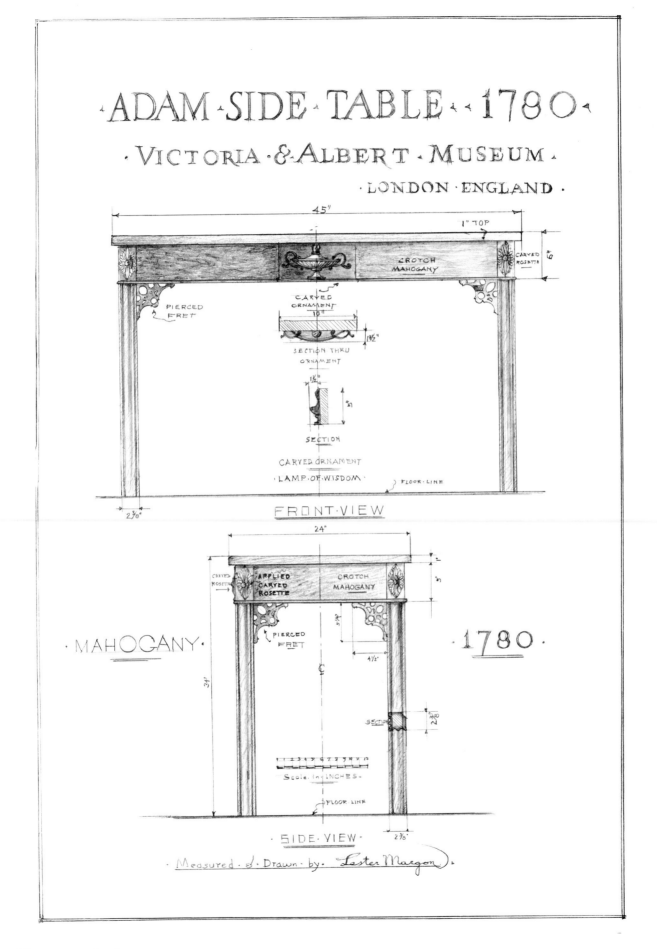

ADAM·SIDE·TABLE·1780·

·VICTORIA·&·ALBERT·MUSEUM·
·LONDON·ENGLAND·

45"

1" TOP

6"

CARVED ROSETTE

CROTCH MAHOGANY

PIERCED FRET

CARVED ORNAMENT 10"

1½"

SECTION THRU ORNAMENT

1½"

3"

SECTION

CARVED ORNAMENT

·LAMP·OF·WISDOM·

FLOOR·LINE

2⅜"

FRONT·VIEW

24"

1"

5"

CARVED ROSETTE

APPLIED CARVED ROSETTE

CROTCH MAHOGANY

·MAHOGANY·

PIERCED FRET

3½"

4½"

·1780·

34"

SECTION

2⅜"

1 2 3 4 5 6 7 8 9 10 11 12

·Scale·in·INCHES·

FLOOR·LINE

SIDE·VIEW

2⅜"

·Measured·&·Drawn·by·Lester Margon·

cannot be conquered readily. After several days of exploring, I gave it up as an impossible undertaking. What interested me most was the Museum of Decorative Arts in a wing of the Tuileries Palace. Here I found a decorator's happy hunting ground: there were 45,000 objects on display including furniture, tapestries and wood carvings, as well as related objects of decoration. I also toured the Cluny

Margon

Museum, one of the most important collections in Paris. It is in a colorful 15th-century structure built by the abbots of Cluny of the remains of a Roman bath. Here is portrayed life as it was in the Middle Ages. Besides Gothic and Renaissance furniture, the collection includes manuscripts and even a chastity belt.

The furniture in these and other museums was so astonishingly beautiful that I was impelled to explore for some way to bring the design elements of these masterpieces of the Old World to the attention of students, designers, craftsmen, decorators and furniture manufacturers over here.

I finally secured an interview with the director of the Museum of Decorative Arts and presented my credentials. I told him what I would like to do—to make measured drawings of some of the furniture. He was interested but suggested that I make one sketch and show it to him. I was glad to do this. He was delighted with the result and gave me carte blanche to proceed as I desired. This reception was repeated in all the other museums. I was on my way to starting a collection of measured drawings of 500 pieces, possibly the largest in existence. Where photographs were available I secured them. Where photographs were not available, special ones could be taken at a moderate cost.

Then followed six European trips traveling thousands of miles in England, Italy, France, Germany, Belgium, Denmark, Norway, Sweden, Rumania, Austria and Czechoslovakia. During World War II some of the furniture in these museums was bombed out and my measured drawings remain the only authentic record of their design. I have on occasion traveled hundreds of miles just to sketch a chair.

Making a measured drawing is not quite as simple a procedure as one might expect. Some previous experience in drafting is essential. A knowledge of the use of drafting materials is taken for granted, such as the T-square, triangles, curves, dividers and the compass, and certainly the ability to use the scale rule.

One must generally know about and have some appreciation of furniture periods and design. Of course, museums have the largest variety of furniture on display, but you must decide what pieces are of interest to you and what particular pieces you wish to sketch. Be selective in your choice. After you have decided, study the piece well before starting on the sketch for the measured drawing.

Of course, permission must be secured from the curator. Find a good spot in the gallery. If necessary, the attendant will rearrange the setting to afford you good light and the necessary privacy while you are working.

You will need your box of instruments, a six-foot folding rule, a good supply of paper, pencils and erasers. Use a legal-size pad of paper. Take measurements of the piece of furniture slowly and carefully. A good scale to use is three inches to the foot. For most pieces this will give ample room. If several sheets are required, so much the better.

Generally, front and side views are required, a seat and top plan, and auxiliary views to show any special aspects of the design. Individual bits of carving can be noted separately. Put down all sizes carefully and check them before leaving. Make notes about any significant features of the design. The title, the period and the name of the designer are important. Be sure to note when the piece was bequeathed to the museum and by whom. Know the woods that have been used, the color and the grains. Don't let anything escape you. You will need all this information when making the final measured drawing. Use a plumb line when necessary and a good, large pair of dividers. Get the correct readings. Then, after all this has been done, you can leave the museum feeling satisfied that the job has been well done. If there are any doubts later, don't hesitate to return to check. It is well to let some time pass between the work at the museum and the actual making of the measured drawing.

This has been the beginning. When you get back to the drawing board, secure sheets of white illustration board, 20 by 30 inches, with a smooth surface. To the scale of three inches to the foot, roughly lay out the entire project. See that it fits nicely on the illustration board. When the layout has been determined, lightly draw in the design. Then use a black pencil, possibly an HB, to make a good clear outline. This is just the beginning. Line drawings are not very attractive. Discover how the piece of furniture has been put together and indicate it on the drawing. These details can be adroitly handled so as not to deface the drawing.

It is important to indicate clearly the measurements in their proper place. Lettering requires careful consideration in its placement. The title, dates and any other relevant facts should be carefully set down. The final step is the rendering. Note the light and shade indicating the grain of the wood. Bring out the moldings and stress the carving. Then the sketch will begin to have life, structure and virility. The result will be far better than any photograph, as the design will be drawn to scale and all the features brought out in proper relationship. It will be the most accurate and complete record of the piece, supplying all the information necessary to reconstruct it.

The designer who has been permitted to make a sketch in the museum is also permitted to make the piece in reproduction, but only for his own use and purpose. Any multiple reproductions for sale or commercial purposes are not to be considered. Occasionally, a manufacturer will be able to arrange with the museum for reproduction of the piece, but this is rare.

My making measured drawings in Europe was a delightful adventure which later found its way into magazines and then into book form. But it is a sad fact that measured drawings of European furniture masterpieces are more welcome in America than in Europe. Europeans seem to dislike having their furniture sketched by an American. I have come to realize that American colonial furniture from 1750 to 1830 is the most rewarding work and finds the greatest audience; my book *Masterpieces of American Furniture* has gone through several printings and continues to be most popular.

Almost every museum in the United States has some furniture on display. Surely there is one with a furniture collection near you. Good Luck! □

Inventing the Coffee Table

Antique tray generates a mahogany "reproduction"

by Eugene Landon

Though I am committed to producing exact American reproductions, I'm sometimes required to make a furniture form that simply did not exist in the 18th century. Recently a client approached me with a mahogany tray, a family heirloom, and asked if somehow it could be used to make a coffee table that would blend with her 18th-century home and other period furniture.

More than likely, the tray was not meant originally to be used as a service tray: it has through dovetails at the corners, and the practice in the 18th century was to hide the joinery. Perhaps it might have been a linen tray from inside a cabinet, where it would have been out of sight behind the doors. The tray's dimensions dictated the size of the tabletop. I stepped the rails back from that, made them 2½ in. deep, a typical size, and chose a table height of 17 in., which would match the usual height for a chair seat.

Despite the fact that there was no original to copy, I still like to call this table a reproduction, because I made it the same way a cabinetmaker would have made it then. The top, for instance, is held on with glue blocks all around. Admittedly, it may split; a lot of tops secured in this manner did, and a lot of them didn't. As far as I'm concerned, it would be nice if it did split, because it then would look old and would be a better match for the tray itself, which is split in two places. For me, doing the job right means doing it the way it would have been done originally—that's implicit in the definition of the word "reproduction." An "adaptation" is something entirely different, where one can certainly try to improve on the old methods and designs. I'm not saying you'll succeed, but you can try. Just remember that for anything you gain, there is something you can lose.

The drawback in making a tray table this long is that its tray is a bit unwieldy to carry through standard doorways. The table's size, however, is properly proportioned to go with most period sofas, and I wouldn't make it too much shorter, because it will lose some of its presence. I also recommend that you retain the lower side on the front of the tray. It gives the table an orientation, thereby adding to its character.

I'd build this table out of mahogany, walnut or cherry, since those were the woods most often used in the 18th century. Even a nice piece of curly maple could be another possibility. There are other options as well. The legs are straight Chippendale, but they could have fretwork knee blocks and other fancy decoration. The stretchers could be more elaborate and pierced, and the rails could be pierced and gadrooned, too. To focus attention on my client's antique tray, I wanted the emphasis placed on it rather than on the table. I guess you could call the effect "country high style."

When building the tray, you can make through dovetails or blind ones, whichever you prefer. For the handle cutouts, drill pairs of large holes, cut between them with a fretsaw, then round all the edges. I attached the bottom with counter-sunk flathead screws, just as the original bottom was attached with handmade ones.

For the table itself, I first cut the leg blanks and the mortises. When laying out the mortises, plan for a shoulder at the top of the rail so that the leg has some strength. The sides also should have shoulders, but you don't need one at the bottom. After making the mortises, I chamfered the inner corners of the legs. Next, I planed the flutes in the legs with an old wooden fluting plane, but you could make them with a router, drill press, tablesaw or carving tools. I like the plane because it always leaves a slight irregularity. This is very difficult to see straight-on, but if you look down the length of the leg, you will be able to spot a little wander. If the legs are too perfect, they won't look right, lacking that very subtle 18th-century character. The same goes for all of the table's rounded edges. It is best to plane them by hand, and where the plane won't reach, pare them with a chisel.

When making the rails, miter the ends of the tenons so that each has the greatest possible purchase to the mortise, but don't allow the tenons to butt against each other. You have to leave some room so that the leg can shrink without splitting.

To make the joint in the middle of the stretchers, I scribed the lines with a knife, cut inside them with a fine-tooth tenon saw, then pared with a chisel to the final fit. Notice how the overlap is offset to leave plenty of material in one stretcher for strength. Cut the tenon shoulders to match the chamfer angle on the legs. Make the tenons a little bit short at first, to establish the angle, then pare the shoulders back to fit.

I left the tray its natural color after stripping and cleaning it, and I stained the rest of the table to match by rubbing in stains and dry powders. The finish is shellac, rubbed on with a rag and some linseed oil—the usual French polish. There was a big dark stain in the center of the tray—a typical sign of an old accident, old age, so I left it. Sometimes I'll add black streaks and marks to pieces, but nothing that would be too noticeable. When I make a reproduction, I expect that my client will be able to set it down in the middle of a room full of 18th-century furniture and have it disappear. This takes a little work. I have a friend who wanted to learn woodworking. So I got him into my shop every Friday from four in the afternoon until about eleven, and we each made identical pie safes. Finally the pieces were done, and it came time to do the antiquing. I handed him a chain and said, "Go to it," and he handed it right back and said, "You first, I can't bear it." So I started beating up my cabinet, then I kicked it across the room until I could hear it crack. I said, "Now we're getting there . . ." And pretty soon he got the idea. You can use your own judgment, but remember that many old pieces have led a hard life, and look it. □

Gene Landon makes and restores period furniture in Montoursville, Pa. See page 6 for more on his methods.

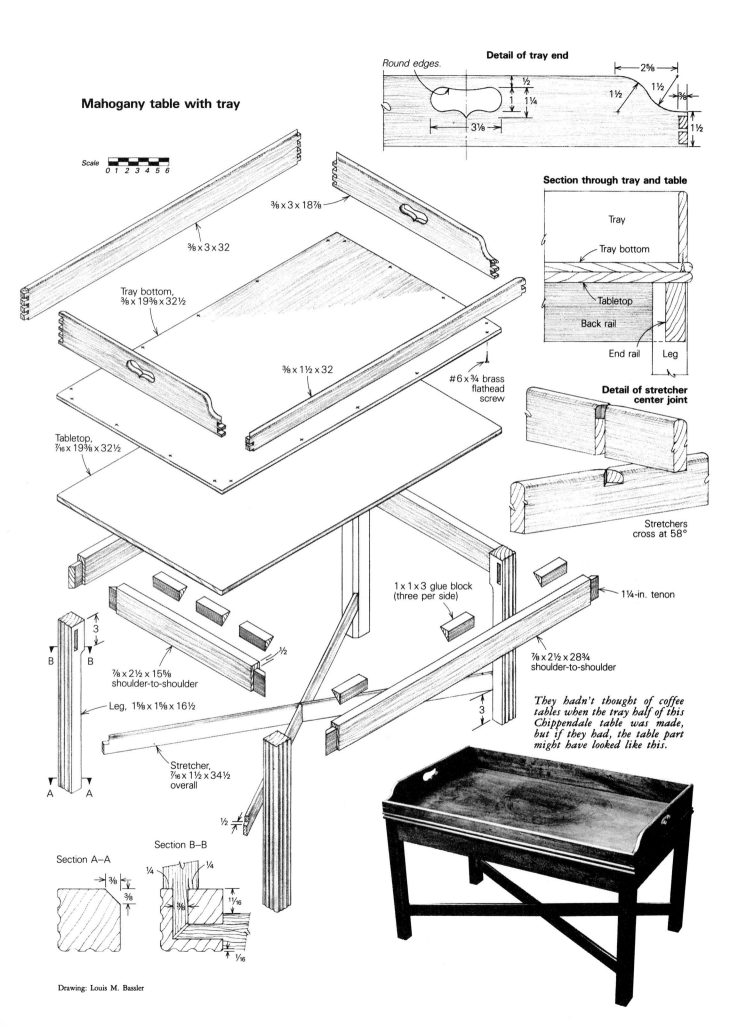

Mahogany table with tray

Scale
0 1 2 3 4 5 6

Detail of tray end

Round edges.

⅜ x 3 x 18⅞

⅜ x 3 x 32

Tray bottom,
⅜ x 19⅜ x 32½

⅜ x 1½ x 32

Tabletop,
7/16 x 19⅜ x 32½

#6 x ¾ brass
flathead
screw

Section through tray and table

Tray

Tray bottom

Tabletop

Back rail

End rail   Leg

**Detail of stretcher
center joint**

Stretchers
cross at 58°

1 x 1 x 3 glue block
(three per side)

1¼-in. tenon

⅞ x 2½ x 28¾
shoulder-to-shoulder

⅞ x 2½ x 15⅝
shoulder-to-shoulder

Leg, 1⅝ x 1⅝ x 16½

Stretcher,
7/16 x 1½ x 34½
overall

*They hadn't thought of coffee
tables when the tray half of this
Chippendale table was made,
but if they had, the table part
might have looked like this.*

Section A–A

Section B–B

Drawing: Louis M. Bassler

Contour Tracer

by Carlyle Lynch

If you have ever tried to copy something as complicated as a cabriole leg, you will appreciate this homemade instrument. A thin edge of clear Plexiglas is simply slid along the profile of the object being copied while the index finger rests gently on top of a pen set into the pylon. Because the pen touches the pattern cardboard at a point immediately under the tracer edge, the dimensions of your tracing will correspond exactly to those of the object.

Each part to be traced must be positioned differently. For example, a piecrust tabletop would be placed directly on the cardboard; the leg of a Queen Anne lowboy would have to be supported horizontally above the cardboard. To trace the post of a four-poster bed, a piece of plywood with smooth cardboard taped to its surface must be clamped vertically to the square part of the post. The tracer, which is held horizontally, is then run up the side of the post against the cardboard.

I used white pine for the upright pylon of the tracer and ⅛-in. birch plywood for the base. The Plexiglas strip is 1/16 in. thick, its long edge beveled to 1/32 in. then sanded smooth. It is inserted into a 1/16-in. by 5/16-in. deep groove in the edge of the pylon—a 7-in. diameter hollow-ground plywood-cutting sawblade cuts the groove for a deliciously snug fit. A 1/16-in. router bit, a machinist's slitting sawblade or a scratch beader made from a ground piece of file tang will also do the job. (To make your own scratch beader, see page 96.)

A 5/16-in. hole is drilled through the lower part of the pylon at an angle of 60° to the base to provide a sliding fit for a no. 25 Scripto medium-point ballpoint pen. If you use the equivalent Bic pen, which is slightly larger in diameter, ream out the hole with a 21/64-in. drill bit. Below and at a right angle to this hole, drill a tapping hole with a no. 9 twist drill, drilling into the hole for the pen. Tap this ¼-20 for a ¾-in. long thumbscrew. (A thumbscrew can be fashioned from a fillister-head machine screw into whose screwdriver slot a piece of 1/16-in. thick metal is sweat-soldered—brass preferred for looks.) The thumbscrew bears against a ½-in. long piece of 3/16-in. dowel, which puts a slight drag on the pen and prevents it from sliding out of place when the tracer is lifted. You may find that you can adjust the pen nicely enough not to have to steady it with your finger when the tracer is in use.

Materials

Pylon	¾ x ½ – 2⅞ x 12	white pine
Base	⅛ x 4¾ x 6¼	birch plywood
Dowel	3/16 dia. x ½ long	birch
Tracer	1/16 x 1 5/16 x 12	clear Plexiglas
Flat-head wood screws (2)	¾ x 5	
Thumbscrew	¼ x 20, ¾ long	
No. 25 Scripto ballpoint pen, 5¾ long		

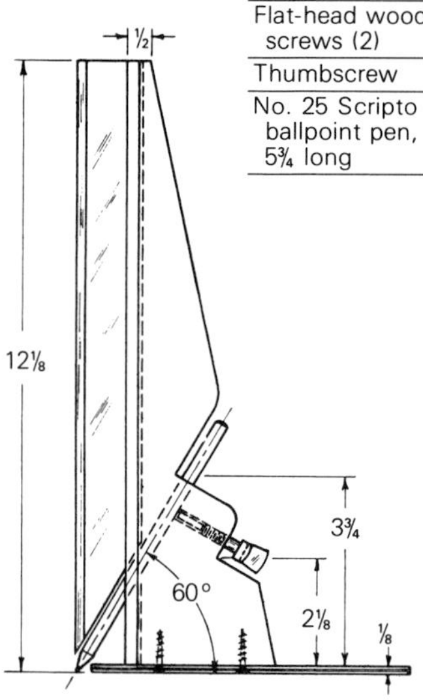

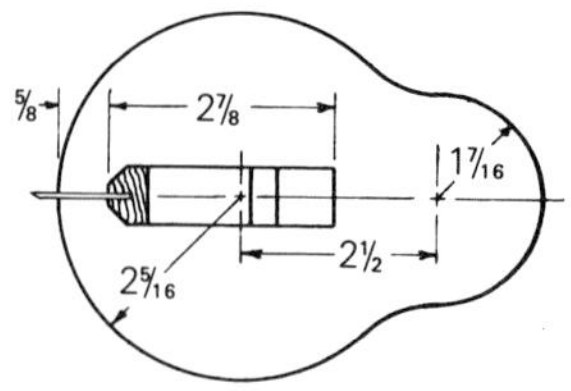

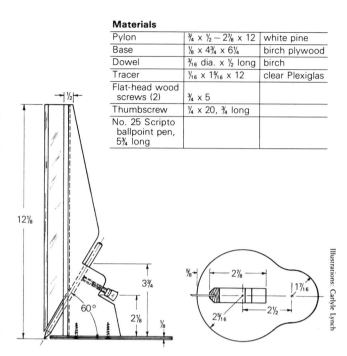

Illustrations: Carlyle Lynch

Fasten the base to the upright with two ¾ x 5 flat-head wood screws countersunk slightly to avoid scratching the pattern cardboard. I recommend light brown mounting board available from picture framers. It is smooth and dense, and can be purchased 3/64 in. thick in sheets 30 in. by 40 in.

Assemble the instrument and adjust the point of the pen to touch the cardboard precisely under the tracer edge. You may have to trim a tiny amount from the base of the pylon. Remove the tracer blade and brush on your finish, keeping it out of the tracer groove. If the groove will not friction-hold the Plexiglas blade, use a couple of dots of epoxy glue. □

Teacher, writer and craftsman Carlyle Lynch, of Broadway, Va., is the author of Furniture Antiques Found in Virginia.

Cabriole Templates

by Charles F. Riordan

Regarding the method of copying a cabriole leg: I secure a piece of stiff, white cardboard so that it cannot move against the side of the leg, and use a point source of light to throw a sharp shadow on the cardboard. The parts that touch the cardboard are traced directly, and where the parts curve away, you have a sharp outline to trace with no fear of a wobbling pencil giving false lines. The light has to be placed far enough away so it has no tendency to magnify the shadow and it has to be on a direct line perpendicular to the leg. Determine the best distance by calipering the leg and measuring the shadow to make sure they are the same. A good source of light is a slide projector, a quartz-iodine bulb or projector bulb.

Another good method is to use the replacement cylinder from a ball-point pen (no pencil-lead wear) fastened with a few drops of epoxy glue to a flat block of wood. The block size is immaterial, since all it does is cancel pen-point wobble.

I use both methods, and both work well. I also have used photography to copy shapes, forms and carvings in making exact copies of antique and other furniture pieces. Nothing like a good

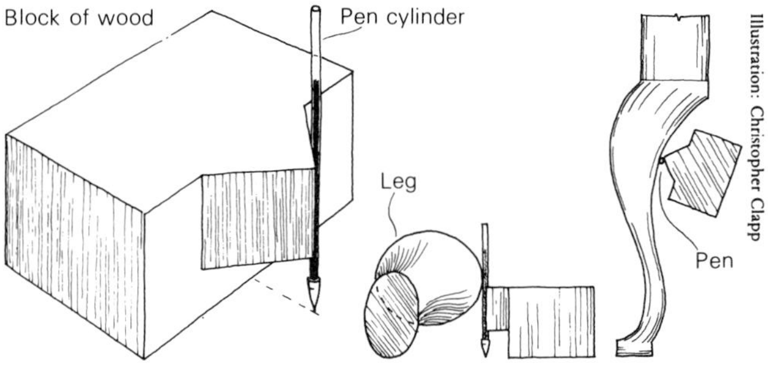

Illustration: Christopher Clapp

camera with a ground-glass view back for making an exact copy of a piece, with a scale included so that one may make an exact-sized enlargement and then chop it up into an exact stencil. □

Charles Riordan restores and reproduces period furniture in Dansville, N.Y.

Applying Classical Proportions
A tea table built to 18th-century rules

by Mack S. Headley, Jr.

After sixteen years of restoring, reproducing and studying 18th-century furniture, I have joined the ranks of those who are convinced that the traditional artisan relied on a geometric proportioning system, based on the five classical orders. As a design exercise to test how the system might have been applied, I built the small table shown here.

Evidence of the system's use is widespread, but vague. Chippendale, quoted below, clearly stated that knowledge of the five orders was basic to the cabinetmaker's art. Some furniture historians insist that Chippendale was exaggerating, but Marcus Wiffen's observations about the character of Virginia buildings, also quoted below, agree with Chippendale. Many 18th- and early 19th-century design books also feature the classical orders, but, like Chippendale, don't tell exactly how the rules were used in designing furniture. This seems to have been privileged information, imparted during apprenticeship. In earlier times, I suspect it was one of the guarded secrets of the furnituremaking and architectural guilds.

I found that the only path toward understanding how the system was used was to go back to the pieces themselves. Surviving examples of period furniture have a great diversity of character, varying with the time and place they were built,

the current style (and how it was evolving), and the environment in which they would be placed. To unravel the complexity, I decided to concentrate on the design work of one man, Peter Scott, a Williamsburg, Va., cabinetmaker from 1722 to 1776. Thanks to Wallace Gusler, curator of furniture at Colonial Williamsburg, I was able to study numerous pieces in the collection. Scott's lifetime production is impressive, and filled with subtle variation, control and flair. Yet all his proportions are derived from the five orders: Tuscan, Doric, Ionic, Corinthian and Composite. Upon scale drawings of many of his pieces I have walked with my dividers for hours, discovering geometric relationships which encompass the whole piece—from its major negative and positive spaces to its actual structural elements, moldings and ornaments.

The origins of this design system reach back at least to the Greeks, from whom the Romans borrowed it. And it later served European craftsmen from the Renaissance to the beginning of the Industrial Age. The earliest surviving writings come from the first century AD, *The Ten Books of Architecture* by Vitruvius. He explains that the proportional relationships used in architecture were derived by "the ancients" from the relationships observed in living things. Leonardo

Of all the arts which are either improved or ornamented by architecture, that of cabinet-making is not only the most useful and ornamental, but capable of receiving as great assistance from it as any whatever.... Without an acquaintance with [the five orders], and some knowledge of the rules of perspective, the cabinet-maker cannot make the designs of his work intelligible, nor show, in a little compass, the whole conduct and effect of the piece. These, therefore, ought to be carefully studied by everyone who would excel in this branch, since they are the very soul and basis of his art.
> —Thomas Chippendale, *The Gentleman & Cabinet-Maker's Director*, 1762

We need not be surprised if we find a high degree of standardization in the design of the eighteenth-century houses of Williamsburg, or of Virginia. The eighteenth century was an age that built according to the rules—the rules handed down in the shops of the various crafts, and the rules set down in the books on architecture. (Which is not to say that the two categories did not overlap, for shop rules were the staple of the authors of many handbooks, and book rules doubtless became the rote-learned formulae of the shops.) But the rules were felt to provide a discipline, not a straitjacket; and always the final appeal, in any disputed question of design, was to the eye.
> —Marcus Whiffen, *The Eighteenth-Century Houses of Williamsburg*, 1960

This walnut tea table isn't a reproduction, but a new design that conforms to classical rules of proportion.

John Westerveldt

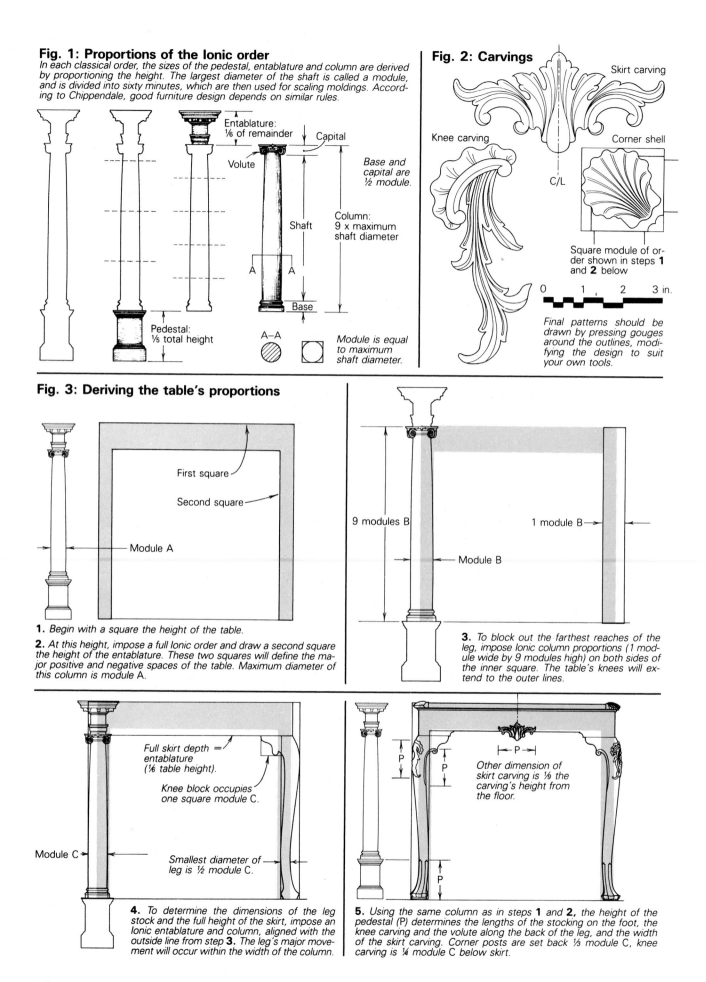

Fig. 1: Proportions of the Ionic order

In each classical order, the sizes of the pedestal, entablature and column are derived by proportioning the height. The largest diameter of the shaft is called a module, and is divided into sixty minutes, which are then used for scaling moldings. According to Chippendale, good furniture design depends on similar rules.

Entablature: ⅙ of remainder

Capital

Volute

Base and capital are ½ module.

Shaft

Column: 9 x maximum shaft diameter

A A

Base

Pedestal: ⅕ total height

A–A

Module is equal to maximum shaft diameter.

Fig. 2: Carvings

Skirt carving

Knee carving

C/L

Corner shell

Square module of order shown in steps **1** and **2** below

0   1   2   3 in.

Final patterns should be drawn by pressing gouges around the outlines, modifying the design to suit your own tools.

Fig. 3: Deriving the table's proportions

First square

Second square

Module A

1. *Begin with a square the height of the table.*

2. *At this height, impose a full Ionic order and draw a second square the height of the entablature. These two squares will define the major positive and negative spaces of the table. Maximum diameter of this column is module A.*

9 modules B

Module B

1 module B

3. *To block out the farthest reaches of the leg, impose Ionic column proportions (1 module wide by 9 modules high) on both sides of the inner square. The table's knees will extend to the outer lines.*

Full skirt depth = entablature (⅙ table height).

Knee block occupies one square module C.

Module C

Smallest diameter of leg is ½ module C.

4. *To determine the dimensions of the leg stock and the full height of the skirt, impose an Ionic entablature and column, aligned with the outside line from step 3. The leg's major movement will occur within the width of the column.*

P

P

P

Other dimension of skirt carving is ⅛ the carving's height from the floor.

P

5. *Using the same column as in steps 1 and 2, the height of the pedestal (P) determines the lengths of the stocking on the foot, the knee carving and the volute along the back of the leg, and the width of the skirt carving. Corner posts are set back ⅓ module C, knee carving is ¼ module C below skirt.*

da Vinci's famous drawing of a spread-eagled man contained within a circle is based on instructions found in Vitruvius, who enumerates other ideal proportions as well. Actual human proportions conform to the ideal more or less for any particular person. By representing the variations, the classical orders portray character from the most masculine, Doric and Tuscan, to the most feminine, Corinthian and Composite. In antiquity, the order chosen for a particular temple or building depended on the character of the god it memorialized, or upon the building's intended use. Vitruvius attempted to codify the ancient proportions, but, as in people, the numbers are not absolute—the rules are guides to be followed with taste and discretion, not scientific formulas.

In each of the five orders, the rules for constructing a column with its pedestal and entablature are based on what its height will be. Figure 1 illustrates the basic directions Chippendale gave for the Ionic order. Similar procedures apply to the other orders as well. In every case, for each part, including the curves of the moldings, a rule is derived from what has gone before. In furniture, the rules appear to be less rigid. Relationships may be based on one of the columns alone or, as I chose for my table, on an order's proportions in various combinations of pedestal, column and entablature.

My plan at the outset was to build a small walnut tea table of moderate decoration. A number of pieces in Williamsburg were influenced by Oriental design. I liked this quality, and suggested it in the shape of the top molding. Many tea tables have knee blocks that run the width of the skirt, from leg to leg. Instead, I applied a small central carving. In addition, I had found a lovely three-million-year-old fossilized shell across the James River from Williamsburg, and decided to add its shape as a block at the corners, to soften them. The carvings on the knee, top and skirt (figure 2) called for something on the foot, so I designed a light stocking. In spite of so many personal design choices, which make the table unlike any single example in the Williamsburg collection, it is, because it was built using the same design vocabulary and the same family of relationships, still something like them all.

The system works whether you apply geometry or numerical measurements. In one surviving piece, Peter Scott used geometry. He drew lines directly on the back of the lower case to proportion the upper section, dividing the back into sixths and projecting diagonals. As an aid to visualizing how my table grew from Ionic proportions, figure 3 shows both the basic square I started with and the three particular sets of proportions I used to determine the actual shape of the table. Instead of a square, I could have begun with a rectangle that was a square-and-a-quarter, a square-and-a-half, or another such simple combination. In end view, for example, the table is twice as high as it is wide, or two squares high. When actually working out the design myself, I found it most convenient to use a calculator to determine the mathematical value of the geometric relationships. I roughly approximated the sizes I wanted the parts to be, then calculated exact sizes by means of Ionic proportions and laid these sizes out on scale drawings. If a part then looked too small, I chose the next larger Ionic relationship and used that instead.

The joinery is simple mortise-and-tenon. The mortises begin ½ in. below the top of the legs to preserve the strength of the upper post. The ends of the tenons are mitered and do not touch each other in the mortise. The ¾-in. long tenons on the top molding fit into the shell blocks, and the molding is grooved to accept the top, which can expand and contract with changes in humidity. The knee blocks are glued in place. The central leaf-element was carved and applied to the skirt, and its projection backed up with secondary wood.

As do the more sophisticated 18th-century examples, the table has an animalistic stance with continuous curves in its legs—no flat, straight spots. Continuous curves are essential to avoid dead spots on legs and carvings. To tune the sculptural curves at knees and ankles, I used my larger, broad-sweep gouges. Sets of carving tools are designed around spiraling curves so that they can be used in various combinations, to control the movement of the spirals and S-curves both in overall sculpturing and in detailing. The larger the variety of gouges, the more control a carver has over the potential movement in a piece. The last master of the original shop in Williamsburg had 94 carving chisels and gouges. Not all would be needed for this table. For the details, you can modify the patterns shown in figure 2 so that they conform to your set of tools. Choose gouges that come close to matching the outline, stamp your pattern according to their curves, and transfer it to the work.

Acquiring experience within this system has been tedious, with lots of new terminology and concepts to understand and integrate. At times I have felt restrained and at other times stretched by where I am being led. But like learning any new language, fluency comes and expression becomes subtler. I no longer feel restricted by it, and in my small shop where diversity of production is important to me, I find that executing a new design is faster, and that the system is an invaluable tool in achieving effective traditional form.

There is another advantage, perhaps more important to the historian than to the furnituremaker. Once the particular classical order to which a piece belongs is understood, its dimensions scale out very close (say, to ⅛ in.) to the hypothetical ideal. The system therefore is helpful in interpreting possible distortions in photographs, as well as aiding in the regeneration of missing parts in restoration work. And despite the freedom of choice enjoyed by the designer, there is more to the modular system than mere coincidence—many outright fake antiques and many modern pieces made "in the style of" can be spotted after just a few measurements have been taken: the system simply isn't there. □

Mack Headley, Jr., makes furniture in Winchester, Va.
For more on the art of proportioning, see "Tall Chests" by Timothy Philbrick on pages 37 to 41.

Further reading

Benjamin, Asher, *The American Builder's Companion,* Dover Publications, Inc., New York, 1969.

Chippendale, Thomas, *The Gentleman & Cabinet-Maker's Director,* Dover Publications, Inc., New York, 1966.

Gibbs, James, *A Book of Architecture,* Arno Press, Inc., New York, 1980.

Herter, Christine, *Dynamic Symmetry,* W.W. Norton & Co., New York, 1966.

Palladio, Andrea, *The Four Books of Architecture,* Dover Publications, Inc., New York, 1965.

Vitruvius, *The Ten Books of Architecture,* Dover Publications, Inc., New York, 1960.

Ware, William R., *The American Vignola,* International Textbook Co., Scranton, Pa., 1904.

Whiffen, Marcus, *The Eighteenth-Century Houses of Williamsburg,* Colonial Williamsburg, Inc., Williamsburg, Va., 1960.

Grand Highboys

Genius in Philadelphia

by Lester Margon

It is remarkable that so many cabinetmakers from various sections of the Colonies gathered in Philadelphia during the latter part of the 18th century. The roster includes such famous names as Thomas Affleck, William Savery, John Gillingham, Benjamin Randolph, Jonathan Shoemaker, Jonathan Gostelowe and a long list of equally skilled artisans. These men worked independently, but produced furniture of similar design and tremendous proportions. The result was a Chippendale-inspired school that was so firmly knit it seems as if they worked together. They made tall cabinets, secretaries, desks, mirrors and dining and living room furniture. But their greatest achievement was the highboy and tall chest of drawers, pinnacles in the history of cabinetmaking.

This extraordinary explosion of talent began around 1680 when William Penn squired a group of craftsmen from the Rhine Valley who settled near Philadelphia. These artisans were not willing merely to copy the European prototypes. They considered them too detailed with many intricacies that were foreign to the free-thinking conceptions of the colonists. Their work was of highest quality, even surpassing their contemporaries in England, and Philadelphia became one of the world's principal centers of cabinetmaking.

One of the foremost Philadelphia cabinetmakers was Thomas Affleck, a Scot, who was trained in England and emigrated to America in 1763. He made furniture for many wealthy and important people, among them the governor, who bought Affleck's beautiful Chinese Chippendale furniture. Affleck was the paramount figure in the cabinet and chair-making crafts and the leader of the Philadelphia Chippendale school.

Dozens of pieces of furniture have been attributed to Affleck. Today his work is considered the finest example of the Philadelphia Chippendale style. During the Revolution he sympathized with the Royalists, but this did not seem to affect the continued demand for his furniture. The important thing was his ability to produce elegant furniture for the stately manor houses then being built.

After Affleck's death in 1795, his son Lewis advertised in the Philadelphia papers that he would carry on in his father's shop. However, Lewis was not successful and soon gave up.

In the latter part of the 18th century, as people became affluent, the manor house found favor in the cities. This stately classical form of architecture featured living-room ceilings that reached a height of 10 ft. or more. The cabinetmakers of the day tried to satisfy the increasing demand for elegant furniture to fit into these interiors. One result was the high chest, which often reached 9 ft. tall, including the carved center ornaments. These cabinets contained many drawers to

This impressive Chippendale-style chest-on-chest, now part of the Philadelphia Museum of Art collection, is attributed to Thomas Affleck, c. 1775. The bonnet top features a double scroll with pierced fretwork. At the center, an arrangement of oak leaves and acorns grows out of a basket. The flamelike pattern of the mahogany veneer is particularly elegant.

hold the necessary service articles for gracious entertaining. The demand for these highboys was tremendous and as they became the center of attention in the fashionable living room, their prices became astronomical. This trend continues today: A highboy recently brought $40,000 at auction. The appraised value of the original Kittinger high chest, which some experts attribute to Affleck and now part of the Yale University collection, is $100,000.

Each part of these Philadelphia highboys was expertly made. Aprons were fashioned in cyma curves; stretchers flowed in graceful lineation. Flowers, rosettes, urns and principal pinnacles were exquisitely turned and often included graceful cartouches. Featured at the top of the crown were pediments perforated at the center to receive flaming torches, turned finials, baskets of flowers or perhaps the bust of a fair lady. Chippendale fretwork was often applied around the upper portion along with carved festoons, drapery effects and stalactites. Pilasters were fluted and corners chamfered or decorated with carved flowers and leaves.

Caribbean mahogany was perfect for carving and the Philadelphia cabinetmakers were masterful carvers. The precise scale and placement of the carving was a matter that received careful study. Restraint was mandatory. Carving is like the icing on a cake: It must be just right or it will appear superfluous. ☐

Lester Margon was widely known for his books of measured drawings; see page 11. His More American Furniture Treasures, Architectural Book Publishing Co., New York, 1971, *contains measured drawings of the tall chests pictured here.*

This high chest from the collection of the Museum of the Rhode Island School of Design is also attributed to Thomas Affleck, c. 1765. The two applied carved panels on the drawers at top and bottom contain concave shell carvings for depth. Convex shell carvings appear at the knees of the cabriole legs.

Tall Chests

The art of proportioning

by Timothy Philbrick

As colors can evoke emotions within us, or combinations of notes and tempos suggest joy or sorrow, so can proportions in furniture produce a desired effect on viewers. Objects built to the same proportions, although different in period, style and composition, can still evoke similar reactions. Proportions set up and define the framework within which the furniture maker expresses himself. The very selection of proportions, or lack of selection, affects the success of the maker's intention as perhaps no other single factor can. In furniture studies, the often-used term "integration of design" must be explained in proportional terms, as well as in terms of structure and decoration.

The esthetics of proportion is today a lost, or at best a well-hidden, science because of the current clinical separation of science from art. The following investigation is an attempt to uncover proportioning systems used by 18th-century cabinetmakers. It should be of use to designers and connoisseurs today.

Most texts on 18th-century furniture contain comments such as, "The old workmen had an instinct for good design." Their authors assume that master cabinetmakers and craftsmen had some mysterious, built-in instinct for proportioning. While this may be true of some country cabinetmakers, great design is not just a "feeling," but a carefully planned and consciously applied system of relationships, learned in a rigorous apprenticeship to an old tradition.

Proving that a system of proportions has been deliberately applied in a piece of furniture is no easy task. In studying a piece of furniture, one can easily be misled into finding those ratios one sets out to find. Unfortunately, little research has been done on the subject and few written records of proportioning systems exist. Ratios were passed on verbally during the cabinetmaker's seven-year apprenticeship. The phrase "Art and Mystery of the trade," seen in the apprenticeship contracts of the period, refers to the study of proportions and geometry, together with skills and techniques. Unfortunately, the "Arts and Mysteries" were a verbal tradition and are now extinct.

Naturally, all furniture has some proportions in common for it must conform to the proportions of the human body. If furniture is to be functional sculpture, its height must relate to its purpose and this measurement will serve as a starting point in calculating proportions. The Danish furniture de-

Timothy Philbrick served a five-year apprenticeship restoring and reproducing 18th-century furniture. He now owns a cabinet shop in Narragansett, R.I., specializing in contemporary furniture based on classical proportions.

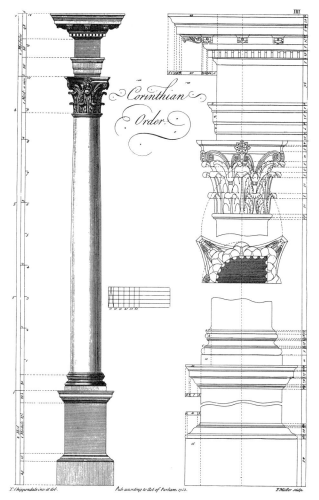

The Corinthian order, from Chippendale (Dover reprint, 1966). Column is scaled in 'modules' that equal its diameter, moldings at right are dimensioned in sixtieths of a module.

signer Kaare Klint has defined optimum chair height at 16 to 18 in., table height 28 to 30 in., standing working height 40 to 42 in., maximum vision height 54 to 56 in., and maximum reach 76 to 84 in. These measurements are not new; they served the 18th century as well as modern society.

Great American high-style furniture designers also used traditional proportions long known in buildings, paintings and furniture. Whole numbers have been important since classical times: Whole numbers and their simple relationships (1:2, 2:3, 3:4, 4:5, 5:6, 6:7, etc, and 3:5 etc) were the expression of perfection and, therefore, the divine. These simple relationships have been the framework for a vast amount of artistic creation. The medieval artist had little mathematical knowledge, but knew well how to use his compass, so the basic division of the square and circle naturally was his proportioning vocabulary.

As Arabic geometry began to permeate the decorative arts of the 13th century, the tools for the Renaissance were provided. A reverence for geometry and mathematics as the ultimate expression of perfection was even more pronounced. The basis of the Renaissance desire for simple, measurable relationships was the concept of universal proportions. These concepts from Renaissance Italy first began to affect American furniture in the late 17th century in the William and Mary

style. The major dimensions are made divisible by a common integer, 5 or 6 usually, in the basic combinations of 2:3, 3:4, and 4:5. Press cupboards for example, tend to be in the ratio of 4:5, width to height (e.g., if the width is 48 in., the height is 60 in.). In the early 18th century, with the advent of the Queen Anne style, visual proportion and geometric ratio are expressed in both furniture and architecture. In Queen Anne chairs, for example, heights to widths of backs, and heights of legs to widths of seats are directly proportional.

The Chippendale style

In the second half of the 18th century, an increasingly pervasive emphasis was placed on the importance of classicism. From James Gibb's *Rules for Drawing the Several Orders* (1731), Chippendale's *Director* (1754) and *The Carpenter's Co. of Philadelphia 1786 Rule Book*, to the work of Thomas Sheraton (1791-1794), the proportions of the five classical orders of columns became one of the most widely written-about topics. Thomas Chippendale, in his introduction to the first edition (1754) of his *Gentleman and Cabinet-maker's Director*, says: ''I have prefixed to the following designs a short explanation of the five orders. These ought to be carefully studied by everyone who would excel in this branch, since they are the very soul and basis of his art.''

Chippendale felt these orders and their proportions important enough to devote the first eight plates of his book to drawings and descriptions of their proportioning. Throughout Chippendale's work, emphasis is constantly placed on the ratio of height to width. Even the contours and form of moldings are worked out by a specific system. In Chippendale's drawings Rococo decoration and ornament are united with disciplined geometrical principles.

In the work of Thomas Sheraton, classical proportion is given an even more elaborate role. His drawings, like Chippendale's, are presented in a precisely proportioned framework. His introduction informs us that the first part of his book ''provides the workman with geometrical lines applied to various purposes in the cabinet branch, (which) can not be subject to alteration any more than the principles of reason itself.'' The first 146 pages of Sheraton's *Drawing Book* are devoted to geometry, including 30 pages on the five orders; the remainder are studies of perspective, showing how to obtain working measurements from perspective drawings.

The importance of the five orders to these men is hard for us to understand today. Sheraton explained it this way: ''Many cabinetmakers are found desirous of having a knowledge of the five orders, and the proportions of the several frontispieces...I believe that the orders are now brought to such perfection in their proportions as will bear the strictest mathematical examination...I consider them incapable of improvement.'' He also wrote that nothing more worthy can appear in a drawing book and that a knowledge of these moldings and proportionings is necessary to any man of culture and to all craftsmen.

The golden section is probably the most ancient and widely revered proportional system. It has been used for such diverse purposes as establishing the date of Easter and proportioning Jacques Villon's paintings and Le Corbusier's buildings. In antiquity, Egyptian and Druid builders alike used the golden section to plan their temples and to proportion other artwork. The golden section represents the division of a line into two parts such that the smaller part is to the larger as the larger is to the whole. In the diagram below, BC : AB = AB : AC. The geometrical division of a line into these proportions is fairly

A————————————————B————————C

straightforward with compass and rule. But if the length BC = 1, algebraic determination of the length AB requires solution of a quadratic equation and produces an endless decimal whose first few terms are 1.61803. A rectangle with sides 1 and 1.618 is known as the golden rectangle. Among its many interesting properties is the fact that if a square is cut off one end, the smaller rectangle that remains is the same shape as the original, that is its short side is still related to its long side as 1 is to 1.618. For most practical purposes, the golden section may be expressed as the ratio 5:8.

Great mysticism surrounded this proportion until recent times. Described as being like God because it is unique, and like the Trinity in that it is one proportion in three terms, the construction of the golden section has always been among the secrets of the Masonic Guilds. Gibbs, Hogarth, Burlington, Thornhill, Washington, Jefferson, Harrison and many other famous men of the 18th century were Freemasons, an order which still claims to have preserved through the ages the secrets of perfect and ideal proportions.

One of the few surviving records of an American cabinetmaker's predetermination of proportions is found on an unclear sketch by Samuel Mickle, who was apprenticed to Philadelphia cabinetmaker Shoemaker in 1765. On the sketch is the notation, ''The Heighth of ye Book Case is 3:6 inclusive of ye top, ye width of ye Book Case is 3:5.'' It is difficult to know just where and how the cabinetmaker is applying these proportions from this cryptic bit of information. However, this sketch stands as a major document, for it conclusively proves the consideration of proportion in the design of a piece of furniture.

Examples of proportioning

In the following study, two drawings from Mickle's sketchbooks and three 18th-century American highboys are examined for proportional relationships. In looking for such relationships, one should not expect to find absolute mathematical precision: A drawing is flat and a pencil line has no thickness, while wooden furniture exists in three dimensions and every piece of wood has thickness. Thus a proportional scheme worked out on paper, no matter how elegant, can't be exactly translated to solid wood. In sketching a piece of furniture, the cabinetmaker would first set up a proportional framework, then detail the drawing within the grid. Once the cabinetmaker has chosen his proportions, nothing compels him to follow them rigidly. Variations would be made for esthetic reasons, and to solve mechanical problems.

Confusion also occurs because immigrant cabinetmakers trained in different national traditions would have used different reference points to set out their proportions, and the style of furniture made in 18th-century Philadelphia would not be exactly the same as that made far away in Newport, R. I. It is nonetheless remarkable that so many definite relationships that reduce to small, whole-number ratios can be found within each piece, and can be found in common among several fine antiques.

I believe the examples on this page and the following two pages demonstrate that 18th-century artisans were well aware of proportions, and provide sufficient evidence for serious

Chippendale dressing table, from Mickle sketchbook, 1765. Handwritten notes are transcribed in the text below.

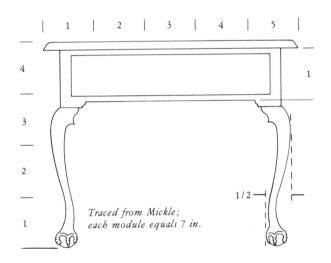

*Traced from Mickle;
each module equals 7 in.*

contemporary study. I cannot describe my own excitement, after studying an antique for several hours and measuring from many points, upon suddenly seeing a relationship.

The photograph above, of a page in Mickle's sketchbook (Philadelphia Museum of Art, gift of Walter M. Jeffords), shows a Chippendale dressing table. The front elevation has been traced from the original to display the proportions. Mickle's notes say, ''Top 2 feet 11 inches long and 17-1/2 inches wide; the draw 2 feet 3-1/2 inches long and 5-1/2 inches wide; the frame 2 feet 6 inches long and 24 inches wide from out to out.''

The drawer width, 5-1/2 in., added to the 3/4-in. thickness of the rails above and below it, produces a module of 7 in. The principal dimensions of the table may be expressed in terms of this module.

The top is 35 in. by 17-1/2 in., or 5 modules by 2-1/2 modules, a 2:1 ratio. The table is 28 in. high (4 modules); its height to its width is as 4 is to 5. The legs are 3-1/2 in. wide, half a module, and thus the height of the table is to the width of the leg as 8 is to 1, exactly the same as the classical Corinthian column pictured on the opposite page.

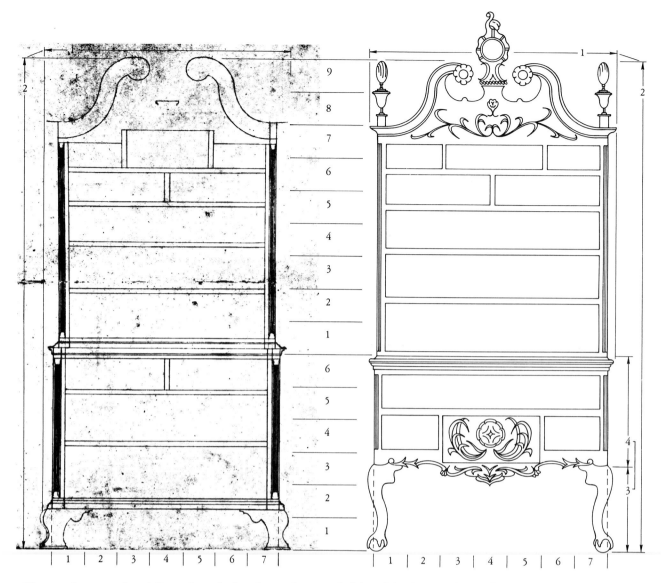

The exactly proportioned front view of a handsome chest-on-chest above is also taken from Mickle's sketchbook (Philadelphia Museum of Art). The original was drawn at 3/32 in. to the inch. The overall height of the chest (from the floor to the top of the pediment) is 90 in.; the overall width (measured at the knees) is 45 in.—a 2:1 ratio. Within this rectangle are two boxes, defined by the mid-molding. The lower chest is 36 in. high, 42 in. wide (from the sides) and 21 in. deep (from an auxiliary view). The upper chest is 42 in. high from molding to cornice, 54 in. high to the top of the pediment, and 40 in. wide. Thus the lower chest is twice as wide as it is deep, and its height is related to its width as 6 is to 7. The upper chest is exactly as high as the lower chest is wide, which is to say the height of the upper is to the height of the lower as 7 is to 6. The height of the upper chest, including pediment, is related to the height of the lower chest to the mid-molding as 9 is to 6, or 3:2. The width of the chest has been divided into seven equal parts (a module of 6 in.) and the height has been stepped off in the same increments.

This drawing, because of its authenticity and lack of confusing detail, is an excellent subject for speculative exploration with a pair of dividers and a scale. For example, the height of the legs is just half the height of the curved braces that form the pediment, and very close to twice the height of the cluster of moldings and rails that divides the chest. The height of the feet plus the bottom moldings is the same as the height of the bottom drawer front. And each drawer front, plus the rail on which it sits, is just as high as the drawer front below it, without rail, except at the mid-molding itself.

The front-view drawing above is a photo tracing of a majestic Philadelphia highboy, now a part of the Mabel Brady Garvan collection at the Yale University Art Gallery. This piece is the original of the well-known Kittinger reproduction and has been appraised at $100,000. Its dimensions and basic proportions are virtually identical to those found in the Mickle drawing: overall 90 in. high and 45 in. wide, a 2:1 ratio. The lower chest is 43 in. wide, 21-1/2 in. deep (2:1) and 36 in. high (width-to-height is almost 7:6); the upper chest is 42 in. high to the cornice and 42 in. wide (1:1), and the upper chest is exactly as high as the lower is wide. The upper chest from mid-molding to the top of the pediment is 54 in., as in the Mickle drawing, a 3:2 ratio to the height of the lower chest. Each increment along the bottom and left side represents a 6-in. module.

Furthermore, the legs are 15-1/2 in. high and the lower case is 20-1/2 in. high, a ratio of 3:4. The small lower side drawers are each one-quarter of the total width between the corner posts, and the central carved drawer is just as wide as the engaged fluted quarter-columns are high. The drawers in the upper case progress as before: Each drawer front, plus the rail on which it sits, is as high as the drawer below it.

The photograph above is of yet another revolutionary-era Philadelphia highboy (Museum of Fine Arts, Boston). At first glance this antique chest appears identical to the previous one, but close examination reveals that not only does it differ in details of ornamentation, but also it is a full 4-1/2 in. shorter. Yet if the overall measurements are taken at the sides of the base rather than at the mid-molding, the proportional scheme is virtually identical. For while the chest is only 85-1/2 in. high, the base is 43 in. wide (2:1) and 21-1/2 in. deep (also 2:1). The height of the base is 36 in., as before a ratio of almost 6:7 to its width, and the height of the leg is related to the height of the lower case as 3 is to 4. The upper chest is 41 in. high to the cornice and 41-1/2 in. wide, a virtual square; its height measures 49-1/2 in. from the mid-molding to the top of the pediment, very close to a 4:3 ratio to the height of the lower chest. If the width of the lower chest is swung up vertically from the mid-molding, it lands at the base of the finials and at the bottom of the pediment cut-outs, while before it landed at the cornice itself.

The central carved drawer is 16-3/4 in. wide and the fluted quarter-columns are 16-3/4 in. high. And once again the drawer fronts seem to progress: Each front, plus the rail on which it sits, is as high as the drawer front below it.

Finally, the photograph of a 1760 Newport highboy at right (Museum of Fine Arts, Boston) has been converted to a

photo tracing, above. While this chest is quite different from the Philadelphia examples, and at 81 in. high is smaller, proportional relationships can still be found. Its overall width at the knees is 40-3/4 in., the usual 1:2 ratio to overall height. But here the similarities end. On one hand, the mid-molding can be considered part of the base, as in the Philadelphia chests, giving a base height of 37-1/2 in. The lower case is 39 in. wide, a height-to-width ratio very close to square, and the leg height, 18-1/2 in., is about half the base height. On the other hand, the mid-molding is actually fastened to the upper case and therefore may be considered a part of it. This assumption makes the base the usual 36 in. high, and the upper case 45 in. high, a 4:5 ratio.

Furthermore, notice that the pediment is three times as wide as it is high, the lower drawers are as wide as the upper case, the small square drawers are a fifth as wide as the case, and the upper drawers follow the familiar progression. □

A Small Highboy
Plans for a Queen Anne charmer

by Carlyle Lynch

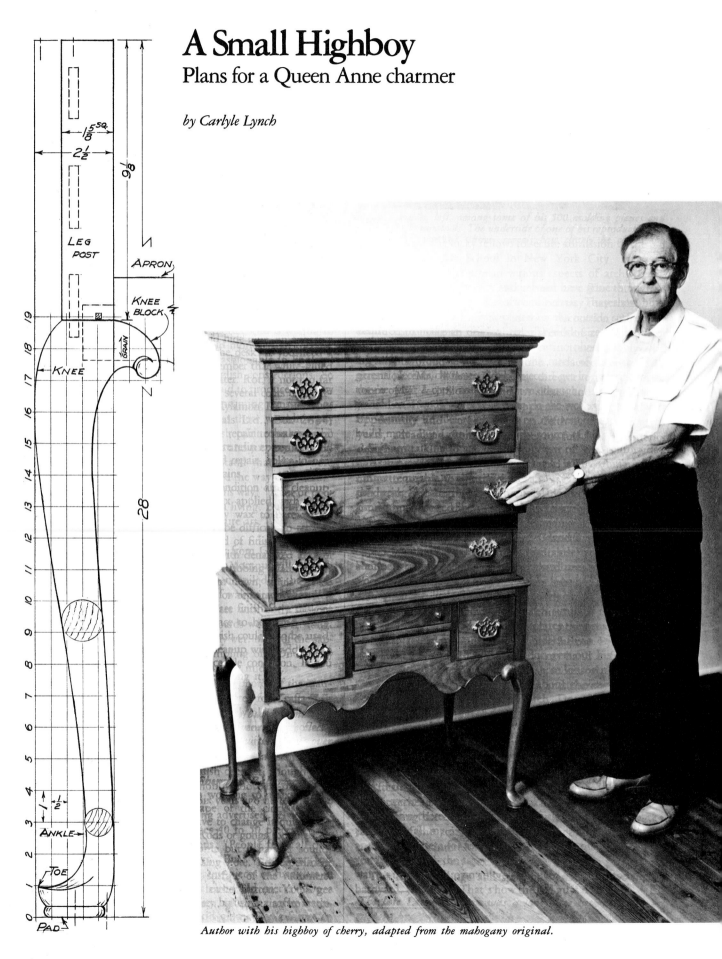

Author with his highboy of cherry, adapted from the mahogany original.

The highboy is an imposing furniture form, too large for the spaces in which most of us live. But 18th-century cabinetmakers didn't always build grandly scaled furniture for stately halls. Shown here is a small, modestly proportioned highboy I found in the home of Mr. and Mrs. Richard P. Lewis in Augusta County, Va. Included in the drawings are a few adaptations—simpler moldings and a less arched front apron that accommodates one more drawer than the original. I built the piece to test these alterations. Here are the basic procedures; a bill of materials is given on page 44.

The legs—Begin by squaring the pieces for the legs. The article that begins on page 46 gives a method for shaping cabriole legs with a bandsaw and hand tools. Here's how the lathe can be used, in addition to the tablesaw, bandsaw and hand tools, to shape the foot and ankle of these cabriole legs: Make a pattern from the drawing on the facing page, and lay out the leg on the two inside faces, so that the apron, sides and back will all fit flush with the post block. Cut the mortises in the post blocks while the leg blanks are still square.

To shape the legs, first draw diagonals on the leg ends to mark their centers, and punch a mark on each end 1 1/16 in.

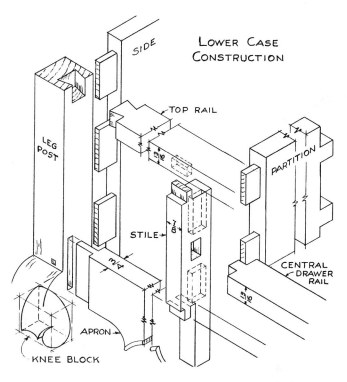

LOWER CASE CONSTRUCTION

SIDE
TOP RAIL
LEG POST
PARTITION
STILE
CENTRAL DRAWER RAIL
APRON
KNEE BLOCK

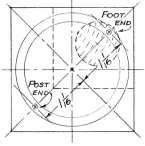

off-center, as shown in the drawing below. Mount each blank in the lathe on its true centers, with the foot end at the tailstock, and turn the foot. Shape it to the top of the pad, but don't finish turning the pad yet, or you will lose the offset center you need to turn the ankles. Remount the blank on the two opposing offset centers and turn the ankles. To someone not used to making cabriole legs, the setup looks forbidding. Use slow speed, and take light cuts with a sharp gouge or round-nose chisel held tight and fed slow. You can turn and sand 2 in. to 3 in. of the ankle, and sand to the top of the foot, before remounting the blank on its true centers to turn and sand the pads.

Take the blanks to the tablesaw, and with a smooth-cutting blade set for maximum height, cut the waste to form the post blocks. Set up a stop block to prevent going too far. In order to keep the post block flat on the table, cut two of the legs with the rip fence to the right of the blade, two with the fence to the left of it. Finish the cuts on the bandsaw and then rough out the rest of the leg. Bandsaw to the pattern line on one face, tape the scraps back in place, turn the leg 90° and saw again to the lines on the scraps. Final shaping is done with spokeshave, rasp and scraper.

The lower case—Mill out the apron, sides and back, then cut the tenons to fit the mortises in the leg. Cut the bottom edge of the sides to shape, but wait to scroll-cut the apron until a gentle fit of its tenons poses no danger of breaking it. Dove-

tail the top rail into the top of the front legs, and test-assemble the frame (drawing, above). Disassemble, and cut the mortises in the apron and the top rail for the drawer stiles, and in the stiles for the central drawer rail. Tenons are 5/16 in. thick by 1 in. long, except the stile tenons, which are 1/2 in. long. Use poplar, pine or other secondary wood for the partitions that mortise into the back edge of the stiles and into the case back. Nail three drawer runners and a kicker strip to each of these partitions.

Now add the cock beading to the apron edge. Cut strips of mahogany or cherry 1/8 in. thick, 15/16 in. wide, long enough to bend around the curves plus enough for cutting the miter joints. Round one edge with a small plane. Use a small gouge to make a groove in a sanding block for smoothing the round. You can use this same block later, to sand the cock beading for the drawers.

Bend the apron beading strips between pairs of plywood forms, shaped to accommodate clamps. Make the curves of the forms a little tighter than the apron radii shown, to allow for springback. Also, make sure the curves on the forms are smooth, as rough or flat places can show up in the bent strips. Boil the strips in a shallow pan of water for ten minutes or so and clamp them in the forms while hot. When they're dry, finish-sand the beading and the apron face, miter the strips, and attach them with glue and small brads. Then fit and attach the short, straight pieces of beading.

Before gluing up the lower case, dry-assemble it to check

TURNING THE QUEEN ANNE FOOT

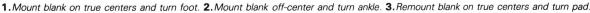

1. Mount blank on true centers and turn foot. **2.** Mount blank off-center and turn ankle. **3.** Remount blank on true centers and turn pad.

for fit and squareness. Disassemble, scrape and finish-sand all parts. Then glue the legs to the sides, clamping the two sub-assemblies together, if necessary, to make them lie flat. You can pin the tenons now, while these subassemblies are in clamps, or after the whole case is glued up. Drill $\frac{3}{16}$-in. holes (four in each side) into the post blocks and through the tenons, coat the inside of the holes with glue, and hammer in $\frac{3}{16}$-in. square pins. A small handsaw with set removed will trim off the pins that protrude, without marring the surrounding surface. Pare flush with a sharp chisel.

While the sides are drying, glue up the front frame, then glue the partitions between this and the back. When these are dry, finish gluing up the lower case, clamping and checking for squareness, and pin the two apron tenons and the four tenons at the corners of the back.

To shape the knee blocks, bandsaw the six blanks and glue each one to scrap wood with paper in the joint. Use the scrap to clamp in the vise while rough-carving the blocks. Match the shape of the blocks to the contour of the leg's knee. When they're shaped, pry the blocks from the scrap, scrape off the paper and glue, and glue the blocks in place. Now finish carving the blocks to fair smoothly into the leg.

The upper case—Begin the upper case by milling the stock and cutting it to length. Along the back edge of each side, cut the $\frac{1}{2}$-in. rabbet for the backboards, and cut the grooves to

receive the buttons that will hold down the case top (detail A, facing page). Mortise the sides to receive the drawer rails—three front and three back. Cut the $\frac{1}{2}$-in. long tenons on the rails—twin tenons for the front, single tenons for the back. For the top and bottom rails, cut the half-sliding-dovetail slots in the top edge of the sides (detail B) and the dovetail mortises in the bottom edge. Fit the corresponding dovetail tenons in the top and bottom rails. Test-assemble the case, then take it apart and plow the slots in the inside edges of the drawer rails to receive the tenons of the drawer runners (detail C). The runners have $\frac{1}{2}$-in. long tenons that fit these grooves, and they will be left unglued; the distance between shoulders is $\frac{1}{8}$ in. short to allow the sides of the case to shrink. The inside edge of the top front rail is also mortised to receive the loose tenon of the top-drawer kicker strip. This does not connect to the back rail, but like the drawer runners will be attached to the side with a single screw. Test-assemble all parts, then take the case apart and glue it up.

The case sides are plain. The top that overlaps them is now molded on three edges and fastened with wood or metal tabletop buttons. Nail the molding strip under the top.

The drawers—All the drawers are constructed alike—dovetailed front and back, with the bottom slid into a groove in the sides and the front, and secured with nails to the bottom edge of the drawer back, as shown in detail D.

BILL OF MATERIALS							
Amt.	Description	Wood	Dimensions T x W x L	Amt.	Description	Wood	Dimensions T x W x L
Lower case				*Drawers***			
4	Legs	mahogany	$2\frac{1}{2}$ x $2\frac{1}{2}$ x 28	2	Fronts	mahogany	$\frac{3}{4}$ x $6\frac{5}{8}$ x $7\frac{7}{16}$
1	Knee block (makes 3 pairs)	mahogany	$\frac{3}{4}$ x $1\frac{1}{2}$ x 15	2	Backs	pine	$\frac{1}{2}$ x $6\frac{5}{16}$ x $7\frac{7}{16}$
2	Sides	mahogany	$\frac{3}{4}$ x $10\frac{1}{2}$ x $15\frac{1}{2}$ s/s	4	Sides	pine	$\frac{1}{2}$ x $6\frac{7}{8}$ x $17\frac{1}{2}$
1	Apron	mahogany	$\frac{3}{4}$ x $4\frac{1}{2}$ x $28\frac{3}{4}$ s/s	2	Bottoms	plywood	$\frac{1}{4}$ x $6\frac{15}{16}$ x $17\frac{1}{4}$
1	Top rail	mahogany	$\frac{13}{16}$ x $1\frac{5}{8}$ x $28\frac{3}{4}$ s/s	2	Fronts	mahogany	$\frac{3}{4}$ x $2\frac{3}{8}$ x $11\frac{15}{16}$
1	Back	pine	$\frac{3}{4}$ x $10\frac{1}{2}$ x $28\frac{3}{4}$ s/s	2	Backs	pine	$\frac{1}{2}$ x $2\frac{1}{16}$ x $11\frac{15}{16}$
2	Drawer runners	pine	$\frac{3}{4}$ x $1\frac{1}{2}$ x $17\frac{1}{4}$	4	Sides	pine	$\frac{1}{2}$ x $2\frac{5}{8}$ x $17\frac{1}{2}$
2	Drawer guides	pine	$\frac{3}{4}$ x $\frac{7}{8}$ x $15\frac{1}{2}$	2	Bottoms	plywood	$\frac{1}{4}$ x $11\frac{7}{16}$ x $17\frac{1}{4}$
2	Kicker strips	pine	$\frac{3}{4}$ x $1\frac{3}{8}$ x $16\frac{3}{8}$	1	Front	mahogany	$\frac{3}{4}$ x $3\frac{5}{8}$ x $28\frac{7}{16}$
2	Drawer stiles	mahogany	$\frac{7}{8}$ x $1\frac{5}{8}$ x 7 s/s	1	Back	pine	$\frac{1}{2}$ x $3\frac{5}{16}$ x $28\frac{7}{16}$
1	Central drawer rail	mahogany	$\frac{13}{16}$ x $1\frac{5}{8}$ x 12 s/s	2	Sides	pine	$\frac{1}{2}$ x $3\frac{7}{8}$ x $16\frac{3}{4}$
2	Partitions	pine	$\frac{7}{8}$ x $8\frac{1}{2}$ x $16\frac{3}{8}$ s/s	1	Front	mahogany	$\frac{3}{4}$ x $4\frac{5}{8}$ x $28\frac{7}{16}$
6	Drawer runners	pine	$\frac{5}{8}$ x $\frac{3}{4}$ x $17\frac{1}{4}$	1	Back	pine	$\frac{1}{2}$ x $4\frac{5}{16}$ x $28\frac{7}{16}$
2	Kicker strips	pine	$\frac{3}{4}$ x 2 x $16\frac{3}{8}$	2	Sides	pine	$\frac{1}{2}$ x $4\frac{7}{8}$ x $16\frac{3}{4}$
1	Apron cock bead	mahogany	$\frac{1}{8}$ x $\frac{15}{16}$ x 40	1	Front	mahogany	$\frac{3}{4}$ x $5\frac{5}{8}$ x $28\frac{7}{16}$
14	Joint pins	mahogany	$\frac{3}{16}$ x $\frac{3}{16}$ x 2	1	Back	pine	$\frac{1}{2}$ x $5\frac{5}{16}$ x $28\frac{7}{16}$
1	Molding	mahogany	$\frac{3}{4}$ x 2 x $32\frac{1}{2}$*	2	Sides	pine	$\frac{1}{2}$ x $5\frac{5}{8}$ x $16\frac{3}{4}$
2	Moldings	mahogany	$\frac{3}{4}$ x 2 x 19*	1	Front	mahogany	$\frac{3}{4}$ x $6\frac{5}{8}$ x $28\frac{7}{16}$
1	Filler strip	pine	$\frac{1}{2}$ x $1\frac{5}{8}$ x $28\frac{1}{2}$	1	Back	pine	$\frac{1}{2}$ x $6\frac{5}{16}$ x $28\frac{7}{16}$
Upper case				2	Sides	pine	$\frac{1}{2}$ x $6\frac{7}{8}$ x $16\frac{3}{4}$
2	Sides	mahogany	$\frac{13}{16}$ x $17\frac{7}{8}$ x $26\frac{3}{4}$	4	Bottoms	plywood	$\frac{1}{4}$ x $16\frac{1}{2}$ x $27\frac{15}{16}$
1	Top	mahogany	$\frac{3}{4}$ x $19\frac{9}{16}$ x $33\frac{1}{2}$	11	Cock bead	mahogany	$\frac{1}{8}$ x $\frac{7}{8}$ x 30
4	Drawer rails	mahogany	$\frac{13}{16}$ x $2\frac{1}{4}$ x $28\frac{1}{2}$ s/s	4	Cock bead	mahogany	$\frac{1}{8}$ x $\frac{3}{8}$ x 30
1	Top rail	mahogany	$\frac{3}{4}$ x $1\frac{3}{4}$ x $28\frac{1}{2}$ s/s		Stops	pine	from 1 x 2 stock
4	Back rails	pine	$\frac{13}{16}$ x $1\frac{1}{2}$ x $28\frac{1}{2}$ s/s				
1	Back top rail	pine	$\frac{3}{4}$ x $1\frac{3}{4}$ x $28\frac{1}{2}$ s/s				
8	Drawer runners	pine	$\frac{13}{16}$ x $\frac{3}{4}$ x $13\frac{1}{4}$ s/s				
2	Drawer kickers	pine	$\frac{3}{4}$ x $\frac{3}{4}$ x $15\frac{1}{4}$ plus $\frac{1}{2}$-in. long tenon, one end				
	Backboards	pine	$\frac{1}{2}$ x $26\frac{3}{4}$ x $29\frac{1}{2}$				
1	Top molding	mahogany	$\frac{1}{2}$ x $1\frac{1}{2}$ x $31\frac{3}{4}$*				
2	Top moldings	mahogany	$\frac{1}{2}$ x $1\frac{1}{2}$ x $18\frac{3}{4}$*				
1	Molding backing strip	pine	$\frac{1}{2}$ x $\frac{1}{2}$ x 76				

Hardware: Ten brass pulls, four $\frac{5}{8}$-in. dia. brass knobs; available from Mason & Sullivan, 586 Higgins Crowell Rd., W. Yarmouth, Mass. 02673.

s/s = shoulder-to-shoulder. Allow $\frac{1}{2}$ in. to 1 in. extra length for each tenon or dovetail.

* Allow extra for final trimming.

** Dimensions include $\frac{1}{8}$-in. vertical allowance for humidity changes.

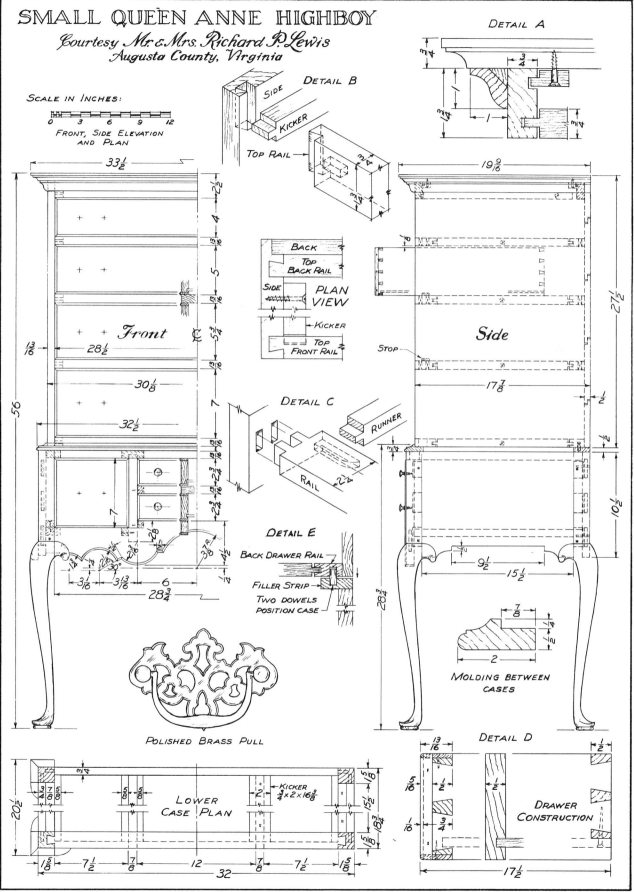

SMALL QUEEN ANNE HIGHBOY
Courtesy Mr. & Mrs. Richard P. Lewis
Augusta County, Virginia

SCALE IN INCHES:

0   3   6   9   12

FRONT, SIDE ELEVATION
AND PLAN

DETAIL A

DETAIL B

SIDE

KICKER

TOP RAIL

Front

BACK
TOP
BACK RAIL

SIDE

PLAN
VIEW

KICKER

TOP
FRONT RAIL

DETAIL C

RUNNER

RAIL

Side

STOP

DETAIL E

BACK DRAWER RAIL

FILLER STRIP

TWO DOWELS
POSITION CASE

POLISHED BRASS PULL

MOLDING BETWEEN
CASES

LOWER
CASE PLAN

KICKER

DETAIL D

DRAWER
CONSTRUCTION

© E.C. Lynch 1983

Making Period Furniture **45**

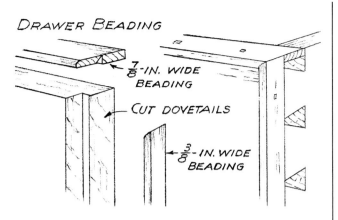
DRAWER BEADING

⅞-IN. WIDE BEADING

CUT DOVETAILS

⅜-IN. WIDE BEADING

The cock beading for the drawers should be ⅛ in. thick and either ⅞ in. or ⅜ in. wide, depending on whether it goes on the top and bottom edges of the drawers or on the sides (drawing, above). Either way, it should stand about ³⁄₆₄ in. proud of the drawer face. Note that the drawer fronts should be at least ¼ in. shorter than their openings, to accommodate the beading, top and bottom, and to allow for possible swelling. When the drawers are glued up, but before the bottoms are slid in, rabbet the drawer sides for the ⅜-in. wide cock beading with a fine-tooth circular saw, guiding the drawer against both the miter fence and the rip fence. Do all final sanding of the fronts, and prepare the top and bottom beading. Cut these full-length and then miter the ends, actually only the front half of their width, to meet the narrower cock beading on the drawer sides. To miter, clamp the cock beading between a 45° angled block of wood and a backing board. Using the wood block as a guide, cut down with a sharp chisel. Apply the top and bottom beading with glue and nails, then miter and apply the beading in the rabbets along the drawer sides.

Finishing touches—Attach the drawer stops to the drawer rails in the upper case and to the drawer runners in the lower case. To ensure a close fit for the rabbeted moldings that provide transition between the upper and lower cases, position the moldings on the bottom of the upper case and miter them to length. Then, using a strap clamp, glue up the three molding pieces using the filler strip to complete the back of the rectangle. Attach this assembly to the top of the lower case. To key the two cases, drill two ⅜-in. holes in the top of the filler strip about 4 in. from each side of the case. Use dowel centers in the holes to mark the position of corresponding holes in the back rail of the upper case when the upper case is set in position on the lower case. Separate the cases, drill the holes, and then insert 1-in. long, ⅜-in. dowels for keys (detail E, page 45).

Rabbet the white pine planks for shiplapping and lay them horizontally in the rabbets you've cut in the back edge of the upper case sides. Space the planks ¹⁄₁₆ in. apart, to allow for expansion, and secure them with small nails. □

Carlyle Lynch, a designer, cabinetmaker and retired teacher, lives in Broadway, Va. After the original publication of this article, he noted that it is difficult to bend mahogany to the tight curves of the highboy's apron; he recommends using cherry or walnut and staining to match.

Cabriole Legs
Hand-shaped, without a lathe

by Philip C. Lowe

Cabriole legs, all characterized by the cyma or S-curve, have taken various styles. The cabriole seems to have evolved from the ancient practice of shaping the legs of furniture after those of beasts, and so in Egyptian furniture you see cabriole legs ending in rather literal animal feet. The Chinese favored more abstract renditions. Chippendale, who borrowed many of his ideas from the Chinese, popularized the ball-and-claw foot, along with carved acanthus leaves decorating the knee. To my eye, the sparest, most pleasing form of the cabriole is the Queen Anne, which terminates in a spoon foot, also called a club or dutch foot.

The leg involves methodical shaping with hand tools. Traditionally, slipper and trifid feet were also hand-shaped. The spoon foot, however, was usually lathe-turned. But there are those who don't have a lathe, and even for those who do, the lathe has a disadvantage: it necessitates carrying the circular perimeter of the foot all the way around, which interrupts the flow of the line down the back of the ankle. Here is how to design, lay out, cut and shape a Queen Anne cabriole, with bandsaw (or bowsaw), spokeshave, rasp and file.

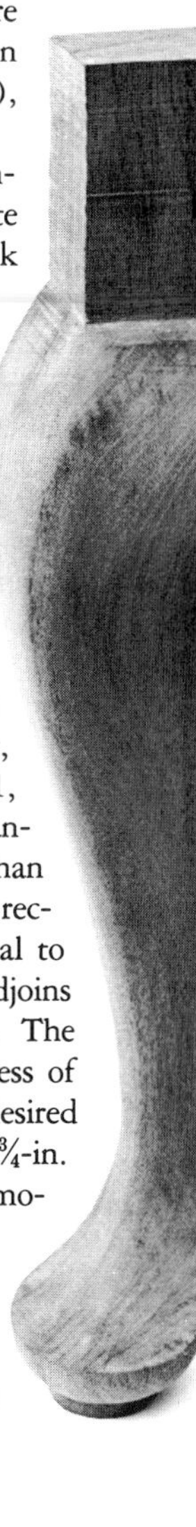

Consider first the rough thickness of the lumber you will use. Solid lumber is best, as laminate lines will interrupt the wood's figure and look offensive when the leg is cut. The most suitable thicknesses for cabriole legs are 10/4, 12/4 and 16/4, depending on the length of the leg and the size of the piece of furniture it will support. I always figure the working thickness of rough stock, after it is planed, to be ¼ in. less than it is nominally. For a typical chair or low table, 12/4 stock, which will yield 2¾ in. of working thickness, is suitable.

You'll need a full-size drawing of the leg, including the post block, knee, transition piece (also called the knee block), ankle, and foot, which is made up of the toe and pad (figure 1, facing page). On a piece of paper, draw a rectangle the length of the leg and ¼ in. smaller than the rough thickness of your stock. Within this rectangle draw the post block first, its length equal to the width of the rail it will join, or, if the leg adjoins a case, the width of the front, back or end. The width of the post block depends on the thickness of the tenons it will receive, as well as on the desired curvature of the knee. For 12/4 stock, a 1¾-in. square post block is common, readily accommodating ¼-in. thick tenons in ¾-in. thick stock.

After laying out the post block, draw the pad and foot. The pad diameter should be about half the width of the blank. Its thickness, from ¼ in. to ⅜ in., depends partly on the thickness of the carpet you expect your piece to stand on. The pad's function is to separate the lines of the leg from the floor. The height of the toe depends on the size of the leg, but on a chair or table leg it's usually ¾ in. to 1 in. from the floor. Sketch in the curves up to the ankle, whose diameter should be about two-fifths the thickness of the leg blank. This narrowest part of the leg should fall at about three times the height of the toe. Next develop the knee, sketching a curve that meets the bottom corner of the post block at about a 45° angle; if it is more horizontal than that, it creates an awkward shelf at the top of the knee. Aim for a tangency point with the outside of the blank a distance from the post block about three times the height of the toe.

Connect the knee to the ankle with a relatively straight line. It is important that you understate any curve here because your drawing is in only one plane, and when the blank is cut in two planes, the curve will be exaggerated. Draw the line of the back of the leg, leading all the way up into the transition piece. Keep this line relatively straight also, and see that the leg thickens gradually and proportionally to the toe, ankle and knee already drawn. The final curve into the transition piece should be relatively tight. If you regard the points of tangency at the knee, ankle and toe, you may be surprised at how much control you have in creating a pleasing shape. Keep in mind, however, that this is only a two-dimensional shape, and its final test will be in a solid piece of wood seen from eye level as part of a whole piece of furniture. Restraint at this stage promises a more pleasing leg in the end.

Next, make a permanent wooden pattern from your drawing. Tape the drawing onto a piece of ⅛-in. plywood, and with a large pin epoxied into a ¼-in. dowel, stipple the outline of the leg onto the plywood, poking through the drawing at ⅛-in. to ¼-in. intervals. Connect the markings on the plywood with a pencil. Repeat this procedure for the transition piece, then cut out both patterns and file their curves smooth.

Prepare the stock next, starting with pieces 2 in. longer than the sum of the two transition pieces (laid out above the post block) plus the leg. Usually the grain of the transition piece runs vertically, like that of the leg. Rip the stock to width at least the dimension of your rough thickness. Joint one face of the blank, either on the jointer or with a hand plane, and then joint an edge square to it. Thickness-plane the blank ⅛ in. larger than the finished dimension, and put the blank aside for a day or so, to give it time to warp in response to any stresses milling may have introduced.

When you have all the leg blanks milled, consider their grain orientation relative to one another. For visual compatibility, either the quarter grain or the flatsawn grain of each blank should face front. Mark the inside corner of each blank, and hand-plane the inside surfaces, removing mill marks and making sure that the surfaces are square to one another. Finish thickness-planing the blanks: plane the outside surfaces parallel to the inside. Crosscut the blanks to their finished length, saving the offcuts for the transition pieces.

To begin layout, set a marking gauge to the width of the post block, and scribe this width on the two inside surfaces (figure 2). Trace the outline of the leg below the post block. To keep the stock from rocking through the second bandsaw cuts, I include in the layout of the leg a pair of bridges—one at the top of the post, the other between the knee and toe. You could also tape the waste from the first cuts back on the stock before making the second cuts, but I find the bridges

easier and more stable. Scribe the position of the mortises on the post block, and cut the mortises while the blank is still square; it's easier to hold square stock.

Now, using a ¼-in. blade, bandsaw the leg: Cut relief kerfs for the bridges first, then saw the post block, staying 1/16 in. away from the scribe line. The post will be planed later, after it is attached to the rail. Saw the curve from knee to ankle, leaving the bridge between. Sawing right on the line will minimize spokeshaving later. Next, define the pad, cutting straight in from the bottom of the blank first, then sawing the curves at the bottom of the foot to meet these relief cuts. Finish sawing the back curve, and save both back-curve scraps. These have the pattern lines for the cut on the adjacent face and should be tacked or taped back in place to saw

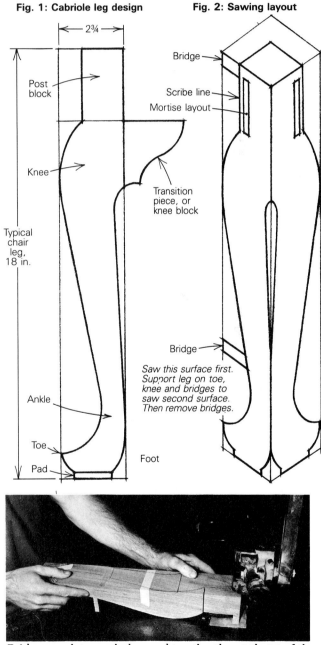

Fig. 1: Cabriole leg design   Fig. 2: Sawing layout

Bridges—one between the knee and toe, the other at the top of the post block—keep the stock from rocking through the second bandsaw cuts. Waste from the first cuts has been taped back in place, to provide layout lines for sawing on.

A pipe clamp mounted in the bench vise, above, makes an ideal holding arrangement for working the length of the leg. Here a spokeshave fairs the bandsawn curves, in preparation for the modeling layout.

To draw modeling lines, the square for the pad is compassed round, and the other four surfaces are divided into quarters, left. Then each leg surface is penciled with lines parallel to the leg edges, above: two inside lines begin at half the ankle thickness and two outside lines begin at one-quarter the ankle thickness.

it. After sawing this second surface, turn the blank back to the first sawing position and saw off the bridges.

The next job is to fair the leg with a spokeshave, removing all the bandsaw marks, bumps and hollows. It is important here that the leg be kept square in section; irregularities are more difficult to see and smooth once you begin rounding the leg. Where the curves are tight and the spokeshave will not reach, you can use a rasp or a file. The leg is now ready to be laid out for final shaping.

Begin laying out the bottom, locating the center of the pad by drawing two diagonal lines from the corners of the square that will contain the pad, and scribing with a compass the largest possible circle the square will contain. Divide each surface of the underside of the foot into four equal sections: first draw a line from the center of each side of the pad to the top edge of the foot, then halve the distance between these lines and the corners of the foot.

To lay out the guidelines for modeling the rest of the leg, position a pencil point at the center of the ankle, and using your middle finger as a depth gauge running on the stock edge, draw lines from ankle to post block parallel to each edge of the leg. There will be a total of eight lines, two on each face. Reposition the pencil point halfway between these lines and the edges, and draw eight more longitudinal lines. Now the leg is ready to model.

Mount the leg bottom up in a vise, and saw the waste away from the pad square to leave a regular octagonal shape (figure 3A, facing page). Similarly, cut the corners off the toe square, but leave the corner at the back of the leg, thus forming only three-quarters of an octagon (figure 3B). Now use a rasp to round the outline of the pad and the foot (figure 3C). Check the shape of the foot periodically by looking down from the knee to see that it is situated symmetrically in relation to the rest of the leg. When the outline is round, use the rasp to fair the underside of the foot, from its perimeter to the perimeter of the pad.

Modeling the rest of the leg requires attention to holding it. As the surfaces become more curved, a bench vise becomes

Fig. 3: Modeling the foot, bottom views

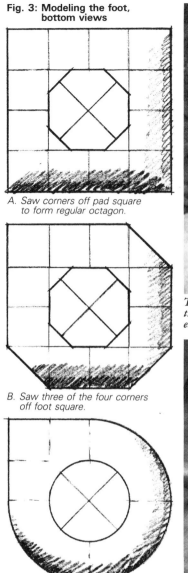

A. Saw corners off pad square to form regular octagon.

B. Saw three of the four corners off foot square.

C. Round outline of pad and foot with a rasp.

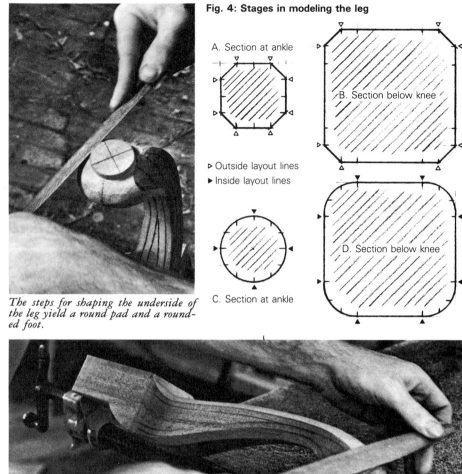

The steps for shaping the underside of the leg yield a round pad and a rounded foot.

Fig. 4: Stages in modeling the leg

A. Section at ankle

B. Section below knee

▷ Outside layout lines
▶ Inside layout lines

C. Section at ankle

D. Section below knee

A rasp chamfers the corners of the leg to the outside layout lines, then rounds the leg to the inside layout lines, as detailed in figure 4.

more frustrating. I clamp the blank lengthwise in a pipe or bar clamp and mount the clamp in my bench vise. This affords access to most of the leg's surfaces, and the blank is easy to reposition. Use a rasp to chamfer all four corners to the outside layout lines, from the ankle to the knee. This yields an irregularly octagonal section of varying proportion, depending on where it is along the length of the leg (figures 4A and 4B). The flat should taper to nothing at the foot and at the curve toward the transition piece. Next rasp the ankle round (figure 4C). Continue rounding the rest of the leg to the inside layout lines. The shape will become a square with rounded corners as you approach the knee (figure 4D). Flare the foot's top and back, to form a smooth-spreading curve.

When the leg is fair, remove the rasp marks with a file, followed by a cabinet scraper. Then sand the leg, except for the surfaces that will be blended into adjoining members.

The leg can now be joined to its aprons or case sides, after which the outside faces of the post block are planed flush, and the transition blocks are shaped and applied. Assuming the rest of the furniture piece is assembled, crosscut the transition block into the two blanks and orient each so that its grain (quarter or face) corresponds to the grain of the leg surface it will become part of. Plane the edge and end of the transition block for a close fit against the leg and the adjoining member (apron or case side). Position the pattern on the block and draw on it the shape of the transition piece. Bandsaw the piece, and glue it to the leg and adjoining member. A sharp, wide bench chisel then shapes the transition piece to the contour of the knee, and the areas that have not been sanded are sanded. □

Phil Lowe operates a cabinet shop in Beverly, Mass., and teaches cabinetmaking at North Bennet Street Industrial School in Boston. For more on cabriole legs, their history, and other techniques for making them, see pages 32 and 51 to 54. Sources for readymade cabriole legs include Fallsview Studios, 165 Fairview Ave., High Falls, N.Y. 12440 and Windsor Classics Ltd., 15937 Washington St., Guernee, Ill. 60031.

Q & A

Reeding on turned bedposts—*I am turning bedposts that I want to reed, and though I have seen articles on the subject, they don't address the problem of cutting the reeds into a curved tapered post. Can you tell me how to do it?*
—*Don Carkhuff, Plainfield, Ill.*
R. PERRY MERCURIO REPLIES: The reeding you see on factory-made furniture is usually done on a shaper with an indexing head, or else on a special machine with automatic indexing and a traveling tool head. In the home shop, you can set up a router on your lathe with an indexing device on the head-stock, and a jig as in the drawing below.

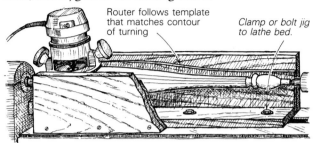

Router follows template that matches contour of turning

Clamp or bolt jig to lathe bed.

Some lathes have a built-in indexing wheel that locks the headstock at 5° increments, or you can jury-rig one by attaching an old sawblade or other toothed wheel to the head-stock spindle. Make the reeding template by bandsawing two pieces of thin stock, say, ½-in., to a contour that matches the cross section of your turning. Then nail or screw these pieces to the stock that will form the sides, and mount the assembly on your lathe. The exact height of the sides will vary from lathe to lathe, and each turning, unless it's a duplicate of an original, will require its own template. This method has limitations. The curve of the column cannot be too radical or else the router base will rock and produce an uneven cut as it's pushed along. No matter how the reeds are cut, the small end of the turning will have narrower, faceted reeds; shape them by hand-sanding or with a flap-wheel sander.

RICHARD HEISEY REPLIES: Straight tapers are a little easier than curved ones. I use the setup shown in the photo below

on my large pattern lathe. When you're setting up, make sure the bit tracks exactly on the radial line along the center of the turning, or else the flutes will be skewed. It's best to make a test turning of the same size to try out the jig before tooling the actual workpiece. Reeds that stop at a bead or other detail must be completed by hand with chisels or gouges. Off-the-shelf router bits don't work very well for this job. They're usually too wide at the tip, or the radius is not quite the right size. I grind my own bits from a commercial steel bit that is close to the profile I need, or from a broken bit.

Here's another method for reeding turnings, be they straight or curved. You need a custom-made router bit, available from Fred Velepec, 71-72 70th St., Glendale, N.Y. 11385. I

mount the router in a plywood jig, as shown in the drawing below. I rig a wooden spring latch to my lathe that engages the holes in the indexing wheel, locking the headstock for the router operation.

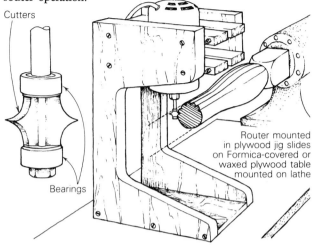

Cutters

Bearings

Router mounted in plywood jig slides on Formica-covered or waxed plywood table mounted on lathe

A cove turned at both ends of the reeded section allows the bit to exit and enter cleanly, so no hand cleanup work is needed. —*James B. Small, Newville, Pa.*

Lustrous brasses—*When we restore antiques the old brasses come to a beautiful patina with a little rubbing but lose that brightness after several weeks. What do manufacturers of brass hardware use to coat their brasses and hold that high lustre?*
—*D. A. Rothenberger, Worcester, Pa.*
Clear lacquer will protect brass and silver from oxidation and tarnishing. Most lacquer manufacturers have special lacquers for this purpose, so specify your need when ordering. The metals to be protected must be absolutely clean.
—*George Frank*

Drawer guides—*What is the best way to make a drawer-guide system? I see a lot of drawers that have grooved tracks on their bottoms, but adding these means that the drawer must be shallower than it could be without them.*
—*John Peterson, Baton Rouge, La.*
The simplest and best way to deal with drawers is to let them slide against the side of the cabinet or chest. If one or both sides of the drawer opening are legs or face frames, you will have to fasten a strip to the inside of the case for the drawer side to ride against. This means you don't have to lose drawer depth to make room on the bottom for a grooved guide.

Cut sides, front and back to fit snugly, then dovetail and assemble the drawer. With a little sanding, it should be a perfect fit. So that it will slide easily, rub the drawer sides and bottom edges with paraffin, as well as the inside parts of the case where the drawer will touch. Never finish the drawer sides on the outside or the case on the inside. —*Tage Frid*

Bonnet top—*I'm about to start a bonnet-top highboy. . . . I'm okay as far as the details of the highboy itself go, but unless I construct the bonnet top like a boat (ribs and planking), I'm stuck.* —*Roy W. Cole, Roswell, N.M.*
A. W. MARLOW REPLIES: You seem to have no problem up to closing in the bonnet—ribs and shiplap planking are correct procedure. Ribs are really ¾-in.-thick panels shaped to follow the front pediment curve but lowered for the planking thickness and based on the case top. Inside closure curves of ribs are your choice, with plank covering. You'll need four: front and back right, and front and back left.

Claw and Ball Feet
Where they came from

by Alastair A. Stair

The claw and ball foot, favored by 18th-century English and Colonial cabinetmakers, is a fascinating furniture ornament that has received little scholarly attention.

The derivation of the form is clear—a dragon's triple claw grasping a sacred, sometimes "flaming" jewel, usually a pearl, or a crystal ball. In Chinese mythology, this motif denotes the guarding of purity, integrity and wisdom from evil demons. It appears frequently on ancient Chinese bronzes and brocades, but the progress of its influence from the East through western Europe to England and its application from one artistic medium to another are not so apparent and imply a rich crosscurrent of influences.

The arts of China and Japan began to impinge on Europe in the Middle Ages, when the first imported specimens of porcelain excited the wonder of craftsmen and collectors. Eu-

Half-walnut ball on mahogany piecrust table allows greater stability. Cabriole legs curve close to ground. Lion clutches ball in Staffordshire pottery figure, c. 1800.

ropeans began trading formally with the Chinese with the establishment of a permanent settlement on Macao by the Portuguese in 1557. Portugal and Spain maintained a virtual monopoly on trade with the East Indies until the turn of the 17th century, when England and the Netherlands entered the trade. In 1588 in England, Packe published *The Historie of the Great and Mightie Kingdom of China* from the Spanish original, and several treatises on China and Japan followed. The East India Company was established in 1600 and its *Court Minutes* and accounts by travelers contain a considerable amount of information concerning the early trade in Eastern wares. Objects in the exotic style aroused widespread interest and admiration in Europe; by 1670 the taste for *chinoiserie* was strongly developed in France, and toward the end of the reign of Charles II (1660-1685) choice collections of Oriental curiosities began to appear.

These collections must have contained a goodly number of bronzes with claw and ball feet that served as prototypes for objects of English silver that appeared in the last quarter of the 16th century. Goldsmiths and silversmiths quickly became familiar with the new exotic ornamentation and reflected their admiration in their work. Some of the finest articles of London silver rested on claw and ball feet, as exemplified by a standing silver gilt salt, hallmarked for London, 1581, and the famed Rogers salt, hallmarked for 1601.

Rogers salt, 22 in. high.

Many Dutch and German immigrant silversmiths worked in Elizabethan England and they played an important role in promulgating this motif, inspired by objects Dutch navigators had brought home in the 16th century.

The claw and ball motif was soon applied in other metalwork. Goldsmiths and silversmiths work in the most precious and costly materials; hence, they are most often in the forefront of decorative experimentation. Craftsmen in other fields—textiles, glass, furniture—were exposed to the same pattern books from which metalworkers drew their ideas. The claw and ball foot found its way into the design books and became a stock ornament, freely used regardless of its original context. The element was slowly incorporated into the vocabulary of the cabinetmaker as an innovative and interesting

Regional Variations

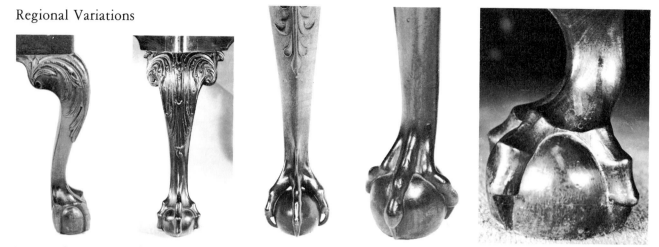

New York: square, box-like foot.

Philadelphia: slightly flattened ball.

Newport: undercut claw and ball.

Boston and Salem: Side talons angle away from center to show more of ball beneath.

way to end the cabriole leg of a chair, table, stool or bureau.

Although the claw and ball foot was not taken directly from Oriental furniture pieces, many features of European chairs may well have been drawn from Oriental sources. Chinese chairs were brought home by European voyagers as objects of curiosity. The outline of the splat of the Queen Anne chair has been likened to the contours of Chinese vases.

18th-century armchair: Tense, exaggerated muscles of ankles and legs disappear at knee curvature.

The spooned effect of the splat on the Queen Anne chair was used on Chinese chairs dating at least 150 years before the reign of Queen Anne (1702-1714). The cabriole leg, another naturalistic form compared to the leg of a leaping goat, may be of Chinese derivation as well. Ball and claw feet did not actually appear on Chinese furniture until the mid-to-late 19th century, when it began to be made for the Western market—an example of reverse influence.

Naturalistic forms have always retained an inherent appeal for the English. For craftsmen in all the arts the exotic birds, animals, sea creatures and flowers that riot over their creations were part of the Elizabethan concept of an ordered world and the dance of life and death. The lion, eagle and oak tree in particular passed into the tradition of English thought and when a silversmith or a cabinetmaker designed an object to please his patron, his themes included the finest flowers, the rarest fruit and the noblest beasts and birds. The claw and ball foot was a worthy addition to this repertoire of ornamentation, and it was natural for the English craftsman to translate the paw of the Chinese dragon into a bird's talons.

The claw and ball foot became quite popular in England around 1710, reached its apex in the reign of George I (1714-1727) and continued through the reign of George II to c. 1750. The style is often mistakenly considered an invention of Thomas Chippendale, although his *Director* (1754) contained no such designs; the vogue was outmoded and no longer eye-catching and had been replaced by scroll feet. The American Colonial craftsman, slower both to adapt and discontinue the fashionable London trends, continued to favor the claw and ball foot well into the end of the 18th century. In the last quarter of the 19th century, when American Colonial furniture enjoyed a revival, this foot treatment was revived, often cast in brass with the claw clutching a glass ball.

In the Colonies, the various ways in which the claw and ball foot was carved became a regional stamp and often a clue to the identification of the cabinetmaker. The use of the claw and ball was almost universal. In New York a large, squared, box-like foot was preferred, while in Philadelphia the claws firmly grasped a slightly flattened ball. The Boston and Salem cabinetmakers angled the side talons away from the center with much of the ball beneath showing through. The talented Goddard and Townsend families in Newport pro-

Tripod table: Long, relaxed paw suggests animal in repose.

Armchair: Tall ball has knobby knuckles.

Gate-leg table: hairy paw carved in relief.

Piecrust table: hairy paw without toenails.

Rectangular table: Toes hug square stock.

duced the undercut claw and ball, with openings carved through between the talons and the ball. This refinement was sometimes employed on the best pieces of English furniture in George II's reign, but was rarely attempted by Colonial cabinetmakers other than in Newport.

English examples also show a rich diversity of carving on the claw and ball foot, both in walnut and mahogany. These feet appear on a wide variety of furniture including wing chairs, side chairs and armchairs; dropleaf, tripod, tea, and console tables; stools, slant-top desks and bureau bookcases. The foot most frequently emulated by New York cabinetmakers is one in which a bird's claw firmly grasps a heavy, square-shaped ball. Just as the dragon's paw symbolized the power of the Chinese emperor, the eagle's claw indicated the social importance of the cabinetmaker's patron. Three claws are stretched across the front and a fourth, and shorter, claw clutches the rear. Varying degrees of tension are expressed in the ankle and the leg, sometimes shown in the muscles right up to the knee curvature. Sometimes a ringlet is carved in relief just above the ankle. For greater realism long talons were often added, and webbing carved between the claws. When both characteristics appear the effect can be striking, almost disquieting. The combined effect of a curved leg, seemingly preparing to leap, and a clutching claw with tension expressed in the muscles can be most realistic.

In England the lion represents authority, and many feet look more like paws than bird claws. In many cases the claws are set so close together that the ball is not visible. The claws multiply—often five and six are carved tightly together. The carving of the paw is quite often highly naturalistic, with hairs shown in relief (commonly known as

Long talons and webbing.

"hairy-paw" feet), long toenails or a series of nodules running along the claws. Sometimes the paws are elongated, rather drooping and without tension, like an animal in repose.

On tripod tables, the ball is altered to improve stability and balance on uneven floors. The ball, referred to as "half-walnut," is more squat and sometimes cut in half. In these instances the cabriole leg curves in closer to the ground and eliminates space for the fourth claw.

About 1755, when English cabinetmakers had exhausted the multitudinous ways in which to carve the claw and ball, they turned to other styles, including the scroll toe, a tapering leg terminating in a spade foot and various turned feet. Variations on the paw foot with ball and a hoofed foot with ball reappeared briefly during the Regency (1811-1820) when they were often gilded, with the ball barely visible beneath the closed paw. □

Many carvers added a ringlet in relief just above ankle, as in this 18th-century upholstered stool.

Some of the antique furniture sold at Alastair Stair's gallery in New York City has claw and ball feet.

Making the Feet
How to carve the ball and claw

by A. W. Marlow

When combined with a cabriole leg, the ball and claw foot is a well-known furniture support dating back to ancient times. The industrial version is hardly recognizable—reason enough for every interested craftsman to develop his own.

Few amateurs are satisfied with their ball and claw carvings. To illustrate the process, I've chosen cabriole legs with ball and claw feet made for a wing chair. To many craftsmen, shaping cabriole legs is an uncertain process, but this step-by-step procedure should be simple to follow. The ball and claw foot on a tripod table requires the same basic carving cuts, but the claw placement is different—the claws come in over the ball horizontally for a more natural look.

1 The average blank size for a cabriole leg, regardless of length, is 2¾ in. by 2¾ in. To make a pattern, follow the line drawing, which is laid out in 1-in. squares. Place the pattern on a blank, as shown in the drawing and the photo at right. Keep the front knee curve toward the right-angled front corner and outline in pencil.

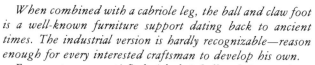

2 Shaping a cabriole leg can be quite simple when done on a band saw. Saw the first surface as shown at right, ending the cut before the waste piece is completely severed. This keeps the second or right-angled surface in place for the second cut. After the second cut has been made, turn the block back to the first surface and finish sawing the short, uncut portions of each curve.

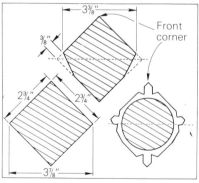

3 The next step is physically a minor one, but of major importance. Without it, the side claws look like wings sticking out. The line drawing shows three full bottom views of a leg as it is shaped. The first view shows the leg as it comes from the band saw. In the center drawing, a ⅜-in. wedge has been removed from each side claw to lessen the total width and give a more pleasing and realistic appearance to the finished foot. In the photo, a ¾-in. #3 gouge is used to chip away the wedge of wood. The third drawing adds the contour of the ball and the veiner cuts made in the next step.

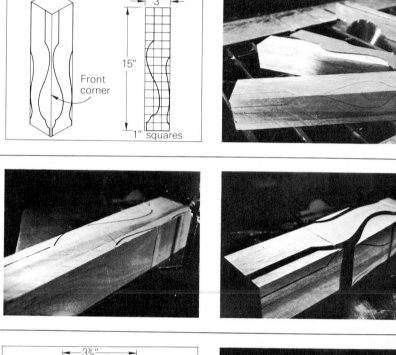

4 Now hold a pencil or ball-point pen as shown in the photo at right. Using your middle finger as a bearing against the wood, mark each side of each corner about ¼ in. in from the edge. These are the guide lines to follow when roughly positioning the claws with a ⅜-in. #41 veining tool. Continue the V-cuts into the angle area (as in the photo at far right), gradually lessening them in depth. If these feet are being cut in mahogany or walnut, you'll need a mallet to cut the rough V's.

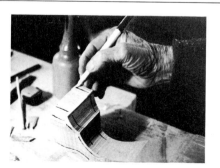

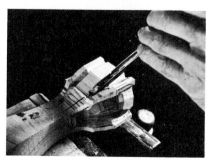

 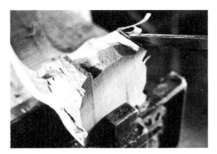 

5 The next step is to shape the ball and claws. In the first photo the claws of the foot have been narrowed closer to the finished width and the ball has been cut about halfway between rough and finished condition. When cutting the ball, check frequently to see that it is reasonably round, because if any adjustment must be made, the depth of the claws must follow

the ball radius. Up to this point, the claws still retain the original band-saw outline and must be trimmed down to an average height of ¼ in. In the center photo the #3 gouge is used to trim the claws. Front and back claws will need more trimming than the sides, and the knuckles, of course, will peak above the connecting bones.

In the last photo the ball of the foot has

been smoothed down to finished size and radius. Also, the claws are another step closer to finished shape, leaving only the work of rounding bones and knuckles. The back claw follows the ball contour until it reaches the apparent knuckle immediately above the cuticle and nail.

---

6 The foot in the photo at right shows real promise of what to expect after a little more work. Take time to carefully round the claws from the ankle down to the knuckle above the cuticle. Now check the length of the nails. This dimension is not crucial, but shoot for ½ in. from the bottom up to the cuticle where they will be about ¼ in. wide by ¼ in. high. Before forming the nail, use a medium-width #7 gouge to press cross-grain over the top for a clean-cut cuticle, shown on the extreme right. Down the sides, instead of continuing to use the #7, choose a medium-width #3 gouge and press to clean-cut the full cuticle. Reduce the nail size so the cuticle appears to overlap the nail and taper the nail to about ⅛ in. by ⅛ in. at the bottom.

Study the lower side claw in the photo. Yours should now look like this except for

the slightly rounded depression between cuticle and knuckle. That slight curve must be made carefully, first from the knuckle down, then from the cuticle upward, still using the #3 gouge.

After nail cutting, pencil in the web curve. As shown in the photo, the arc starts and ends just above the lower knuckles, although the placement is not critical. Some carvers of old felt that the web should start halfway between the knuckles.

Forming the web is a repeat performance of cuticle cutting. A #4 gouge about ½ in. wide should be close to the needed radius. Because of the larger area, tap the gouge with a mallet for a clean parting cut. Make tapered shaving cuts with a #3 gouge in the area of the web line to raise the web about ¹⁄₁₆ in. above the ball. Look at and feel the ball for any bumps that should be removed

or any adjustments in contour that would improve its appearance.

---

7 So far, carving has ended at the ankle. Use a spokeshave to round the leg corners. Start at nothing where the curve swings into a wing block, to be attached later. Increase the radius as the tool descends, ending at the ankle in a near round. Round the high point of all knuckles.

Sanding may be done thoroughly, or slightly, leaving some tool marks. A smooth-looking job calls for a first sanding with 80-grit garnet paper followed by 120 grit. Wear rubber gloves to protect your finger tips and nails. If carving is planned for the knee, sand only to above the ankle. Should the knee be plain, sand to it now.

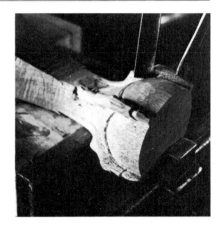

---

8 Infinitely varied foliage patterns are used on the knee for decoration. Lay flexible pattern board over the knee surface and outline the curves on the board as shown at right. Then pencil in your choice of design for carving. The photo at far right shows what to strive for. □

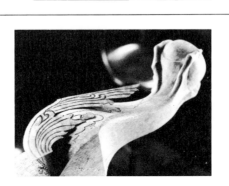 

The late Andy Marlow was a designer of traditional furniture and a consulting editor for Fine Woodworking *magazine.*

Q & A

Gooseneck molding—*I'm building some reproductions of old Norwegian cabinets, and they have some pretty fancy crown molding at the top, which for the life of me I can't figure out how to make. I'm sending along a sketch and I'd appreciate any help you can give me.*

—*Dean E. Madden, Decatur, Ill.*

NORM VANDAL REPLIES: The type of cornice you describe is found on scrolled pediments, an important motif in period architecture and cabinetwork. The molding itself is sometimes called a gooseneck.

The traditional way to make this cornice is to hand-carve the curved section, a process that seems more difficult than it actually is. The first step is to make the straight returns that are nailed to the top of the cabinet sides. You can make these by hand with a molding plane, with a shaper or with a molding head mounted in your tablesaw. Make sure to mill them long enough to allow for cutting the miters later.

Next, make a full-size cardboard template of your gooseneck section that's exactly as wide as the return molding, as shown in the drawing below. Transfer the shape to your stock and bandsaw the gooseneck. With the gooseneck blank held against the cabinet pediment, mark the point at which the miter will meet the cabinet corner.

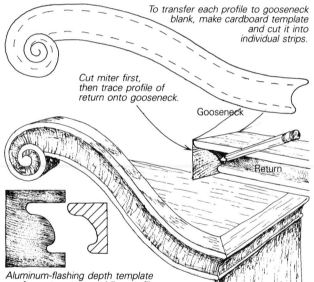

To transfer each profile to gooseneck blank, make cardboard template and cut it into individual strips.

Cut miter first, then trace profile of return onto gooseneck.

Gooseneck

Return

Aluminum-flashing depth template conforms to return molding profile.

Remove the blank and cut the miter. It may seem improbable to cut the miter before carving the molding, but it will prove to be helpful later.

Next, cut a matching miter on the return, leaving it long at the unmitered end to allow for fitting later. Fasten the return to the cabinet temporarily and then place the gooseneck section on the pediment, butting the miters together. With a sharp pencil, trace the contour of the return onto the mitered face of the gooseneck. This represents the exact profile that the gooseneck must be where it joins the return. The layout lines for each separate profile of the molding should now be traced onto the gooseneck shape. Do this by first drawing lines representing the profiles on your template, then cut up the cardboard to make individual templates for each contour.

Before you begin carving, make another template out of aluminum flashing, using the contour of the return as a guide. As you carve the gooseneck, check the shape and depth of the profile with your aluminum template. Final shaping and truing should be done with a gooseneck scraper. Two important things to remember are that gooseneck mold-

ings don't need to be as perfect or as consistent in profile as do straight sections, as long as they look correct, and that the only critical points are where the miter joins the two sections. (See page 100 for an article on cutting curved moldings with the radial-arm saw.)

Detachable highboy legs—*I want to reproduce a highboy made in Newport, R.I., circa 1760, but I can't figure out how the cabriole legs were mounted. On this piece, the legs are detachable. I can't inspect the original, and would appreciate any help on this construction technique.*

—*Robert T. Granger, Mustang, Okla.*

PHILIP C. LOWE REPLIES: Detachable legs were probably used so that a piece could knock down easily for shipping. When the highboy was delivered to its owner, the legs were attached with glue and screws.

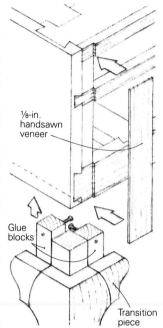

⅛-in. handsawn veneer

Glue blocks

Transition piece

The legs are rabbeted at the top where the knee meets the case. For the front legs, the rabbet across the front of the leg is as thick as the apron; the rabbet across the side is as thick as the case end. For the rear legs, it's the case end and back that determine the rabbet edges. Glue blocks are attached to the legs after rabbeting, then the transition pieces are glued on, shaped and carved.

To give the illusion of a stronger leg-post construction (see pages 42 to 49), a piece of ⅛-in.-thick veneer is glued in the rabbet cut in the front of the case, to cover the joinery.

Locks on drawers—*Why did the designers and builders of yesteryear put so many locks on their drawers, desks and cabinets? Did strangers come snooping in bedrooms more readily in the 18th century than now? Were socks and shirts and bow ties so valuable? Were people more afraid of thieves, or less able to keep their own kids and cousins out of the silverware or other private goods? Such questions arise every time I repair some old piece with the inevitable lock on every door or drawer.*

—*Stephen Sidora, Albany, Calif.*

A few aspects of 18th-century life contributed to the proliferation of the security devices you describe. Yes, textile goods and tableware were more valuable then; they were handmade and expensive. The finer households, whose furniture was what most was modeled after, often contained matching pieces of clothing, jewelry and arms, difficult to replace. Since houses as a whole were not so secure as today's, the furniture had to have locks. Often the keys to drawers, closets, larder and wine cellar would be kept in one drawer, and the key to that carried by the master of the house, to be passed on to servants or guests when necessary. The need for secure case furniture is one reason for dustboards; they prevented access to other drawers by forcing open only one.

Pillar-and-Claw Table
Designs and methods for a period piece

by John Rodd

There is always a demand for small tables to put beside an easy chair or in a bare corner. One of the handiest types of these has been traditionally known as the pillar-and-claw table. The name is confusing, because the term claw refers to the whole leg and not to the foot, which may or may not be an actual claw of the sort that most of us are accustomed to seeing. So to avoid confusion hereafter, the claw will be called the leg. Before describing how to make one of these step by step, let's consider some of the historical variations on the three principal elements of the basic design—the legs, the pillar and the top.

The earliest and most common form of this table is the Queen Anne version shown in figure 1A. Fashionable from about 1700 to 1760, it's never entirely gone out of favor. Most of these were made of walnut and often had a shell carved on the knee. Instead of plain pads, the feet might be ball and claw as in figure 1B. Occasionally, tables with pad feet were "improved" by craftsmen who glued cheeks on the feet and then recarved them in the ball-and-claw style. This left the foot wider than the leg at the pillar and the result was horrible. Later, when mahogany became popular, paw-and-scroll feet were introduced.

Tables shown in Sheraton's drawing book have legs with continuous concave curves that sweep from pillar to foot. Examples of these often end in a brass paw carrying a caster (figure 1C). In America this form was perfected by Duncan Phyfe, whose designs combine beauty and strength in a most satisfactory way and should be studied by anyone who plans to work in the style. If you choose to make one of these, you may have difficulty trying to cut the reeds on the legs so they taper in the same proportion that the leg tapers. See the box on page 61 for my cutting method. The table shown in figure 1D is typical of those fashionable during the Regency (1811-1820). The legs are tapered, rectangular in section and terminate with involuted scrolls.

The lower end of the pillar is always a cylinder to which the legs are attached, usually with sliding dovetails, but sometimes with dowels instead. Above this there is usually a shoulder, next a waisted section and then an urn, which may be decorated with reeds, carved leaves or other ornament. The member between the urn and the top should be the longest part of the pillar, and spread to the maximum diameter at the top to give adequate support. It is often fluted and, in Victorian tables, worked with a tapered twist, a rather attractive detail that's fun to make. Examples of that period also may include a boss and pendant at the base, covering the dovetails and showing a bead at its junction with the pillar.

A common weakness in pillars of this type is that the waist

John Rodd's book, Restoring and Repairing Antique Furniture, *is available from the Van Nostrand Reinhold Co., 450 W. 33rd St., New York, N.Y. 10001.*

section below the urn has been turned too narrow. Not only is there danger of its breaking across the grain, but also any strain on the legs can cause splitting along the sides of the dovetail housings. These housings should be supported by a substantial amount of wood on either side and at the top. The fat pillar shown in figure 1B is less common, but in some respects to be preferred for its strength. Also, it shows classical details, as does the pillar for the table whose construction is described on the following pages (figure 2). The base of the pillar, like an Ionic column, consists of two beads with a hollow between, or as it was called, an upper and lower torus with a scotia between. The base of the shaft, in classical fashion, curves outward to meet the fillet above the torus. Turning a perfectly tapered shaft is more difficult than turning beads and coves. I once asked an old turner whether a pillar should have an entasis (a slight bulging in the shaft), thinking this was a feature that belonged only on a large architectural column. I was surprised when he answered that to be correct it should, and added that explaining the classical derivation of the entasis made a good excuse if the customer complained that the shaft was barrel-shaped.

Unlike a classical column with its 20 or 24 flutes, table pillars have only 12, but the ratio of one part land or fillet to three parts flute is correct. However, having repaired so many

Fig. 1: Four basic table designs

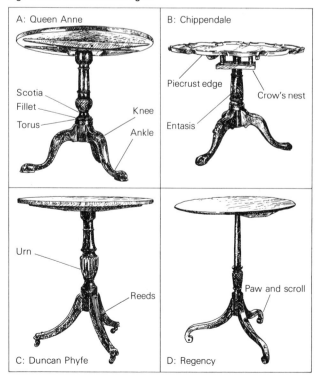

A: Queen Anne — Scotia, Fillet, Torus, Knee, Ankle

B: Chippendale — Piecrust edge, Crow's nest, Entasis

C: Duncan Phyfe — Urn, Reeds

D: Regency — Paw and scroll

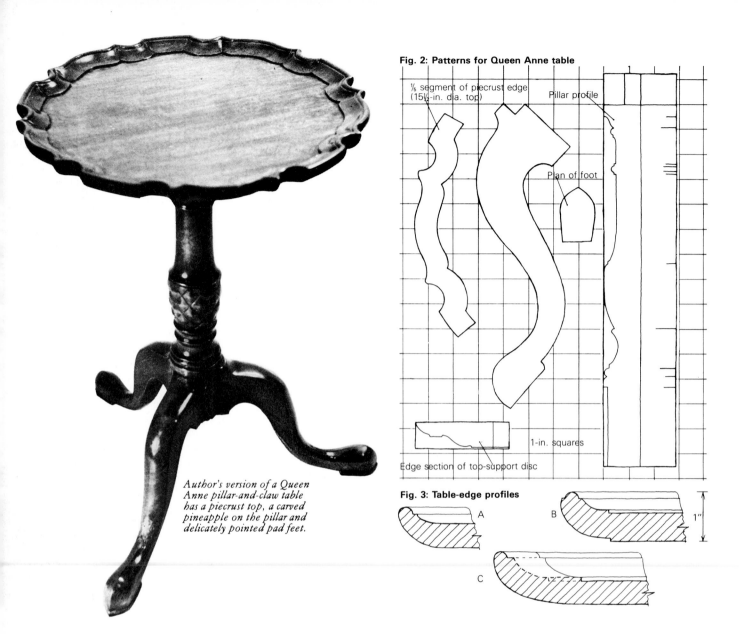

Author's version of a Queen Anne pillar-and-claw table has a piecrust top, a carved pineapple on the pillar and delicately pointed pad feet.

Fig. 2: Patterns for Queen Anne table

⅕ segment of piecrust edge (15½-in. dia. top)

Pillar profile

Plan of foot

1-in. squares

Edge section of top-support disc

Fig. 3: Table-edge profiles

A

B

C

1"

thin fillets where they have been chipped out, I usually make them more substantial, sometimes as much as one part fillet to two parts flute.

A plain top with a slightly rounded edge is quite satisfactory, or with a double or triple bead around the edge. Dished tops (figure 3) are nicer, but should be turned from stock at least ⅞ in. thick, unless they are quite small; then the edge is usually like the one in figure 3C. The best of all, in my opinion, is the piecrust edge, about which I'll say more later. A top that is not intended to tilt should be supported by a turned disc that could be as much as half the diameter of the top. The disc will reduce the tendency of the top to warp and strengthen its attachment to the pillar. It's best to make the disc of the same wood as the top, and to orient its grain in the same direction. Tilting tops have a crow's nest, as in figure 1B.

Making a table—The style I like best is the Queen Anne table with pad feet and a piecrust top. Figure 2 shows the patterns for the legs, pillar, top-support disc, the foot and a one-fifth segment of the piecrust edge. Cut the patterns from ¼-in. plywood, hardboard or solid wood. Take care to fair and smooth all the curved edges, and make sure that the bottom of the foot is square to the back of the leg (what will become

the dovetail tenon). Next prepare the stock for the parts, using the dimensions given in figure 2. The top is 1 in. thick, the legs 1⅜ in. thick, and the pillar 3 in. in diameter. Bandsaw the top and the top-support disc to rough circles, ignoring the shape of the piecrust edge at this stage.

The legs—Now cut the three legs, having made sure that the grain in each runs at about a 45° angle from the foot to the back where it will join the pillar. Stack the three legs one atop another, align them carefully and clamp them together in a vise. Then plane the rear edges flat and flush. These surfaces will become the backs of the dovetail tenons, and the shoulders are gauged from them, so having all three in the same plane ensures that the legs will be square to the pillar when the dovetails are seated in their housings.

Gauge in from the backs ½ in. and score a line on all four sides of each leg to mark the shoulder lines of the joint. Then lay out the dovetail tenons. The accepted slope is 1:7, and they should be no narrower than ½ in. where they meet the shoulders. Saw right to the lines to minimize cleaning up of the cheeks with a chisel, but you must pare the end grain carefully to form the shoulders of the joint. Cut the top of the dovetail tenon back about ⅝ in., as shown on the pattern.

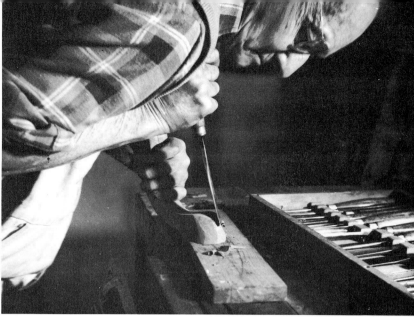

With the leg secured to the bench with a holdfast, author, above, spokeshaves the leg in a gentle curve to form one side of the ankle. The penciled line on the leg marks the limit of cut. The other side (down) has already been shaved to the line. At right, holding the leg in one hand, a wide-sweep gouge in the other, Rodd pares the foot to bring it to a point. Note how the butt of the gouge is seated in the hollow of his shoulder and how his arm is locked in position, so the cutting force comes from the body rather than from the arm.

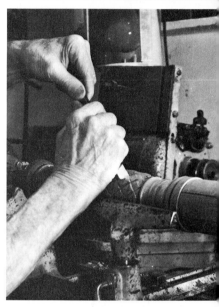

Author uses this marking jig, left, on his lathe to lay out complex patterns for carving and for turning, like this stylized pineapple. The jig consists of a base which sits flat on the ways, plus a post for holding a pencil. Attached to the outboard mandrel is the wooden indexing wheel and pin stop. At right, having set the diamond pattern for the pineapple, Rodd uses a shallow gouge to form the pyramid-shaped elements. The horizontal lines on the base of the pillar delineate the areas to be later flattened and mortised for dovetail housings which will receive the dovetail tenons on the legs.

This will make the housing stronger by leaving more wood at the top of the joint.

Now begin shaping the legs by fairing and smoothing the sweep of the curves top and bottom with a spokeshave. To make the ankle area about two-thirds to three-fourths the thickness of the foot and upper leg, pencil in a line from each side to mark the depth of cut. Hold the leg to the bench with a holdfast, and spokeshave it in a curve down to the line (top left photo). The curve should begin about midway between the shoulder and the foot and continue onto the foot itself. The ankle gets fully rounded, while the sides of the leg remain flat. The top surface of the knee is rounded, leaving a distinct corner at the top which fades about one-third of the way down. The spokeshave does most of the final shaping, though rifflers and large half-round files are useful in small, concave surfaces.

The pointed toe is roughed out with a large gouge (photo, top right). You can do this by eye or use the pattern provided and lay out the shape on the bottom of the foot. Note that the sharp ridge from the pointed toe dies out on top of the foot. Complete the shaping of the foot by carving a groove around the bottom with a V-parting tool and rounding the sides of the toe into it.

The pillar—Except for decorating the urn, turning the column is pretty straightforward and needs no comment. Urns were commonly ornamented with reeds, but I chose to carve a pineapple instead, and I'll describe how it's done. If your lathe is not equipped with an indexing wheel, make one out of wood, along with a pin stop. The wheel should fit friction tight on the outboard end of the mandrel. Laying out the pineapple calls for 18 equally spaced horizontal lines along the circumference of the urn, so bore a ring of 18 holes (each 20° apart) in the indexing wheel. To mark the 18 horizontals, make the simple jig shown above, at left. It consists of a base which sits on the lathe bed and a vertical post which holds a pencil, whose point is aligned precisely with the turning axis.

The next step is to mark the spiral lines on the urn. First draw on a single spiral line using a short length of flexible metal tape to guide the pencil. At each point where this initial spiral intersects the horizontal lines (there are five intersections in the example shown) you will draw a circle around the circumference of the urn, using the marking jig and rotating the stock into the pencil. Now you have a framework on which you can accurately mark out the rest of the spiral lines in both directions. Once this is done, you will have a grid of uniform diamond-shaped elements, and you can to set them

Used for cutting dished-out tops to final depth, after most of the stock has been wasted with a gouge, this depth cutter, above, is basically a hefty stick with a hole in it, through which protrudes a ½-in. gouge. The stick rides against the raised rim of the revolving top while the tool cuts the relieved area to a uniform depth. Below, for turning round tabletops, author made this tool rest from steel bar stock. It can travel laterally on the horizontal bar below, and is provided with an auxiliary rest for getting at the rim of the rotating stock.

in, cutting grooves along the spiral lines with a V-parting tool.

When these cuts are finished in both directions, start shaping the individual diamonds. With a fairly flat gouge, pare away the wood on the four sides of the center point to form a pyramid. Cut close but not quite to the bottoms of the grooves, and try to leave the intersections of the spirals plainly visible. Once the gouge work is finished, you should clean up the grooves with a small parting tool.

While the stock is still on the lathe, you will need to lay out the base of the pillar to receive the legs. This involves cutting three flat areas and the dovetail housings. First mark out the boundaries for the flats; these are 1⅜ in. wide and as long as

the shoulder on the legs. Use the indexing wheel to find the centerline for each land, and measure over 11/16 in. on either side to establish the shoulder lines. Cut the flats by sawing a series of kerfs almost to the shoulder lines, then remove the waste between with a chisel. Finally, pare to the lines with a wide chisel or rabbet plane, and check for flatness using a piece of glass with crayon smeared over its surface. The color will rub off on the high spots, and you can level them.

To cut the dovetail housing, first bore a ⅝-in. hole on the centerline so the top edge of the hole is ⅝ in. below the top of the land. This area is not mortised because the dovetail tenon has been cut back ⅝ in. from the top. Position the end of the dovetail tenon as though it were going to enter the pillar, and trace around it with a sharp pencil or scriber. Carry the marks up across the face of the flat to the outer edges of the holes. With a dovetail saw or tenon saw, cut down the walls of the housing, finishing the cuts with the point of the saw. The hole at the upper end makes this job easier. Chisel out the waste between the cuts, making sure that the bottom of the housing is cut to full depth and is absolutely flat. Slightly bevel the two outside corners, then try the fit by inserting the tenon to about two-thirds its length and moving it in and out a couple of times. Check the walls of the housing for shiny spots to pare down. Repeat this until the leg can be driven home with a few light blows. The fit should be snug, and the shoulders should pull up tight.

At this point I find it convenient to glue the rough-sawn top-support disc to the pillar (you can reinforce the joint with a dowel), and turn it as part of the spindle, rather than as a separate faceplate turning. Then I sand the finished turning, taking care to avoid the urn. You'll ruin its appearance if you sand the points off the pyramids.

The top—The roughsawn blank for the top should be 1 in. thick and 15½ in. in diameter. The dished area will be ½ in. below the carved rim. Screw the top to a faceplate and mount it on the outboard side of the lathe. You will need a wide tool rest like the one shown at left, which you can fabricate from steel bar stock, or simply make out of wood for an occasional turning. To dish out the top I first remove most of the wood with a ½-in. gouge; then I use the depth cutter shown above, which I made myself. It consists of a long bar about 1½ in. square and three times as long as the radius of the largest top to be turned. The ½-in. dia. hole for the cutting tool, an ordinary ½-in. turning gouge, is bored about one-third the way from the one end, and the back of the bar should taper slightly from this area to the ends. The cutter (wedged in place) projects through the hole in the amount you want to dish out the top. In use, the bar is tilted back for the initial cuts and slid back and forth across the rim. Finally, the face of the bar rides flat against the rotating rim.

Before removing the top from the lathe, prepare a wooden straightedge of suitable length, cover it with crayon and hold it against the top as it revolves. High spots will show up as rings. The center portion can be leveled with a finely set block plane, and the outer part can be smoothed with a flat 1½-in. wide gouge which has been ground to an angle of 65° and honed absolutely sharp.

Next comes the piecrust edge. With a compass, describe a circle 15 in. in diameter and use it to register the pattern for the outside scalloped edge, which is marked out and cut with a bandsaw. Next fair all the curves with a large half-round file. This outer edge serves as a guide for making two more such edges, one within the other—the line to mark the upper edge of the cove, and the one to mark the lower edge of the cove. The curves and proportions of the piecrust pattern change as you move inward, and some freehand drawing is necessary to get things right. Once you do, make a cardboard template for these inner edges.

With the two inner edges marked out, begin setting in and grounding the cove, taking care to cut it to no more than half its final depth, and observing how the grain responds to your direction of attack. This is followed by a second setting in, us-

ing an almost flat 1¼-in. gouge, until the cove has been fully grounded. Both care and control are needed to avoid tearing the wood during final grounding, so remember how the grain behaved during the first stage of carving and adjust your direction of cut if necessary. Next cut the inside corners of the rim with a parting tool, using an easy sweep from top to bottom; then complete the cove, cutting into the corners with the flat gouge.

Use a small parting tool to set in and ground the little fillet that separates the cove from the bead which forms the top edge of the rim. Work the intersections (inside corners) with a spade firmer chisel. Finally round the bead with the concave side of a ¼-in. carving gouge, whose sweep should conform to the curve. These cuts are made from both directions with a rolling motion. This is particulary good exercise in handling carving tools because the angle of the grain is constantly changing, and cuts to both the left and the right are necessary. In doing this you will appreciate the small inner bevel you get if you sharpen your gouges properly.

Little now remains to be done. The underside of the outer edges must be rounded, the inner curve being started with a large gouge and finished with file and spokeshave. Lastly, the grounded areas of the top are smoothed with a cabinet scraper, and then the entire top is sanded before attaching the top-support disc with woodscrews. □

Cutting tapered reeds

Tapered table legs, whether curved or straight, are often decorated with reeds, which for a correct appearance must also be tapered in the same degree as the leg. Reeds can be tapered freehand with carving tools, but getting accurate and uniform results is tedious and difficult. The only specialized tool involved is a scratch stock, which you will find useful for other molding jobs. Mine is similar to Henry Kramer's scratch beader (see page 96), but has an adjustable fence, like a marking gauge, instead of a fixed fence. The adjustable fence isn't necessary; on a conventional scratch stock, you simply move the cutter in its slot and tighten the setscrews to reset the distance between the cutter and the fixed fence.

Two cutters are needed. One is ground to cut the vein between two reeds and half the profile of each (cutter A, shown at right). The other is ground to cut only the outside half of the outer reeds and the relieved area between it and the border on the leg (cutter B). You can make these from bits of hacksaw blade or other thin, suitable steel.

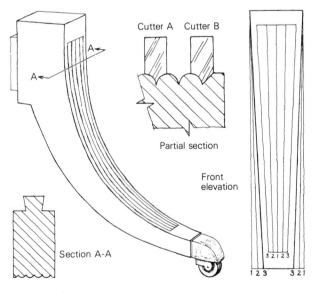

Cutter A Cutter B

Partial section

Front elevation

Section A-A

I'll describe how to cut four tapered reeds on a curved tapered leg; the principles can be adapted to handle other legs or furniture parts and more or fewer reeds. First dimension the leg blank, bandsaw it to its proper profile and fair the curve, leaving the sides yet untapered. With a flexible metal tape, lay out the lines of the finished taper on the face of the stock. Now look at the wedge of wood on either side that will become

waste; at the bottom of the leg divide the wide part of both wedges in two. Draw a line from this midpoint to the top of the leg, bisecting the wedge of waste. Do this on both sides of the leg.

Install cutter A to take a cut down the center of the leg. Hold the fence against the side of the leg and cut in the middle vein and the two inner halves of the two middle reeds. Then handplane the taper on both sides to the first line. You now have a new edge on which to register the scratch-stock fence. Reset the fence to cut the veins between the two outer reeds and the two inner ones. When done you will have formed two tapered central reeds and the inner halves of the two outer reeds. Now plane the leg to its finished taper, install cutter B and form the outer halves of the outer reeds.

Cutting more reeds means tapering the leg in more increments. Cutting an odd number of reeds requires tapering the center reed by planing first to half the depth of the first taper line on both sides. To stop reeds, square off the ends of the veins with a parting tool. —J.R.

A Southern Huntboard
Cock bead is an elegant touch for doors and drawers

by Carlyle Lynch

"With the Southern forests rich with game and the housewife eager for the results of the day's hunt," wrote Paul Burroughs in *Southern Antiques,* "the sport was engaged in by all classes. The hunting boards around which the owners of Southern plantations gathered before and after the hunt resemble the sideboard. They were often simple in design.....As a general rule, they were taller than sideboards ...and were used chiefly in halls, where members of the hunt could stand and partake of wine and food in the fashion of a buffet lunch." Besides serving as informal hall furniture, huntboards helped keep the muddy hunters off the chairs.

This huntboard is adapted from one that I measured and drew in 1952 while it was on loan to the Museum of Fine Arts in Richmond. It's like most of those illustrated in Burroughs' book in that it has four legs instead of the six usually found on sideboards, and it's of a convenient size. Within reason, the piece can be made longer, deeper or taller without destroying its appearance. When I built the huntboard, I put doors on the two end compartments instead of the deep drawers of the original. The center compartment could be fitted with doors or with two drawers of differing depths.

The edges of the doors and drawer fronts of the original were decorated with a plain, but elegant, molding called cock bead and I recommend retaining this detail. Though cock bead is defined as any beading that stands proud of the surface it is meant to decorate, it is best applied as a strip glued to the edges, as shown in the drawer detail in the drawing, rather than merely stuck on the front. Cock bead is common on drawer fronts and door edges of furniture of the Chippendale, Hepplewhite and Sheraton styles. I see no reason why it couldn't be used to good effect on more contemporary furniture. Because cock bead is an applied molding, it can be of a different wood than that of the drawer or door, giving the maker an opportunity to experiment with colors and textures. I made the cock bead of cherry, which contrasts subtly with the walnut used for the rest of the piece and with the holly inlaid in the doors and drawer fronts.

Building the huntboard is straightforward. The carcase consists of two solid wood sides and a back mortised into the four tapered legs. Openings for the doors and drawers are formed by rails attached to the front legs. Two solid wood partitions, mortised into the front stiles and nailed through the carcase back, divide the case into three compartments. Except for plywood doors veneered with walnut, I built with solid wood throughout. But you could substitute plywood for the drawer bottoms and the carcase bottom.

Start by making the legs. They are rectangular in section, $1\frac{1}{2}$ x $1\frac{5}{8}$, as on the original. Lay out and cut the joints to join the sides, back, and front rails to the legs. Then cut and fit the stiles, the center rail, the drawer runners and the two partitions. Dry-clamp the carcase before gluing it up. Before assembly, groove the bottom front rail to accept the bottom; the bottom itself, though, can be fitted later. For added strength, the leg, back and rail tenons should be pinned after assembly.

So they won't warp or swell, the doors should be made of $\frac{3}{4}$-in. plywood veneered on both sides. Don't forget to allow for the thickness of the cock bead when sizing the doors. If you squeeze the leaves of the hinges a bit in a vise, you can mortise them entirely into the legs instead of into both leg and door edge—this makes a neater appearance.

Drawer construction is conventional. I allow for the cock bead on the top and bottom edge of the drawer fronts by making the fronts narrower than their sides by an amount equal to twice the thickness of the cock bead. Or, you could glue up the drawer and cut down the drawer front after assembly. In either case, cock bead on the drawer sides is let into a $\frac{5}{16}$-in. wide, $\frac{1}{8}$-in. deep rabbet. The rabbet should be cut after assembly so that the rearmost edge of the bead will just touch the tapered ends of the dovetail pins.

I make cock bead by ripping thin strips and then using a jack plane to remove the sawmarks and shape the small radius on the bead's front edge. Once made, the bead is simply mitered to length and then glued in place so that it projects about $\frac{1}{16}$ in. You'll have to cut a stopped miter where the wider bead along the top and bottom edges of the drawer fronts meets the narrower bead on the drawer sides.

Carlyle Lynch is a retired designer, cabinetmaker and teacher. He lives in Broadway, Va. More of his drawings are available from Garrett Wade or Woodcraft Supply.

┌─ **Materials List** ────────────────────────────

4 Legs: $1\frac{1}{2}$ x $1\frac{5}{8}$ x 38
2 Sides: $\frac{13}{16}$ x $12\frac{1}{8}$ x $13\frac{7}{8}$, shoulder to shoulder (s/s)
1 Top rail: $\frac{7}{8}$ x $1\frac{1}{2}$ x $43\frac{3}{4}$ (s/s)
1 Bottom rail: $\frac{7}{8}$ x $1\frac{1}{2}$ x $43\frac{3}{4}$ (s/s)
1 Back: $\frac{3}{4}$ x $12\frac{1}{8}$ x $43\frac{3}{4}$ (s/s)
2 Stiles: $\frac{7}{8}$ x $1\frac{1}{2}$ x $10\frac{3}{8}$ (s/s)
2 Partitions, pine: $\frac{13}{16}$ x $11\frac{1}{4}$ x $14\frac{1}{2}$ (s/s)
1 Center rail: $\frac{3}{4}$ x $1\frac{1}{2}$ x 16 (s/s)
1 Bottom, pine: $\frac{3}{4}$ x $14\frac{3}{4}$ x $46\frac{1}{8}$

1 Top: $\frac{7}{8}$ x $18\frac{1}{4}$ x 49
2 Doors: $\frac{3}{4}$ x $10\frac{5}{16}$ x $12\frac{15}{16}$ plywood, plus veneer of desired species
2 Drawer fronts: $\frac{13}{16}$ x $4\frac{1}{2}$ x $15\frac{15}{16}$
2 Drawer backs: $\frac{1}{2}$ x $4\frac{1}{8}$ x $15\frac{15}{16}$
4 Drawer sides: $\frac{1}{2}$ x $4\frac{3}{4}$ x $15\frac{5}{8}$
2 Drawer bottoms: $\frac{3}{8}$ x $15\frac{7}{16}$ x $15\frac{3}{8}$
4 Drawer runners, pine: $\frac{5}{8}$ x $\frac{3}{4}$ x $14\frac{1}{4}$ (2 are kickers)
15 linear ft.: $\frac{1}{20}$ x $\frac{1}{16}$ x 36 holly inlay

14 linear ft.: $\frac{1}{8}$ x $\frac{7}{8}$ cock bead
2 linear ft.: $\frac{1}{8}$ x $\frac{3}{8}$ cock bead
14 Joint pins, walnut: $\frac{3}{16}$ x $\frac{3}{16}$ x $1\frac{1}{2}$ (2 in front, 4 each end, 4 in back)

Hardware: 2 pairs brass butt hinges, $1\frac{3}{4}$ x $1\frac{3}{8}$ open; 4 bright brass drawer pulls, $3\frac{1}{4}$-in. bore; 2 brass thread or inlay escutcheons; 2 cupboard locks, $\frac{3}{4}$-in. selvage to key pin, with barrel keys.

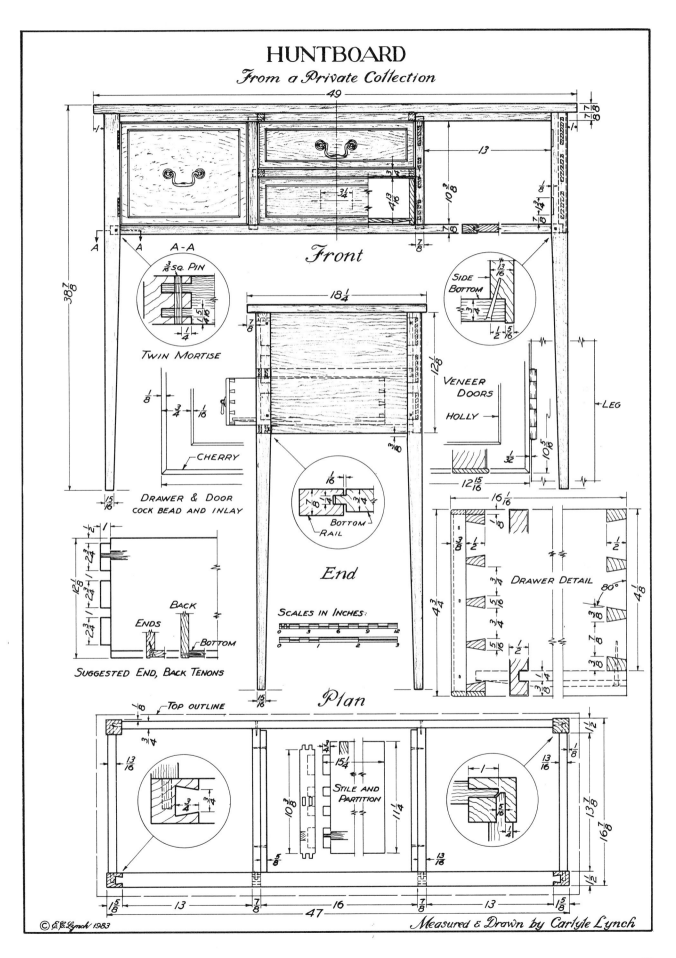

HUNTBOARD
From a Private Collection

Front

A-A

⅜ SQ. PIN

TWIN MORTISE

DRAWER & DOOR
COCK BEAD AND INLAY

CHERRY

SUGGESTED END, BACK TENONS

ENDS

BACK

BOTTOM

End

SCALES IN INCHES:

VENEER
DOORS

HOLLY

LEG

SIDE
BOTTOM

BOTTOM
RAIL

DRAWER DETAIL

80°

Plan

TOP OUTLINE

STILE AND
PARTITION

Measured & Drawn by Carlyle Lynch

© E. E. Lynch 1983

Q & A

S-curved panel tops—*I'd like to make raised-panel doors with S-curved panels like the ones shown in the drawing.*
—*Michael Mohr, Williamsville, N.Y.*
You should start by milling rails and stiles to completion, leaving enough wood on the top rails for the cyma curves.

Make a plywood or hardboard pattern for these curves, mark the top rails and bandsaw them.

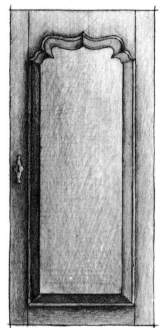

To get the exact outline for the panel, assemble the door frame dry and set it on top of the panel blank, which you may have to glue up from narrower boards so that it is at least ½ in. larger each way than the inside dimensions of the door frame. Center the frame over the panel, letting the ¼-in. excess on each side and bottom provide wood for the tongue. Now pencil the curves on the top of the panel and add ¼ in. to this to form the curved tongue on top.

You can form the straight bevels of the panels on the table saw in the usual way, though the curved bevels must be shaped entirely with chisels and carving tools. However, if you have access to a spindle shaper, the curved bevels can be cut with panel-raising knives and the appropriate collar, but the inside corners on the bevels must be cleaned up with hand tools because the knives will create an arc at the juncture.

The inside edges of the frame can be molded with a router, using the proper bit with a ball-bearing pilot, but you will have to form the angles of the inside corners with hand tools. If you do it this way, you'll have mason's miters where rails meet stiles.
—*Andy Marlow*

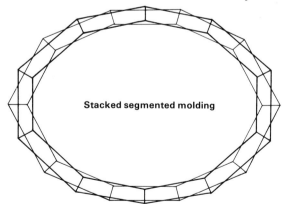

Stacked segmented molding

Oval molding—*I would appreciate your advice on the best method for joining segments of an oval molding that is to surround an oval marble slab for a coffee table. The marble is heavy, and the table will undoubtedly be moved by lifting the edge molding, so strength is important.*
—*W.J. Ripley, Clayton, Calif.*
The strongest way to make the oval molding is to use a method of bricklaying, which can be very attractive. First, draw the oval full scale, and decide upon the number of

layers you'll need and upon the number of segments required for each layer. The thickness of the "bricks" is determined by the final thickness of the molding and by the number of layers you want to stack. Use at least three.

In the drawing the dark lines represent one layer, and the light lines represent another. When you've mitered all the blocks to proper length, rub the joints together using hot hide glue, which will set up as soon as it cools, allowing you to assemble these joints by hand, without having to use clamps. When the rings are complete, glue them together, one on top of another so that they are staggered like bricks. Once the outside is smoothed into an oval, you can veneer the edge if you've made the molding from a utility wood like poplar. If you've made it from the same wood as the rest of the table, then you might like the stacked look it has already.
—*Tage Frid*

Tea table tops—*In Volume I of his* Furniture Treasury, *Wallace Nutting illustrated tea tables with delicately molded tray tops. How were these tops constructed, and were they always attached to the table rails, or could they be removed for use as a serving tray? Was the tabletop ever protected with a sheet of glass?*
—*Earl M. Wintermoyer, Niceville, Fla.*
CARLYLE LYNCH REPLIES: The tops of the rectangular Queen Anne tea tables you refer to invite being picked up, but I've never seen such a table with a removable tray top. The wide rails sometimes housed a wide drawer or pullouts—one table I saw recently had pullouts that showed signs of a hot teapot having been set on them. Though some of these tables appear to have been rabbeted for glass, I don't think it was used. The tops were usually made of a single, wide board, thick

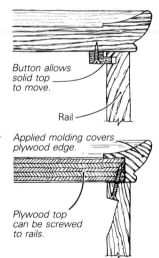

Button allows solid top to move.

Rail

Applied molding covers plywood edge.

Plywood top can be screwed to rails.

enough to allow the table surface to be dished out and its edges molded. There was good reason to make the tops in one piece: if the molding were applied cross-grain, seasonal comings and goings would have warped or cracked the top.

In the traditional cabinet shop, a hand router plane and chisels would have been used to scoop out the table surface, followed by a scratch stock, molding planes and perhaps gouges for the molding. We have an option not available to our forebears, however. We can make the top of plywood faced with the veneer of our choice. I know that purists cringe at the thought of plywood, but our cabinet-grade is a good product that adequately replaces the large slabs of hardwood which are becoming scarce and expensive. If early cabinetmakers had had plywood, I don't think they would have scorned its use. With stable plywood for the tabletop, the molding can be applied with no worry about grain direction. To hide the edges of the plywood, the molding should have a rabbeted skirt, as shown in the drawing. It can be joined by splined miters at the corners. You can attach the top to the rails with the traditional buttons in mortises, or, since seasonal wood movement isn't a problem, with screws driven through the rails and into the top at an angle.

The Blockfront
Its development in Boston, Newport and Connecticut

by Margaretta M. Lovell

Blockfront casepieces (chests of drawers, slant-front desks, kneehole desks, high chests, chest-on-chests and desk-and-bookcases) were made in great numbers in New England during most of the 18th century. There are many variations, even within regional characteristics, but all of these block-fronts exhibit an undulating facade made up of three vertical blocks: two of them convex and one concave. These act visually (along with a proportionate decrease in drawer widths from the bottom to the top of the piece) to give these casepieces a sense of lift as well as a sense of plastic complexity. The blockfront is an expensive and showy design (the blocking is usually carved out of a single piece of primary wood) and many of the pieces are among the finest American cabinetmakers have produced.

Characterized by sweeping curves, rational symmetry, closed composition and a general richness of effect, blockfronts represent a distinctly native interpretation of Baroque (or Queen Anne) aesthetic ideals. Although the generating design principles originated in Europe, and a number of English casepieces exhibit a thin and tentative variety of blocking (see M. M. Lovell, "Boston Blockfront Furniture" in Walter Muir Whitehill, ed., *Boston Furniture of The Eighteenth Century*, Colonial Society of Massachusetts, Boston, 1974), no specific prototype exists. The block-front, it seems, is an American invention.

Three areas are noted for their blockfront case-pieces—Boston, Newport, R.I., and the Colchester region of Connecticut. Each of these areas produced a distinct "school," represented by a fairly consistent set of compositional principles, decorative motifs and habits of construction. The dynamics of regional characteristics are not well understood but clearly the ties of kinship, the phenomenon of specialist craftsmen and the force of apprenticeship training encouraged the establishment and repetition of distinct regional design vocabularies.

Boston seems to be where the blockfront originated, for the earliest signed and dated example (1738) was made there. Although noted for their richly varied forms and decorative features, Boston blockfronts nevertheless have basic things in common. The example illustrated in figure 1 will serve as an archetype. Its primary wood is West Indian mahogany (usually darker in Boston examples than in those made to the south), and its secondary wood is white pine (native to Massachusetts and imported from Maine since early in the

Figure 1.

Figure 2.

Figure 3.

Fig. 1: *Boston chest, mahogany, pine and poplar, 31½ in. by 33¾ in. by 20⅛ in., 1755-1790. Courtesy Yale University Art Gallery, Mabel Brady Garvan collection. Fig. 2: Newport chest, mahogany and tulipwood, 34½ in. by 36¾ in. by 19 in., made by John Townsend, 1765. Courtesy The Metropolitan Museum of Art, Rogers Fund, 1927. Fig. 3: Connecticut chest, cherry and pine, 35¾ in. by 40 in. by 20 in., 1765-1790. Courtesy The Henry Francis du Pont Winterthur Museum.*

Boston pieces, as at left, follow the English practice and typically cover the sliding dovetail that joins drawer divider to carcase side with a thin strip of molded wood nailed on. In most pieces the drawer divider does not go all the way through the carcase side, and so the joint is completely concealed. Newport pieces, as at right, display the sliding dovetail. The pins of the drawer dovetails are thin and precise. Courtesy Yale University Art Gallery, Mabel Brady Garvan collection.

18th century). Its feet are of the straight bracket type (although short cabriole legs with claw-and-ball feet are almost equally common on Boston examples). A decorative drop, which is not found in pieces from other regions, usually punctuates the bottom line of the piece at its midpoint. (This feature, which is absent on the piece pictured in figure 1 on page 65, is shown in the drawing below, right). The drawer dividers are joined to the carcase sides with a full sliding dovetail, sometimes cut all the way through so that the end grain of the dividers is visible on the sides of the chest. Usually a thin strip of mahogany, bead-molded on its inner edge and nailed to the front edge of the carcase side conceals the joint. With the bottom drawer removed, a giant dovetail is visible behind the central concavity where the mahogany bottom molding is joined to the white pine carcase bottom. The juncture between these two parts is in one plane.

By contrast, Newport blockfronts are usually made of lighter, redder mahogany, and the grain of the wood is an im-portant feature of the design (figure 2). Secondary woods are characteristically chestnut (on the back of the carcase) and tulip poplar (the drawer interiors). The feet are invariably of the ogee bracket type; its gentle waving line complements the three-dimensional curves above. Carved shells, a feature not found in Boston examples, terminate the columns of blocking. The convex shells are almost always applied. Rather than conceal the joint between the drawer dividers and the case, the neat and precise dovetails that anchor the case together are clearly visible on the facade—one of the rare instances of joinery being used for decorative effect in an 18th-century design. And instead of the thin, abrupt top common to Boston chests, Newport cabinetmakers modified this transition from vertical to horizontal by a series of wide compound moldings. Behind the mask of these moldings two boards of secondary wood run under the top, one at the front, the other at the back, half-blind dovetailed into the carcase sides. The top is glued to the front member and cleated to the back member by means of a neat, sturdy butterfly, visible from the back of most Newport chests of drawers. This method of construction fixes the top at the front, allowing it, without warping or cracking, to expand and contract at the back. (The tops of Boston pieces are put on in a variety of less ingenious ways, including glue blocks, nails, and, in some cases, sliding dovetails at the top of the carcase sides.) Another obvious difference from the Boston pieces is that Newport blockfronts have no giant dovetail in the carcase bottom. The lower rail, shaped in front to repeat the line of the blocking, is straight on its back and often buttressed with a 2-in. or 3-in. wide straight piece of secondary wood in the same plane. The actual carcase bottom is about 2 in. below this piece, flush with the bottom of the molding.

In general, Newport blockfronts are renowned for the neatness of their construction. Impeccable drawer dovetails have thin necks, and the complicated moldings and the beading in the dovetailed drawer dividers are finely mitered. The consistency in quality of craftsmanship is matched by an almost equal consistency in design. The Newport school was obviously a tight network of individuals who—once the original Newport formula was established—stuck to variations on the major theme from the 1760s until the early 1800s. Although almost a hundred cabinetmakers worked in Newport during

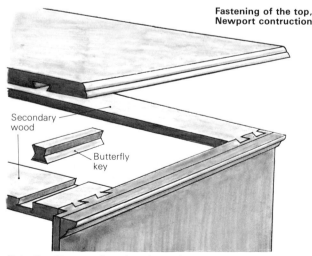

Fastening of the top, Newport contruction

Secondary wood

Butterfly key

Note: Few Newport pieces have been taken apart for examination. This drawing is partly conjectural.

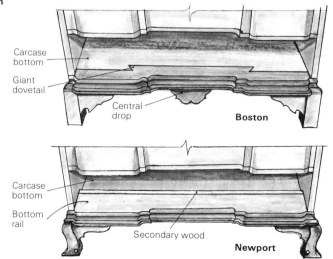

Bottom-rail/carcase-bottom construction

Carcase bottom

Giant dovetail

Central drop

Boston

Carcase bottom

Bottom rail

Secondary wood

Newport

Illustrations: Ric Lopez

this time, all the signed or labeled blockfronts that have survived were made by members of the Townsend family. There is evidence that Edmund, John and other family members collaborated on blockfronts—either side-by-side in their small shops or separately, each man working on his specialty in his own shop. Almost all the Newport blockfronts bear elaborate directions (in 18th-century calligraphy) indicating "front top," "left side," etc., on the designated member, or *A, B,* and *C* on drawer series. Perhaps the craftsman needed to remind himself of his parts, but it is more likely that these notations were made to communicate between craftsmen. Such assembling instructions are absent from the interiors of Boston blockfronts, which—judging by the seven signed and documented examples—were made by individual craftsmen in widely separated places and not linked by the tight kinship system that characterized the three generations of Newport's premier cabinetmaking family.

Such cohesive cooperation is not evident in Connecticut blockfronts (figure 3), which, if we may judge from surviving examples, were exercises in eccentric individual interpretation. In general, Connecticut blockfronts follow Newport, not Boston, in design and construction. The Newport shell capping the blocked areas, the ogee bracket feet, the wide top molding, the straight, internal front of the carcase bottom, are all carry-overs from Newport to neighboring Connecticut. However, significant differences are even more apparent. As in most Connecticut furniture, even for these expensive, showy pieces, the primary wood is cherry stained to resemble mahogany rather than the imported mahogany favored in Massachusetts and Rhode Island. The secondary woods are chestnut and tulip poplar as in Rhode Island, but pine is also used. Together with ogee bracket feet, short cabriole legs with claw-and-ball feet are common. Drawer dovetails are more widely spaced and less elegantly made, and secondary pieces (such as drawer bottoms) are often heavy and chamfered at their edges. But most characteristic of Connecticut is the variety of forms and arrangements attempted within the basic tripartite blockfront arrangement. The piece shown in figure 3 has, for instance, heavier feet than the Newport type with an extra energetic curve on the bracket. The classical vocabulary of Palladian architecture, which underlies the proportions and motifs of all the furniture of this period, has been stretched here to produce a non-Renaissance effect. The flanking pilasters lack both base and capital while the dentil course at the top is doubled; oddest of all, the base molding is also ornamented with a dentil course.

Made by and for a pragmatic people, blockfronts exhibit an unusual disregard for expensive materials and time-consuming labor. That they existed in such numbers and developed such complex forms over such a long period of time and over such a wide geographical area attests to the power of the design to satisfy the self-image of a large number of customers, both rural and urban. The style went through an adventuresome investigative period in Boston (1730 to 1780), moved into its classic phase in Newport (1760 to 1800) and then experienced a second, more mannered, inventive stage in Connecticut (1770 to 1815). Throughout, it retained its original appeal as a design based on rational symmetry and plastic, tactile richness of form. □

Margaretta Lovell teaches in the Art History department at Yale University.

Building Blockfronts
Improving traditional constructions

by E. F. Schultz

Blockfront furniture has always been regarded by antiquarians and craftsmen alike as a unique, beautiful and important American decorative-arts creation. Students of furniture and design admire the blockfront for its boldly sculptured form, its fine proportions and its superlative moldings. This article attempts to deal with some of the demanding constructional features particular to Boston and Newport (R.I.) blockfront furniture. The cabinetmaker today can construct period reproductions either exactly like the original in every detail or with modifications, incorporating contemporary improvements in the joinery without visually altering the piece's magnificence. I choose to improve the construction where time has shown the originals to have shortcomings.

Before beginning, it is important to note the complexity of these designs and the meticulous execution they warrant. Be prepared to spend several months in a well-equipped shop to complete a blockfront like the ones discussed here. A time-consuming, but indispensable, first step is to draft full-scale plans. They indicate the relation of all the parts, their joinery and detailing, and thus prove whether or not your planned method of construction will work. In effect, once you have successfully completed a set of plans, you will have mentally assembled the piece of furniture. The plans are then a record of information often not easy to recall in the midst of actual construction. They also can be elaborated upon in designing more sophisticated pieces. I prefer full-scale plans when the size of the piece permits, as you can measure from them directly and use them to make and check templates.

Much of the beauty of blockfront furniture is attributed to

Joseph Benenate

Schultz's reproduction of a Boston blockfront chest of drawers, 40 in. by 35⅜ in. by 22½ in., Honduras mahogany. Plans for this piece and for the Newport blockfront slant-top desk shown on the next page appear on pages 70 to 73.

Fig. 1: Newport case construction

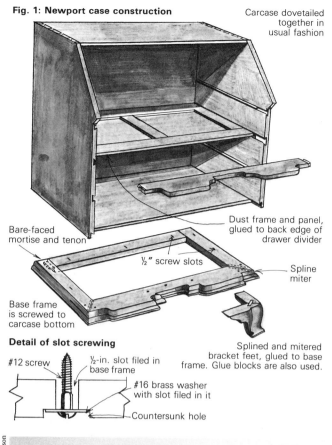

Carcase dovetailed together in usual fashion

Bare-faced mortise and tenon

Dust frame and panel, glued to back edge of drawer divider

½″ screw slots

Spline miter

Base frame is screwed to carcase bottom

Splined and mitered bracket feet, glued to base frame. Glue blocks are also used.

Detail of slot screwing

#12 screw

½-in. slot filed in base frame

#16 brass washer with slot filed in it

Countersunk hole

Newport blockfront slant-top desk in construction. One-piece mahogany side is 20¾ in. wide.

From the back, base frame (left) shows bare-faced mortise and tenon, and half-blind dovetails between back feet and braces. Segmenting the bracket-foot glue blocks (right) minimizes the chance that the bracket pieces, which run crossgrain, will crack.

the wide, one-piece ends and top. A mahogany board of the required width will usually display quite diverse visual grain characteristics: flame figure, dark (almost black) stripes, rich swirls and beautiful iridescent colors. To make a visually accurate blockfront reproduction, the cabinetmaker must first deal with the problem of locating suitable and worthy stock, and then plan his construction to cope with the constant movement of even well-seasoned boards. However they move, they must provide a stable carcase for the sculptured drawers they contain. With both Boston and Newport furniture, these wide boards must also attach to a sculptured base molding and to bracket feet. Because the grain direction of the carcase sides is perpendicular to that of the base molding, the traditional construction techniques—gluing and nailing this molding to the carcase side—is troublesome. Many cases have loose moldings and/or cracks originating from the molding because it constrained the movement of the sides and thus caused them to relieve their internal stresses through checking. Also, the ogee bracket feet were glued across the grain of the wide boards, so this joint too loosens in time.

One possible solution to this problem is to allow the wide boards to move, but to direct their movement. The aim is to have the exterior remain visually perfect, so we construct the piece for the movement of the wide boards to occur from front to back. The visual facade of the piece remains tight while expansion and contraction occur "behind" its exterior surface. This can become somewhat of an engineering job.

The construction that I suggest for the Newport case is shown in figure 1. In simplified terms, a dovetailed carcase is attached to a molded base frame. The front corners of the base frame are mitered and splined, with bare-faced tenons cut on the back rail and mortises on the sides. The front and sides of the base are glued up first, the back rail afterward. Remember when gluing up the miters that only the outermost edge shows; therefore, this edge should be tightly fitted even if the inner edge of the miter is not.

Next, the front two ogee bracket feet are splined and glued together while the back feet are half-blind dovetailed to the back braces (photo, above). All four are then glued directly to the base frame. Glue blocks are used as well. For the bracket feet themselves, cutting several short glue blocks instead of one long one should keep the deleterious effect of wood movement to a minimum.

The entire base has now been assembled as a separate unit. The bottom surface of the case and the top surface of the base frame should now be trued with a plane and straightedge prior to slot-screwing the base into place. I use a Starrett 36-in. straightedge because of its heft and resistance to bending. Slot the screwholes in the center and rear of the base frame only; thus the carcase is fixed to the base frame at the front and allowed to expand and contract at the back.

With Boston blockfronts the suggested construction for attaching the base molding must differ somewhat from the Newport style because of the absence of a drawer divider between the bottom drawer and the molding. This, along with the absence of a drawer divider between the top drawer and the carcase top, gives the Boston chest a more starkly linear appearance. The joinery for constructing and attaching the base on the Boston blockfront is more complicated than with the Newport style, but the principles are the same (figure 2). A major difference here from the Newport construction is that the base, once installed, is not removable. The molded base front, incorporating its giant dovetail, is glued permanently to the case bottom's leading edge. The base sides are then glued to the front of the base with a lap miter joint. Thus the base molding is held secure to the front of the case, allowing the carcase to move in slotted screwholes from front to back. The rear rail of this base "cradle" is fitted and lap-joined to the base molding sides *after* the sides are screwed to the bottom of the case. This sequence is followed to ensure a tight fit between the case sides and the L-shaped, molded base sides. The bracket feet are applied to the base in the same manner as in the Newport blockfront, using segmented glue blocks. When completed, and even with the bottom drawer removed, unless one looks underneath the Boston case, it is not possible to differentiate this type of construction from the original.

Because the wide boards, whose movement we have been taking into account in our construction, must also be an integral part of a sturdy carcase for supporting the large, sculptured drawers, the joinery between drawer dividers and carcase sides deserves attention. Newport pieces traditionally have exposed sliding dovetails with cockbeading on both drawer dividers and carcase sides. Boston pieces usually cover the drawer-divider dovetails with thin cockbeaded strips of wood the length of the carcase sides. In both Boston and Newport blockfronts there are no dust panels. The period pieces, for the most part, have drawer runners dadoed and glue-blocked to the carcase sides, a crossgrain construction that can result in cracked sides.

I prefer to incorporate dust panels whose frames provide more than adequate drawer support while allowing the runners to float free of the carcase sides (figure 1). The extra time and stock required for this construction is negligible when compared to the sturdier, more durable and more finished piece that results. Figures 3 and 4 contrast the Newport and Boston-style joints between carcase side and drawer divider. The cockbeading and its mitering in both cases present a special challenge in fine joinery.

Gene Schultz builds custom furniture at Boston Cabinet-Making, Inc., in Boston, Mass.

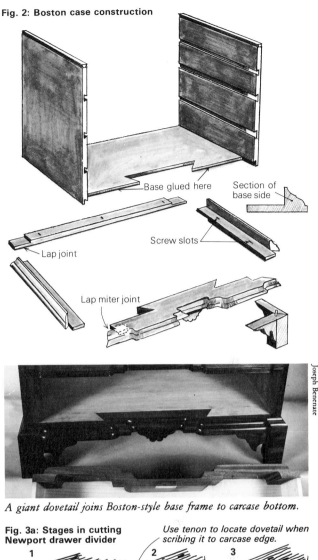

Fig. 2: Boston case construction

Base glued here

Section of base side

Screw slots

Lap joint

Lap miter joint

Joseph Benerate

A giant dovetail joins Boston-style base frame to carcase bottom.

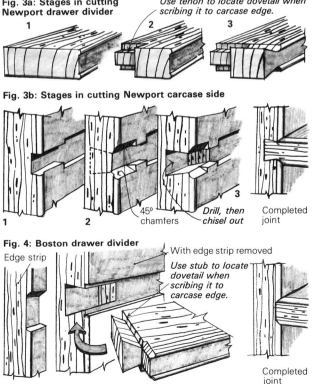

Fig. 3a: Stages in cutting Newport drawer divider

Use tenon to locate dovetail when scribing it to carcase edge.

1   2   3

Fig. 3b: Stages in cutting Newport carcase side

1   2   45° chamfers   Drill, then chisel out   3   Completed joint

Fig. 4: Boston drawer divider

Edge strip

With edge strip removed

Use stub to locate dovetail when scribing it to carcase edge.

Completed joint

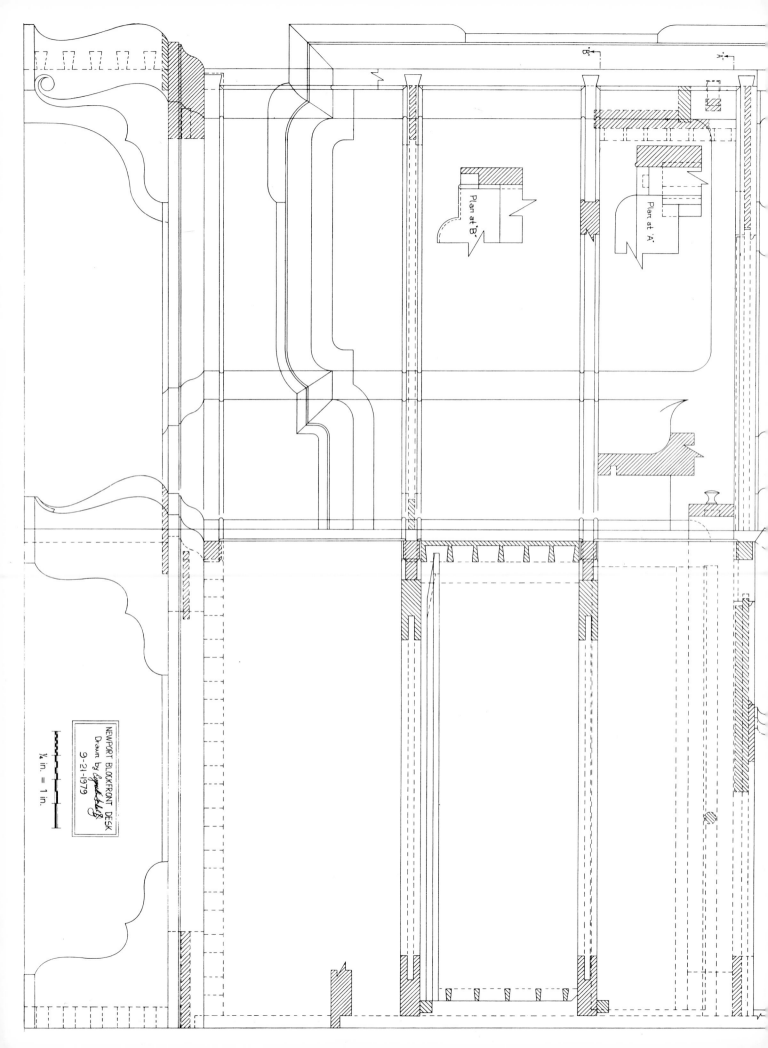

Plan at 'B'.

Plan at 'A'.

NEWPORT BLOCKFRONT DESK
Drawn by *[signature]*
9-21-1979

¼ in. = 1 in.

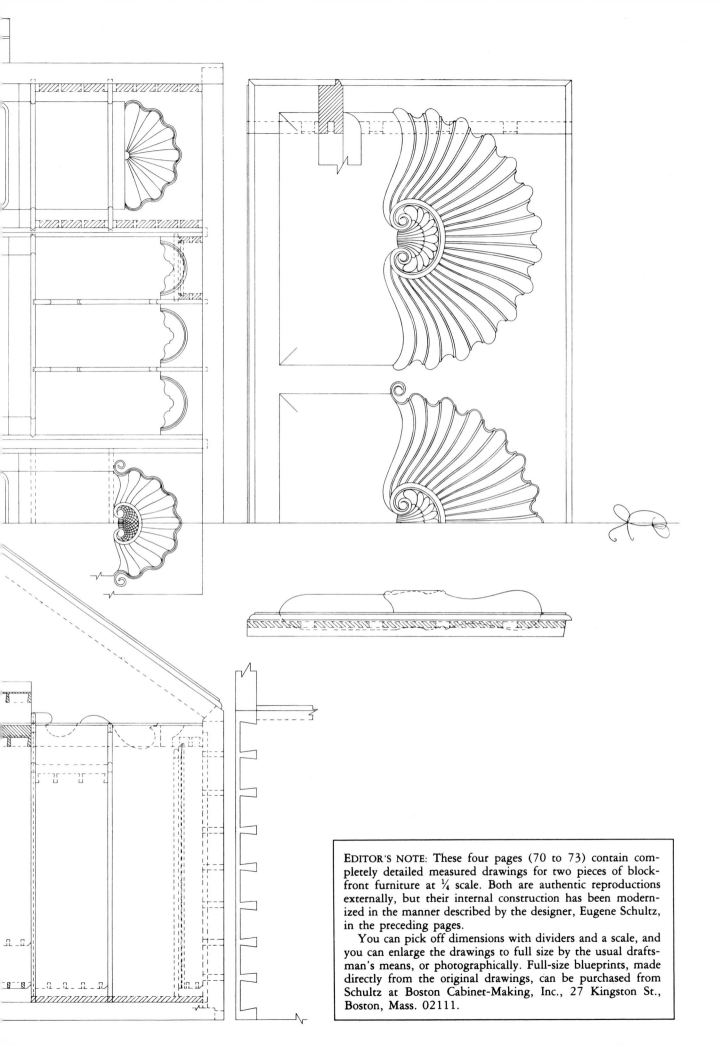

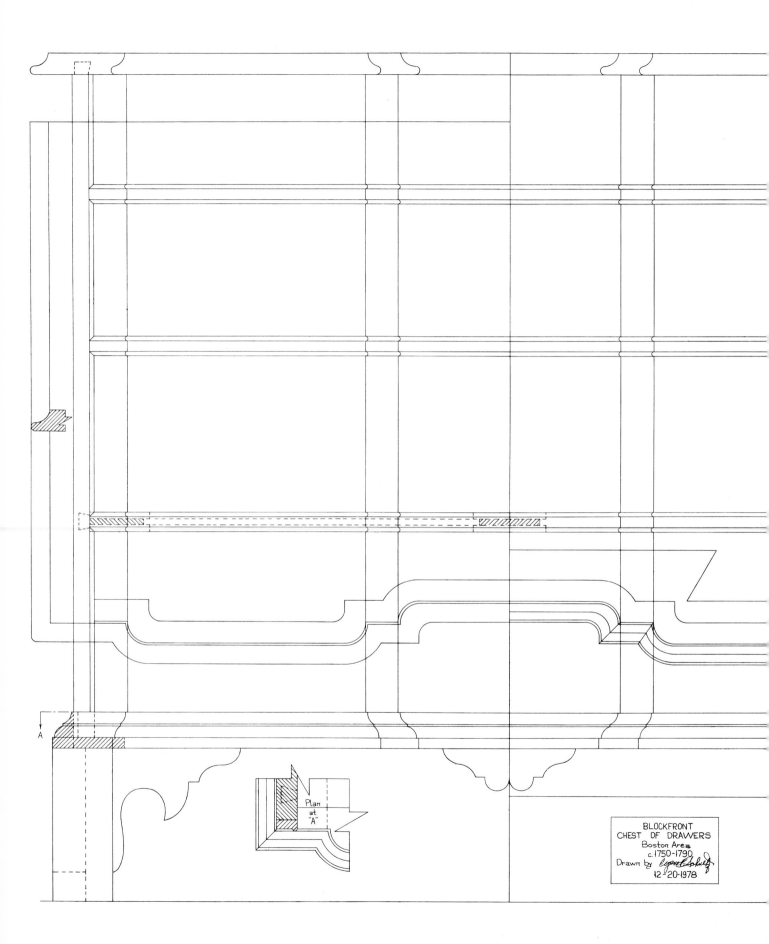

Plan
at
"A"

BLOCKFRONT
CHEST OF DRAWERS
Boston Area
c. 1750-1790
Drawn by *[signature]*
12-20-1978

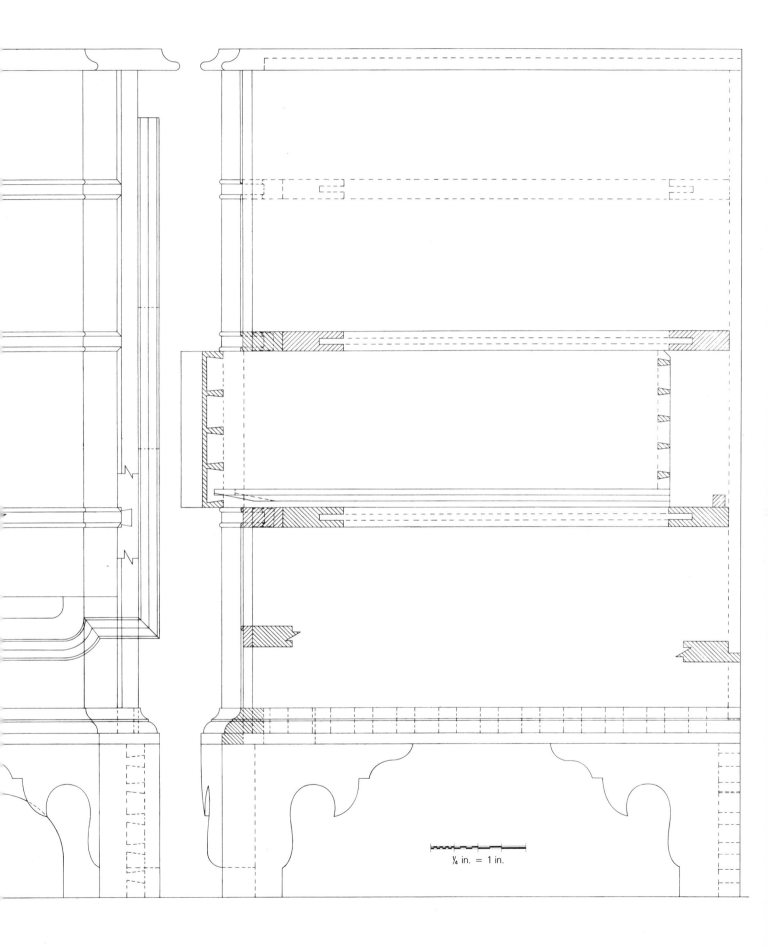

¼ in. = 1 in.

Boston Bombé Chest
Bulging drawer fronts are all shaped at once

by Lance Patterson

More than 50 pieces of American bombé furniture made in the last half of the 18th century still exist. Surprisingly, all were built in or around Boston. The kettle-shaped bombé form (the term is derived from the French word for *bulge*) is characterized by the swelling of the lower half of the carcase ends and front, with the swell returning to a normal-size base. This shape is, I think, directly related to English pieces such as the Apthorp chest-on-chest, which was imported to Boston before 1758 and is now at that city's Museum of Fine Arts. Bombé was popular in England for only 10 to 12 years, but remained the vogue in Boston for nearly 60 years.

In America, the carcase ends were always shaped from thick, solid planks of mahogany. In Europe, the ballooning case ends were most often coopered—3-in. to 4-in. pieces of wood were sawn to shape, glued up, contoured and then veneered. Instead of veneering, the Americans worked with sol-id wood. I think the magnificent grain patterns of this shaped mahogany are a major attribute of Boston furniture. The bombé form, I believe, also shows the enthusiasm that 18th-century cabinetmakers must have felt when wide, clear mahogany first became available to them.

There was also an evolution in the treatment of the case's inside surfaces and, consequently, in the shape of the drawers. On the earlier pieces, the case ends are not hollowed out and the drawer sides are vertical. Some transition pieces have lipped drawer fronts, the lip following the curve of the case. The fully evolved form has hollowed-out ends and drawers with sides shaped to follow the ends. Some of the later pieces have serpentine drawer fronts.

I will describe how I built a small bombé chest with four shaped drawers, ball-and-claw feet and a serpentine front. I didn't take step-by-step photos while building, so I'll have to

Patterson's bombé chest, based on an 18th-century design, has four dovetailed drawers and ball-and-claw feet. Side view, right, shows shape of serpentine front.

Fig. 1: Patterson's plans for a Boston bombé chest

BILL OF MATERIALS

	Rough Dimensions				Finished Dimensions			
Description	Amt.	T	W	L	Amt.	T	W	L
Case								
Top	1	1	20¼	39½	1	⅞	19¾	38½
Bottom	7	1¾	3	36¾	1	1½	19¼	35¾
Ends	2	12/4	20½	25	2	⅞	20	24½
Rail I	1	1	4	38	1	13/16	3½	34
Rail II	1	1	4	38	1	13/16	3½	35
Rail III	1	1	4	38	1	13/16	3½	38
Drawer runners I	2	4/4	2	15⅜	2	13/16	1¾	14⅞
Drawer runners II	2	4/4	2	16	2	13/16	1¾	15½
Drawer runners III	2	4/4	2	17½	2	13/16	1¾	17
Runner supports	2	4/4	3½	19½	2	¾	3	19
Feet with one ear	2	12/4	8	16	4	2⅞	7	7½
Ears	1	12/4	4	14	4	2⅞	3⅞	2½
Backboards	3	⅝	6¾	38	3	⅜	6¼	37½
Back cleat strips	4	⅝	2	38	4	⅜	1½	37½
Drawer I								
Front	1	12/4	4¼	38	1	⅞	3⅞	32¼
Sides	2	⅝	4¼	17	2	½	3⅞	16¼
Back	1	⅝	4	33	1	½	3⅜	32¼
Bottom	1	⅝	16½	32	1	⅜	16⅛	31⅝

	Rough Dimensions				Finished Dimensions			
Description	Amt.	T	W	L	Amt.	T	W	L
Drawer II								
Front	1	12/4	6	38	1	⅞	5¾	33⅜
Sides	2	⅝	5¾	17	2	½	5⅜	16⅞
Back	1	⅝	5	34	1	½	4¾	33⅜
Bottom	1	⅝	17¼	34	1	⅜	16¾	33
Drawer III								
Front	1	12/4	7	38	1	1	6½	36⅜
Sides	2	4/4	6½	19	2	⅝	6⅛	18⅜
Back	1	⅝	5½	37	1	½	5⅛	36⅜
Bottom	1	⅝	18¾	37	1	⅜	18¼	36
Drawer IV								
Front	1	12/4	8	38	1	1⅜	7¾	36⅜
Sides	2	5/4	7½	19	2	1	7	18⅜
Back	1	⅝	6	37	1	½	5⅝	36⅜
Bottom	1	⅝	16½	32	1	⅜	16⅛	31½

All measurements include length of tenons and dovetails.

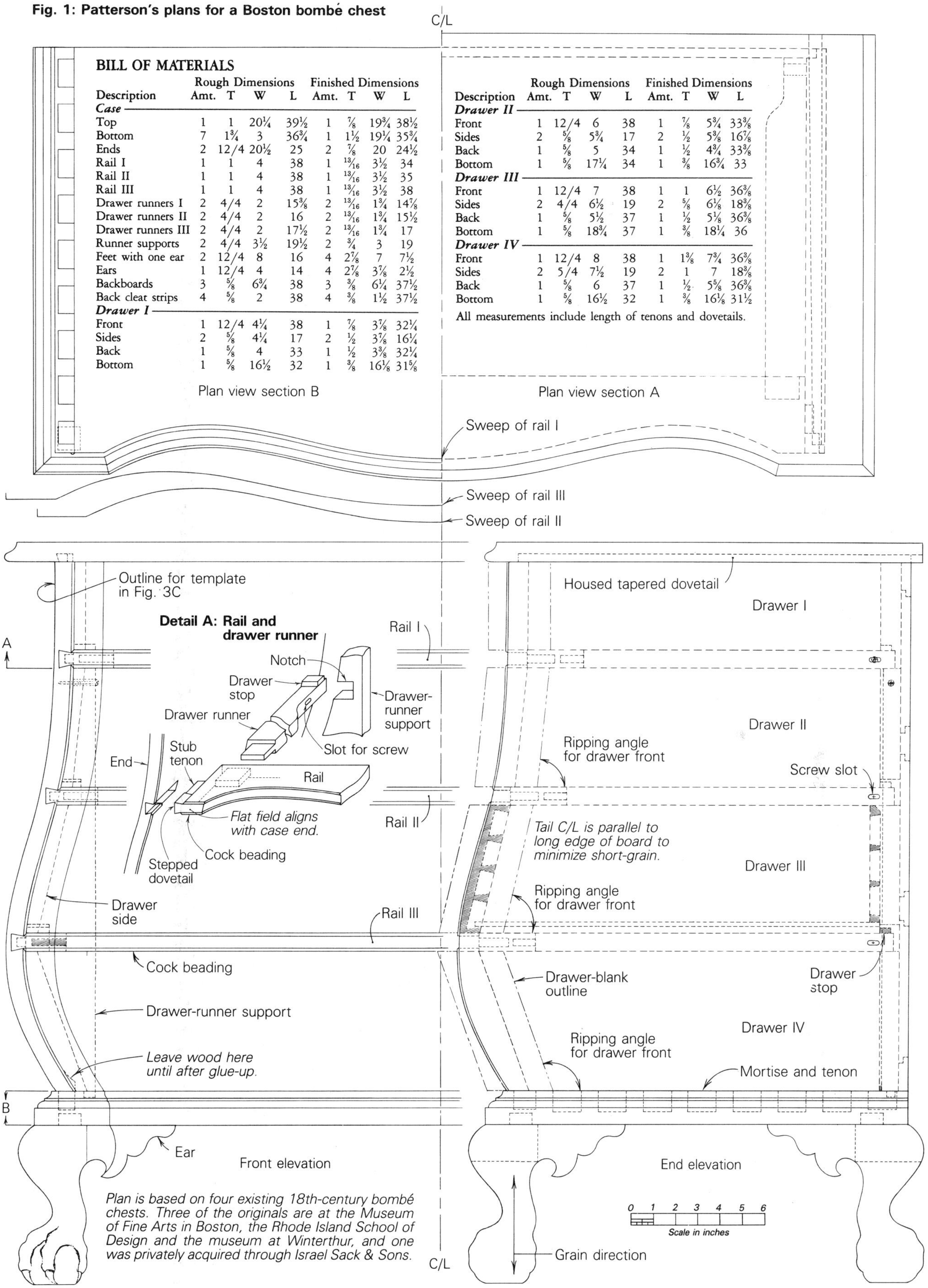

C/L
Plan view section B
Plan view section A
Sweep of rail I
Sweep of rail III
Sweep of rail II
Outline for template in Fig. 3C
Detail A: Rail and drawer runner
Notch
Drawer stop
Drawer runner
Drawer-runner support
Slot for screw
End
Stub tenon
Rail
Flat field aligns with case end.
Cock beading
Stepped dovetail
Rail I
Rail II
Rail III
A
B
Drawer side
Cock beading
Drawer-runner support
Leave wood here until after glue-up.
Ear
Front elevation
Housed tapered dovetail
Drawer I
Drawer II
Ripping angle for drawer front
Screw slot
Tail C/L is parallel to long edge of board to minimize short-grain.
Drawer III
Ripping angle for drawer front
Drawer-blank outline
Drawer stop
Drawer IV
Ripping angle for drawer front
Mortise and tenon
End elevation
0 1 2 3 4 5 6
Scale in inches
Grain direction
C/L

Plan is based on four existing 18th-century bombé chests. Three of the originals are at the Museum of Fine Arts in Boston, the Rhode Island School of Design and the museum at Winterthur, and one was privately acquired through Israel Sack & Sons.

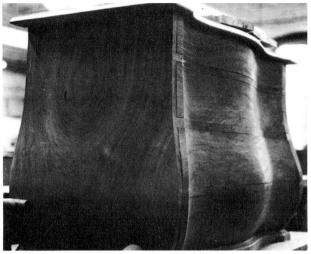

Vivid grain patterns are exposed when thick mahogany is shaped. Making the board's bark side convex yields a hyperbolic figure, as in the author's chest, above; cutting into the other side produces elliptical patterns, shown in the photo on page 78.

illustrate some operations with photos of Jerry de Rham building his bombé desk at Boston's North Bennet Street School, where I teach. His version is of the basic bombé form: the front is not serpentine, but bulges to match the ends.

It's unclear how early cabinetmakers made the shaped drawers, but it probably was done by trial and error, then angle blocks and patterns were made for future reference. There are graphic methods for figuring the angles, and mathematical methods are quick and accurate, too, as explained on page 79. These same techniques can be applied when you are designing anything with canted sides and ends, such as a cradle, dough box, or splayed-joint stool or table.

The first step in any project of this scope is to make full-size orthographic drawings, primarily to facilitate making patterns for shaped parts. This also helps you work out joinery dimensions, and preview the actual size and look of the piece. In developing drawings, I like to gather information from all the sources I can find. I know of four original chests similar to mine—one was privately acquired through Israel Sack & Sons, and the others are at the Museum of Fine Arts in Boston, the Rhode Island School of Design, and Winterthur. Measured drawings of the chest at RISD can be found in *Masterpieces of Furniture* by V.C. Salmonsky (Dover Publications). After building the chest, I revised my drawing by adding ½ in. to the bottom drawer height. Because this drawer recedes from the common viewing angles, it appears narrower than it is. Usually I follow the rule of thumb that drawer height plus

rail height should equal the height of the next lower drawer.

The wood for my chest was a 12/4 plank of South American mahogany, 12 ft. by 22 in., and a 4/4 mahogany board, 40 in. by 21 in., with secondary parts of poplar. For effective use of grain, the symmetry of the ends and the continuity of the front are the most important considerations. I laid out the ends book-fashion, with the bulge toward the wider annual-ring pattern (figure 2). Either face of the plank can be used as the outside; both elliptical and hyperbolic annual-ring patterns are beautiful. I chose the bark side of the plank, producing a hyperbolic pattern at the bulge, as shown in the photo at left. De Rham's desk shows the characteristic elliptical pattern of the heart face, seen in the photo on page 78.

To avoid conflict between the long grain and the cross grain around the case, and to eliminate applied moldings, I departed from traditional construction. I used a thick mahogany bottom with the base molding cut into it. Thus the end base molding is end grain, but so is the molding on the top's end, and there's a lot of end grain in the serpentine front molding as well. I especially like end-grain molding.

To shape the chest, first rough-saw all the parts according to the rough stock list, page 75. Note that the final dimensions differ considerably in many cases, but the parts should be cut oversize to ensure that they can be shaped with the setups shown in figure 3. Next, rip the front pieces for the three lower drawers at the angles shown on the side-elevation drawing in figure 1 so that they can be canted to provide the necessary thickness for the serpentine shape. Mark out the rails from the centerline and bandsaw them to shape.

I shaped the front as a unit, the method I recommend for any serpentine or oxbow casework. Mount the drawer fronts and rails on the benchtop jig shown in figure 3A, made with two 2-in. wide supports cut to match the rail and drawer-front profile. I tack-glued the parts to each other at the ends and added two bar clamps for support during shaping.

Using the full-size patterns, trace profile shapes on all four edges of the assembly. These lines, with the bandsawn rails, are your guides for the compound curves. With a large, shallow gouge, I first roughed out the concave areas and then the flat fields at the ends. Now spokeshave to the profile lines, using a square from the end surface to check the front. I used a bandsawn three-dimensional pattern, shown in figure 3C, to draw the line of the corner in to where the flat fields meet the serpentine shape. The rest of the front was shaped from this line. I did most of the gouge work across the grain, following up with spokeshaves, cutting from high to low in various directions. I sawed an inch off the handle of my No. 151 round-bottom spokeshave to reach all the concavities.

The front should be symmetrical and free of lumps,

Fig. 2: Plank-cutting diagram

End		End	Rail II	Two pieces of bottom		Five pieces of bottom		Foot	Foot
				Drawer front III					
						Drawer front I			Ears
Center of annual rings			Rail III	Drawer front IV	Rail I	Drawer front II		Foot	Foot

Most of the major parts were cut from a 12/4 South American mahogany plank, 12 ft. by 22 in. The case ends were laid out book-fashion with the bulge toward the wider annual ring pattern.

Fig. 3: Shaping the curves

A: Contouring the front

A benchtop jig positions all the drawer fronts and rails together so that they can be shaped as a unit. The drawer fronts shown here are in various stages of completion. The two supports are cut to conform to the slope of the backs of the drawer blanks, shown in Fig. 1, and are notched to receive the rails.

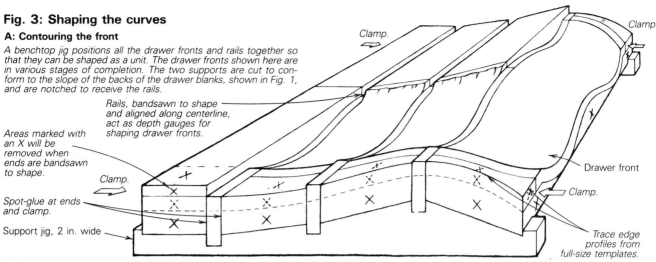

Clamp.

Clamp.

Rails, bandsawn to shape
and aligned along centerline,
act as depth gauges for
shaping drawer fronts.

Areas marked with
an X will be
removed when
ends are bandsawn
to shape.

Clamp.

Drawer front

Clamp.

Spot-glue at ends
and clamp.

Support jig, 2 in. wide

Trace edge
profiles from
full-size templates.

B: Shaping the ends

Carcase ends are rough-shaped by making tablesaw cuts every 2 in. about ¼ in. short of the profile lines traced on the edges. These parallel sawcuts allow the waste to be removed quickly with a wide chisel. The contours are smoothed with planes, spokeshave and scraper.

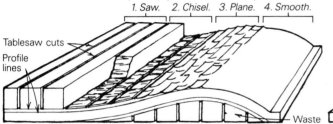

1. Saw. 2. Chisel. 3. Plane. 4. Smooth.

Tablesaw cuts

Profile
lines

Waste

C: Matching the curves

Three-dimensional pattern, bandsawn to match chest outline in Fig. 1, allows you to draw a fairly accurate pencil line over the contoured surface to define the corner where the case ends meet the front.

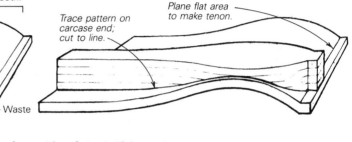

Plane flat area
to make tenon.

Trace pattern on
carcase end;
cut to line.

smoothly curved in all directions. The final scraping and adjusting of the field lines can't be done until the case and drawers have been assembled, yet before the cock beading is carved. The gouge work goes quickly and is fun. It's important to stay relaxed, and I try to keep a rhythm to my mallet blows. Hollow the backs of the drawer fronts individually, but leave enough flat area at both ends to pass each piece over the tablesaw, to mark out the dovetails, and to check for any movement after shaping. If there is any winding or other movement, first plane it out of the back of the drawer front, thus making a reference surface for correcting edges and ends.

Now put the front assembly aside, and turn to the case ends. Cut them to their finished width of 20 in., but leave the length and thickness rough. With the flat patterns, trace the shape of the long-grain edges. Rough out the contours by making tablesaw cuts about every 2 in., as in figure 3B. I stopped the cuts about ¼ in. away from the profile line to allow for the inevitable movement: the top of my ends cupped outward, though I suspect that the bulge prevented significant cupping at the bottom. The sawcuts allow the bulk of the waste to be chiseled away quickly, after which it's best to let the wood settle for a couple of days. Then plane the inside areas near the top and bottom edges flat and parallel, and retrace the pattern. Now scrub-plane across the grain down to the line, and finish up with smooth plane and spokeshaves. Place the three-dimensional pattern over the contour and trace the profile of the long edges. Bandsaw the ends to shape, and true up the top and bottom edges.

To join the case, first attach the ends to the top with housed tapered dovetails. When fitting the joint, I tapered the square

side of the half-dovetail with my shoulder plane because I don't have a dovetail plane that will taper the angled side, as is usually done. Otherwise I used traditional methods of sawing, wasting with a chisel, and cleaning up with a router plane. When drawn home, these joints establish the width of the case, and thus locate the mortises in the base.

I made the case bottom from seven pieces, 36¾ in. by 3 in. by 1¾ in., ripped from waste sections of the plank. The thickness lets you shape the base itself, rather than having to use applied moldings. The moldings on the top and base are cut on a spindle shaper, as are the rabbets in the ends. I grind my own cutters. Nine tenons join each end to the base, allowing a lot of grain to run through to the molded edge. There is a short-grain problem inside the case ends between the tenons, so leave extra wood here until after glue-up to prevent a crumbled edge.

Rails on 18th-century Boston cases are typically 4 in. to 6 in. wide, with secondary wood often joined to the primary wood. I think that 3½ in. to 4 in. is wide enough to keep the rails straight. Assemble the case dry, position the rails (aligning the center marks), and cut them to length. Slide the rails in on the stub tenons, scribe the stepped dovetails and cut the mortises for the runners in the rails (figure 1, detail A). The case is ready to be glued up. To avoid friction between parallel edges, the dovetails joining the top and ends must be slid in individually before the rails and base are added.

Glue blocks or screws usually support the runners in bombé cases. To provide support while allowing movement, I used a vertical strip of poplar, notched to support each runner, at the back of the chest. Stub tenons hook these two vertical supports to the base, and screws through slots hold them at the top. The runners are screwed to the case ends through slots at the back. De Rham used oak supports and fastened them both top and bottom with screws, as shown in the photo at right. I didn't glue the runner tenons in until later, after some finish had been applied to the inside of the case.

Notched vertical members support drawer runners at back.

Bevel dovetails are needed for the lower three drawers, since both their sides and fronts are angled. Following the directions on the facing page, cut the drawer parts to length at the proper end and bevel angles, and then before shaping the drawer sides, cut the dovetails. Next, to fit each drawer front into the case, position it over its opening and scribe the curve of the case ends onto the dovetail pins from inside the case. Trim the pins to the scribe line to get the drawer front started in the opening and to check the fit. Then trim the rest of the drawer front to the pins. The grooves for the drawer bottoms are cut on the shaper wherever possible; the rest is done by hand. Assemble the drawers and plane the drawer sides down to the curve of the drawer-front ends. The drawer bottoms are solid wood, with the grain running from side to side and three sides beveled from underneath to fit the grooves.

With the case on its back, block up the drawers flush with the rails. I established the line of the corner between the flat fields and the serpentine shape by running a compass along the curve of the ends. Scrape the entire front to smooth all the contours, taking care to leave the flat fields at a uniform width that is crisp and clean. Then, after removing the drawers, use a scratch stock to make most of the cock beading on the rails and the case ends. The scratch stock will have to be adjusted for the middle rail, because of the angle of its face. The beading at the corners is carved.

The back of the chest is made of wide and narrow horizon-

Jerry de Rham, a student at North Bennet Street School, scrapes his desk front smooth. Note the alternate traditional design—the front is not serpentine, but matches the curve of the sides.

tal boards with overlapping rabbets. The narrow boards are screwed into the rabbets at the case ends, but the wide boards are free-floating and can move.

The grain runs vertically in the feet and their ears. I bandsawed each foot with one ear as part of it and the other ear applied. This uses a little more wood, but it eliminates half the glue joints, and the grain match, of course, is perfect. The feet are stub-tenoned to the base, and I put a screw through a sloppy hole in each ear into the base. The feet are carved as large as possible in the 12/4 pieces. (See A.W. Marlow's article on how to carve ball-and-claw feet on pages 54 to 55.) The side toes are angled slightly forward, but the tips of the claw extend to the diagonals of the square blank. I also keep the knuckles of the rear, side and front toes different distances from the floor, to avoid a box-like appearance. The bones of each toe get progressively longer as you go back from the nail, and the number of knuckles is anatomically correct. The ball itself and the claws are smooth, but I left tool marks on the rest of the foot up to the ankle. The case is designed so that the line formed where the flat field ends and the serpentine shape begins runs across the base molding and around the transition as a miter corner, and ends at the point representing the fetlock. I think knee carving suits this design if the mahogany is highly figured. But if the wood is straight-grained, as mine was, then a less fancy style is better.

Bombé chests deserve the best traditionally made hardware: I spent more money for the hardware than for the lumber. My thin cast brasses with separate posts are from Ball and Ball, 436 W. Lincoln Highway, Exton, Pa. 19341. I shaped a pine block to help bend the plates. To seat the posts properly, I drilled post holes perpendicular to the tangent of the curve, then I adjusted the bails to fit the posts. I used #0 by 1/4-in. round-head brass screws to attach the keyhole escutcheons, so they are easily removable. All the locks needed 1 1/8 in. to the selvage. I used a slant-top desk lock on the lowest drawer and made strike plates for all the locks.

To finish the chest, I gave it one very thin wash coat of orange shellac, to set up the grain for its final sanding, then used boiled linseed oil. If applied in very thin, hand-rubbed coats, linseed displays the grain with depth, clarity and warmth. I don't thin oil greatly with turpentine (never more than 1 part turpentine to 20 parts oil), nor do I apply soaking coats. I don't think these methods significantly increase penetration, and I suspect that not all of the oil oxidizes, so you risk bleed-out problems. I do add a little Japan drier. I store my oil in a colored glass bottle placed in direct sunlight—I think this helps polymerization and drying. It is most important to apply the oil in the thinnest layers possible and to give it adequate time to oxidize between coats. Each coat should be rubbed hard to build up enough heat to force the oil into the pores and to level the surface. Carvings and moldings should be brushed vigorously to remove excess oil. Instead of waxing, I prefer to build up the oil slowly to a high gloss.

Like most 18th-century furniture, each Boston bombé piece is a complete design in itself, independent of its environment. It has character and warmth which are a joy to live with. Its shape continually invites you to run your hand over its curves, or even to tickle its carved feet. □

Lance Patterson is a cabinetmaker and shop instructor at the North Bennet Street School in Boston, Mass.

Photos this page: Brad Mayo

How to make slope-sided boxes

Plans for slope-sided boxes, such as the drawers in the bombé chest on page 74, aren't in the perspective we're used to. In a front-elevation drawing, the front measures less than its true height because it is tilted out of the plane of the drawing. Here is a method for reading tilted plans, laying the pieces out, and setting the tablesaw to cut the elusive angles involved. In this particular hopper, the front and the back could be cut with the same saw settings, but for clarity, let's consider just the front.

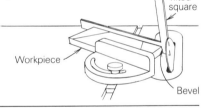

Plan view

Side

Front

90°

├── True length of top edge ──┤

Front elevation

Distorted end angle · Reference line

├── True length of bottom edge ──┤

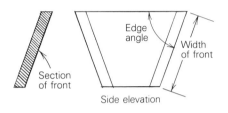

Edge angle

Width of front

Section of front

Side elevation

With no math at all

1. *The side elevation, above, shows the true cross section of the board that will be the front of the hopper. Use a bevel gauge to transfer the edge angle to the tablesaw, then rip the front to width.*

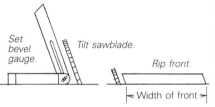

Set bevel gauge.

Tilt sawblade.

Rip front.

├── Width of front ──┤

2. *The end angle shown in the front elevation is distorted, but the drawing does show the true length of the top and bottom edges. Measuring out from a perpendicular reference line, transfer the edge lengths to the workpiece. Then connect the edges to draw the true end-cut lines. This method also works for asymmetrical pieces—where end-cut lines are at different angles.*

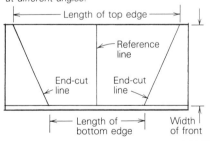

├── Length of top edge ──┤

Reference line

End-cut line

End-cut line

├── Length of bottom edge ──┤ Width of front

3. *With a straightedge, set the miter gauge so the end-cut line is parallel to the blade.*

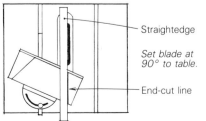

Straightedge

Set blade at 90° to table.

End-cut line

4. *As shown in the plan view, above, the cut has to be at 90° to the beveled edge of the workpiece, not at 90° to the face. To determine this tilt angle, place a carpenters' square flat against the beveled edge of the workpiece and crank the blade over until it lies tight against the arm of the square.*

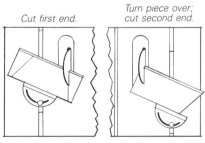

Tilted square

Workpiece

Bevel

5. *Lower the blade to a safe height and cut to the line. If the piece is symmetrical, you can switch the miter gauge to the other side of the blade, turn the work over, and saw the other end. If asymmetrical, repeat steps 3 and 4. Repeat all five steps for the other sides.*

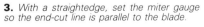

Cut first end.

Turn piece over; cut second end.

The problem of the hopper joint is traditionally solved by projection and measurement on full-size drawings. Lance Patterson derived the mathematics at right from the graphical method, then picture-framer Jim Cummins devised the no-math method shown above. For a photocopy of Patterson's mathematical proof, send a self-addressed stamped envelope to Hopper, c/o *Fine Woodworking*, Box 355, Newtown, Conn. 06470.

The ends of hopper pieces are cut at compound angles by tilting the sawblade and setting the miter gauge. You can use trigonometry to calculate the tangents of the angles, then from the tangents set a bevel gauge with which to set the saw, as follows.

Here's the math

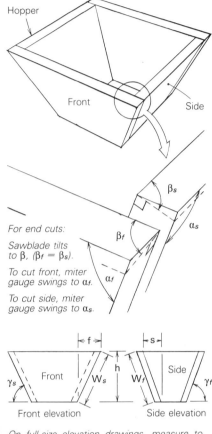

Hopper

Front

Side

β_s

β_f

α_s

α_f

For end cuts:

Sawblade tilts to β, ($\beta_f = \beta_s$).

To cut front, miter gauge swings to α_f.

To cut side, miter gauge swings to α_s.

├─ f ─┤ ├─ s ─┤

γ_s Front W_s W_f Side γ_f

h

Front elevation

Side elevation

On full-size elevation drawings, measure to 1/32 in. or better:

h = hopper height
f = front 'overhang'
s = side 'overhang'
W_f = width of front face
W_s = width of side face

Now calculate γ_s, the edge angle of the side: $\tan\gamma_s = h \div f$. Calculate γ_f, the edge angle of the front: $\tan\gamma_f = h \div s$.

Then $\tan\alpha_f = W_f \div f$ and $\tan\alpha_s = W_s \div s$. And $\tan\beta = \tan\gamma_f \div \cos\alpha_f$, or $\tan\gamma_s \div \cos\alpha_s$. Or $\tan\beta = h\sqrt{f^2 + W_f^2} \div (f \cdot s)$.

Having figured the tangents, you can look up the actual angles in trigonometric tables, punch them on a scientific calculator (arctan or tan⁻¹), or directly set your bevel gauge as below:

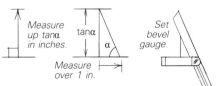

Measure up tanα in inches.

tanα

α

Set bevel gauge.

Measure over 1 in.

To tilt the blade for a mitered hopper, such as a shadow box, when sides and fronts are of equal thickness: $\beta_m = (180° - \beta) \div 2$.

Building a Secretaire-Bookcase
Lots to learn from this 18th-century case study

text and drawings by Victor J. Taylor

It's not often that you come across a piece of English antique furniture that can be dated precisely, but glued to one of the drawer linings of this handsome secretaire-bookcase is the following receipt: "B. Milward [the purchaser]. Jan 25. 1787. Bought of Mr. Evans, Broadmead, Bristol. Price £15.15."

Today the piece stands in the Withdrawing Room of the Georgian House, Bristol, which is a real treasure store of late 18th-century household goods ranging from fine furniture and priceless paintings down to kitchen utensils. It is officially described as Hepplewhite style, but it seems to me that the date is too early for Hepplewhite, and that the piece is more likely late Adam. In drawing this complex piece, I was struck

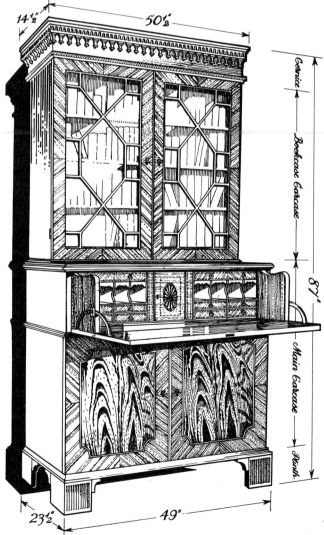

by how instructive it can be of various features common to much simpler furniture. Rather than follow a strict (and probably oppressive) how-to-do-it formula, I have attempted to present the piece as a tour of period construction practices, with side-trips into alternatives for the present-day craftsman.

As can be seen in the drawing on this page, the piece is composed of five sections: from the floor upwards these are the plinth, the cupboard (containing cutlery and linen drawers, and two butler's trays), the secretaire, the bookcase and the cornice. These sections were usually made as complete, separate units, then fitted together, although in this piece the bookcase and cornice are combined as one unit.

Often the sections merely rested on each other so that they could easily be dismantled if they had to be moved—indeed, quite often the main cupboard section had handles fitted to it to make lifting easier. Usually the weight of each section kept it in place, with various sorts of blocks and keys serving to keep things from shifting.

Mahogany is used for all show-wood parts, with oak and pine for the hidden parts and groundwork, normal practice for the time. The mahogany is almost certainly Cuban, and the superb "Spanish Feather" veneer is virtually unobtainable these days. All veneer is laid on without benefit of counter-veneer, which would be risky with today's central heating.

In the following drawings, each part of the secretaire-bookcase is illustrated and its construction explained, beginning with the plinth and working upwards, which is not necessarily the order in which it would be built. All pieces are numbered to correspond to the list in the bill of materials on page 86. In each figure, there is a small diagram of the full cabinet—the shaded part of the diagram is shown exploded in the drawing.

In drawing the piece, where it was impossible to see the joints, I have followed orthodox cabinetmaking practice. Doweling, incidentally, was a very common method in the old days. Craftsmen made their own dowels by trimming down a suitable piece of scrap wood, and then hammering it through a dowel plate, a piece of ⅛-in. thick metal in which holes of various sizes had been drilled—¼-in., ⅜-in. and ½-in. were usual. Dowels were often shaped from offcuts from the parts they were intended to join, minimizing uneven shrinkage. Willow was also used; its stems could be made into dowels with hardly any trimming.

At the time this piece was made, French polishing had not been invented (it did not become widespread in England until about 1820), so the piece was probably originally finished with linseed oil and wax, then French polished at a later date.

Victor Taylor, of Bath, England, spent many years in the furniture industry. He has written several books, and was editor of the British magazine Woodworker.

Figure 1: Plinth. The basic members of this subassembly are the four corner posts *(1)*, which are connected at the front and back by rails *(2 & 3)*, and at each end by a rail *(4)*. The cupboard rests on this base and is almost certainly keyed to it with blocks screwed beneath the cupboard bottom *(5)*, though I couldn't see them.'

The feet *(8)* are not weight-bearing, but are merely glued as decoration around the corner posts. The ear pieces *(9)* are glued and doweled to the feet, then the moldings *(10)* are pinned and glued on. Brackets are glued and screwed into each corner to strengthen the whole framework. Screws (hand-made) were first introduced in the late 17th century and by 1720 were common. Nails and pins (brads), of course, have been used for centuries, and there is even a reference from 1343 on using an adze to smooth "old timber" full of nails. On the arris of the foot there is a staff bead, whose profile makes any opening of the joint less obvious. A central frame rail *(11)* is mortised flush into the front and back rails. Following the usual practice of the time, the main carcase ends *(7)* are lap-dovetailed to the cupboard bottom *(5)*. There is a filler strip *(6)* beneath the cupboard doors, and this is shown in section at *A*.

Figure 2: Cupboard and drawer framing. The doors overlap the upright ends of the carcase, therefore the carcase ends have to be stepped back by ¾ in. below the point where the front secretaire separation rail *(15)* meets them.

The front and back drawer rails *(12)* are tenoned into the main carcase ends *(7)*, as are the top separation rails *15* and *38* (visible in figure 4, overleaf). Muntins *(14)*, drawer bearers *(13)* and a central bearer *(16)* connect these four rails. The two upper drawers are supported by this conventional framing, while the lower single drawers run on bearers *(30)* glued to the cabinet ends. This ignores wood movement, but the bearers are still secure. The drawer construction is orthodox, with lapped dovetails on the fronts and through dovetails on the backs. The bottoms are solid wood, grooved into the sides and fronts without being glued in, so that they can expand and contract. You could, of course, use plywood for the bottoms instead. The handles on the drawers are solid brass and match those on the fall front; they are shown at *A* in figure 10.

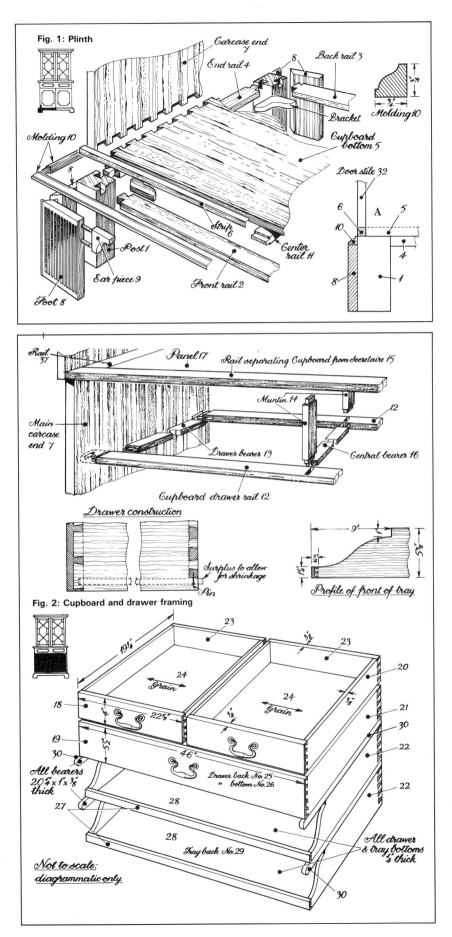

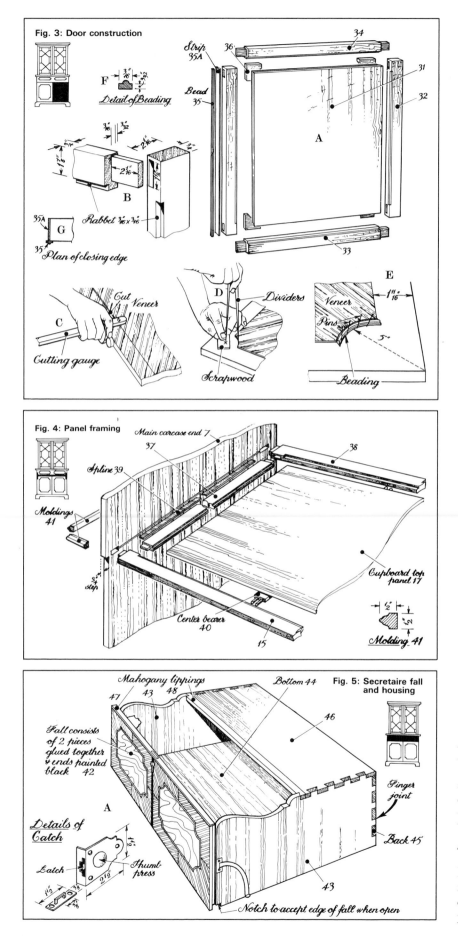

Fig. 3: Door construction

F $\frac{3}{16}''$ $\frac{3}{32}''$
Detail of Beading

Strip 35A
Bead 35

34
36
31
32
A
33

B
Rabbet $\frac{3}{16}'' \times \frac{3}{16}''$
$2\frac{1}{16}''$
$\frac{3}{16}''$ $\frac{3}{32}''$
$2\frac{1}{16}''$

35A
G
35 Plan of closing edge

C
Cutting gauge
Cut Veneer

D
Dividers
Scrapwood

E
Veneer
Pins
$1\frac{11}{16}''$
5°
Beading

Fig. 4: Panel framing
Main carcase end 7
37
Spline 39
38
Moldings 41
Cupboard top panel 17
$\frac{3}{8}''$ step
Center bearer 40
15
$\frac{1}{2}''$ $\frac{1}{2}''$
Molding 41

Mahogany tippings
47 43 48
Bottom 44
Fig. 5: Secretaire fall and housing
46

Fall consists of 2 pieces glued together & ends painted black 42
A
Details of Catch
Latch
Thumb press
$2\frac{1}{8}''$
$1\frac{1}{2}''$
$\frac{1}{4}''$
Finger joint
Back 45
43
Notch to accept edge of fall when open

Figure 3: Door construction. The doors are hung by pairs of brass hinges. As you can see at *A,* the frame is a straightforward mortise-and-tenon job with a rabbet for the panel, which lies flush, glued and pinned. The rabbets on the rail run the full shoulder length, while those on the stiles are stopped, as at *B.* The tenons on rails *33* and *34* go right through the stiles, and their ends can be seen on the outside edges. On the closing edges, however, a thin strip (*35A*) has been glued to the edge to mask them. Blind tenons would do just as well here, and the cover strips could thus be omitted. A thin astragal beading (*35*) is fixed as shown at *G.*

The corner brackets (*36*) appear to have been glued behind the panel merely to add rigidity.

The doors were constructed entirely of oak, with no veneer on the inside. At the time the piece was made, veneers were sawn and consequently were much thicker than our present-day veneers. The central part of the veneered panel would have been laid in a press, while a veneering hammer would have been employed to put down the border. Workmen trimmed the edges of the veneer, after laying, with a cutting gauge (*C*), simply a marking gauge with a small, sharp blade instead of the usual marking pin. A pair of dividers, with one point sharpened, was used to scribe the corners, as at *D,* and the cut was finished off with a knife.

Detail *E* shows the small ovolo beading being glued—almost certainly, it was steamed first. Both this and beading (*35*) are a blond color and could be birch, sycamore or holly. The left-hand door has brass bolts top and bottom, and a false escutcheon that matches the lock on the other door.

Figure 4: Panel framing. This panel (*17*) appears to be $\frac{3}{8}$-in. thick pine, but I'd suggest birch plywood instead. It is pinned and glued into $\frac{3}{8}$-in. by $\frac{3}{8}$-in. rabbets worked on the edges of rails *15,* *37* and *38.* Although the frame lines up at the front with the front edge of the carcase end (*7*), it falls $\frac{3}{4}$ in. short of the back edge, to leave room for the back framing. The moldings (*41*) are glued and pinned on, corners mitered.

Figure 5: Secretaire fall and housing. The pigeon-hole section has a clever feature that I have not seen on other pieces from this period. It is contained within a fall-front drawer, shown at right and at the bottom of the previous page, that pulls out to provide knee room for writing. The fall front (42) is made up of two pieces face-glued together to form a lip that fits into a notch cut into the side (43) when the fall is down (see B and D). The fall has three hinges, and is fitted with two brass handles, shown at A in figure 10. Two mahogany lippings (47 & 48) mask the drawer front's top edge and the exposed pine edge of the drawer top.

The quadrant stay was made from solid brass, with a small fixing flange brazed on. Cut out a $\frac{3}{16}$-in. channel in the drawer side for the stay to run in. You might wish to install a lock in the fall front and catches fitted into the sides (see A and B).

The fall front is veneered similarly to the cupboard doors, with the addition of a black inlaid line running from top to bottom in the center. Lippings are applied after veneering so that the top edge of the veneer is protected. The ends of the fall are painted black—not an attractive feature—and you may wish to substitute another thin lipping.

Figure 6: Secretaire unit. This is a real work of art, as all the parts are only $\frac{1}{8}$ in. thick, except for the drawer fronts, which are $\frac{1}{2}$ in. thick (including the veneer). All parts are mahogany. With such thin partitions, a practical joint is the interlocking joint shown at C.

The main structure comprises the bottom (50) and the two ends (49), which can be butted together and glued to the "drawer" side and bottom (43 & 44). The remaining partitions (51, 52, 53, 54, 55 & 68) can be connected with interlocking joints. Construction of the drawers is shown at D.

The veneer is enlivened by black and white stringing about $\frac{3}{32}$ in. wide, and the cupboard door is further embellished with an inlaid fan.

Now we come to an intriguing item: the secret compartments (B). Frankly, they are rather obvious and clumsy compared to some I have seen, and you may wish to elaborate upon them. They are built in behind the two pilasters (see A). Once you have opened the door, the two inner walls can be pulled inward and taken out completely. I had to pry them out with the point of a penknife, but probably a leaf spring had originally been fitted behind the tray to help push it out.

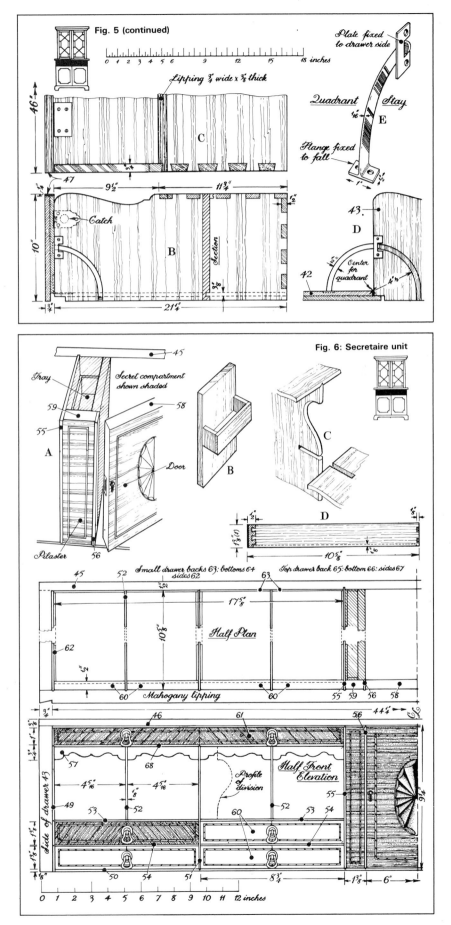

Fig. 5 (continued)

Plate fixed to drawer side

Lipping $\frac{3}{4}$ wide x $\frac{3}{8}$ thick

Quadrant Stay

Flange fixed to fall

Catch

Section

Center for quadrant

Fig. 6: Secretaire unit

Tray

Secret compartment shown shaded

Door

Pilaster

Small drawer backs 63: bottoms 64 sides 62

Top drawer back 65: bottom 66: sides 67

Half Plan

Mahogany lipping

Side of drawer 43

Profile of division

Half Front Elevation

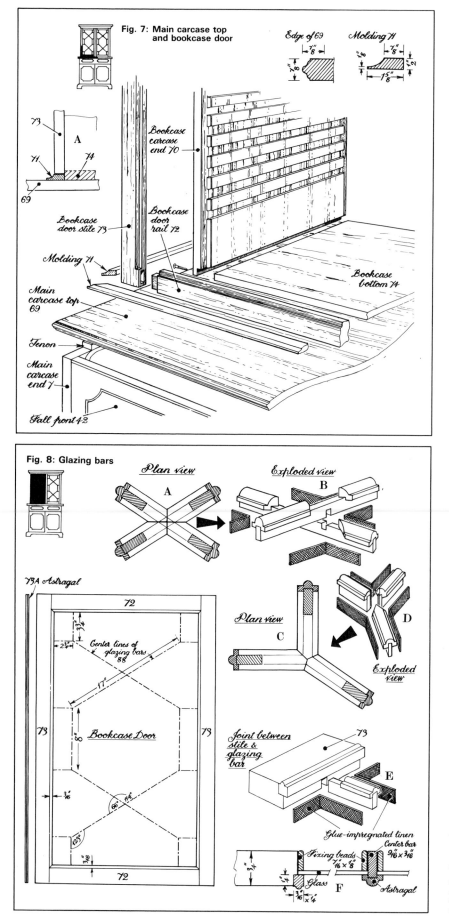

Fig. 7: Main carcase top and bookcase door

73

A

71

74

69

Bookcase carcase end 70

Bookcase door stile 73

Bookcase door rail 72

Molding 71

Main carcase top 69

Tenon

Main carcase end 7

Fall front 42

Bookcase bottom 74

Edge of 69

⅞"

⅞"

Molding 71

⅞"

⅛"

½"

1⅝"

Fig. 8: Glazing bars

Plan view

A

Exploded view

B

Plan view

C

D

Exploded view

73A Astragal

72

3¼"

2¾"

17"

8"

³⁄₁₆"

66° 11¼°

105°

³⁄₁₆"

73

73

Center lines of glazing bars 88

Bookcase Door

72

Joint between stile & glazing bar

73

E

Glue-impregnated linen

Center bar ⁹⁄₁₆ × ³⁄₁₆

¾"

Fixing beads ⁷⁄₁₆ × ⅛

¼"

Glass

³⁄₁₆ × ¼

F

Astragal

Figure 7: Main carcase top and bookcase door. The top of the main carcase (69) is fixed to the carcase ends by means of blind tenons on the main carcase end (7). Moldings (71) are attached to the top (shown in section at A) so that the removable bookcase section does not shift. The bookcase is made up of the two ends (70), the bottom (74), and the top. The ends extend up to include the cornice, and we shall be dealing with the upper part, including the top (76), in figure 9.

The bottom (74) is housed in a rabbet formed at the foot of the end. The joint is glued and then strengthened with wood screws driven in from the outside—the surrounding molding (71) will conceal the screw heads. The shelf supports (70A) are glued and pinned to the carcase end—these supports are made from a piece of ⁵⁄₁₆ in. stock which first has a small thumb molding worked on its front edge, and is then sawn into separate strips. Note that their back ends must stand ¾ in. away from the rear edge of the bookcase end to allow for the fitting of the back frame.

On the actual piece, the corners of the bookcase doors have through tenons, but I have drawn blind tenons, on the assumption that you will prefer them.

Figure 8: Glazing bars. Once the bookcase door frames are made, lay them on a flat board so that you can pencil the centerlines for the glazing bars on it, following the pattern and measurements shown. Leave off the astragal beadings until you have gotten the center bars fitted. Delicate joints such as these (A–E) can be reinforced with strips of linen soaked in glue.

In the original piece, the glass is fixed in place with putty instead of the fixing beads shown at F. I cannot recommend putty, as it has no resiliency, and consequently the glass will crack easily if the wood swells or shrinks—in fact, several of the panes have done so.

The last step is to hang the doors with three 2-in. hinges per door, and if you wish, you can fix a closing bead on to the right-hand door to match the one on the cupboard door. Door stops can be fitted beneath the top, where they will be out of the way.

As with the cupboard doors, the right-hand door has a lock and an escutcheon, while the left-hand door has just an escutcheon plus a brass bolt at top and bottom.

Figure 9: The cornice and top. The cornice *(75)* consists of a piece of mahogany lap-mitered to the top of the bookcase end *(70)*. It is rabbeted along its lower edge to house the bookcase top. Note the dado for the top in the bookcase end, as shown at *A*.

The carcase top *(77)* laps over the back framing (shown in figure 10), and it also laps over the bookcase ends *(70)* and the cornice *(75)*. In the original, it is screwed down all around, which does not allow for wood movement.

The piece will look best if you reproduce the original moldings instead of substituting lumberyard patterns.

The top molding *(78)* is quite straightforward, but the one below it *(79)*, which comprises the dentil motif with a cavetto beneath it, is not so easy. Probably the best way to tackle it is to run off the outline profile first on a spindle shaper, and then use a router to take out the slots for the dentils. Then you will need to chop out the rounded end of each slot with a small scribing (in-cannel) gouge.

Now for the bracket molding *(80)*. On many designs of the period this was a straight run of molding with the brackets joined together at the top. In our model, however, they will need to be sawn out separately with a fretsaw or jigsaw, and the small pieces of beading glued on beneath them. These small pieces were turned on a lathe as "split" turnings—two small blocks were glued together with a sheet of paper between them and then turned; it was easy to split them apart afterward.

Lastly, we have to deal with the Grecian key motif *(81)*, and the best way, again, is to use a router, squaring up with a chisel.

Once the brackets are glued on, it will be difficult to polish into all the nooks and crannies, so you can adopt the method employed by the old-timers. First they would have polished the cornice and the brackets as separate pieces, then they would lay the brackets on the cornice to scribe around them. When they removed the brackets, an outline was left and the polish was scraped away from this. Next they warmed up a metal plate (called a sticking board), so that the glue would not chill when it was spread on it. They would draw the backs of the brackets lightly across the sticking board so that each received a thin coat of glue, enabling them to be fixed with no fear of gummy crevices.

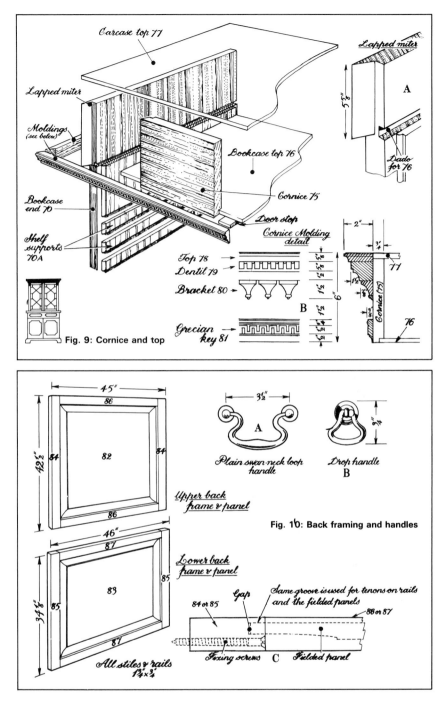

Fig. 9: Cornice and top

Fig. 10: Back framing and handles

Figure 10: Back framing and handles. Chances are that the framed panels in this piece were screwed into place, not glued. This would have allowed their removal, considerably lightening the piece if it had to be moved. It was difficult to see how the back frame was constructed, so I am giving details of typical framings that you can use. Those on the original were of solid oak, although you may wish to use pine. In any case, the frames are made up with conventional mortise and tenon joints. The fielded panels *(82 & 83)* are grooved in all around *(C)*—remember that solid panels must be loose to shrink or swell, not pinned or glued in place—leave some space, too, in the groove.

If you make the groove ¼ in. wide by ⅜ in. deep, you can then use it to accept the tenons as well as the panels. You may stop the grooves on the stiles *(84 & 85)* to avoid their running through the top and bottom edges when the frame is made up, although when everything is in its place, finally, these edges won't show.

See page 86 for the bill of materials.

Bill of Materials

The dimensions given below are net, and you should allow extra for sawing, planing, etc., at the rate of about 1 in. in length, ¼ in. to ½ in. in width, and ⅛ in. in thickness. Where I have shown shoulder lengths you will need to add extra length for tenons. I have left the tenon dimensions mostly up to you, and you may, of course, use whatever joinery you prefer throughout the piece.

I have not included parts for the secret compartments, as no doubt you will wish to use more ingenious devices (see pages 87 to 89) or design your own.

In measuring a complicated piece like this, one often finds that many of the parts were scribed from other parts or cut to fit, rather than laid out with a ruler. I found I had to adapt some of the measurements in order to get things to add up. Although I have made every effort to ensure accuracy, parts of the cabinet were inaccessible—cooperative as the folks at Georgian House were, no one was about to let me move it, let alone take it apart. I suggest that you temper haste with a bit of caution, and cut to fit as you go along. □

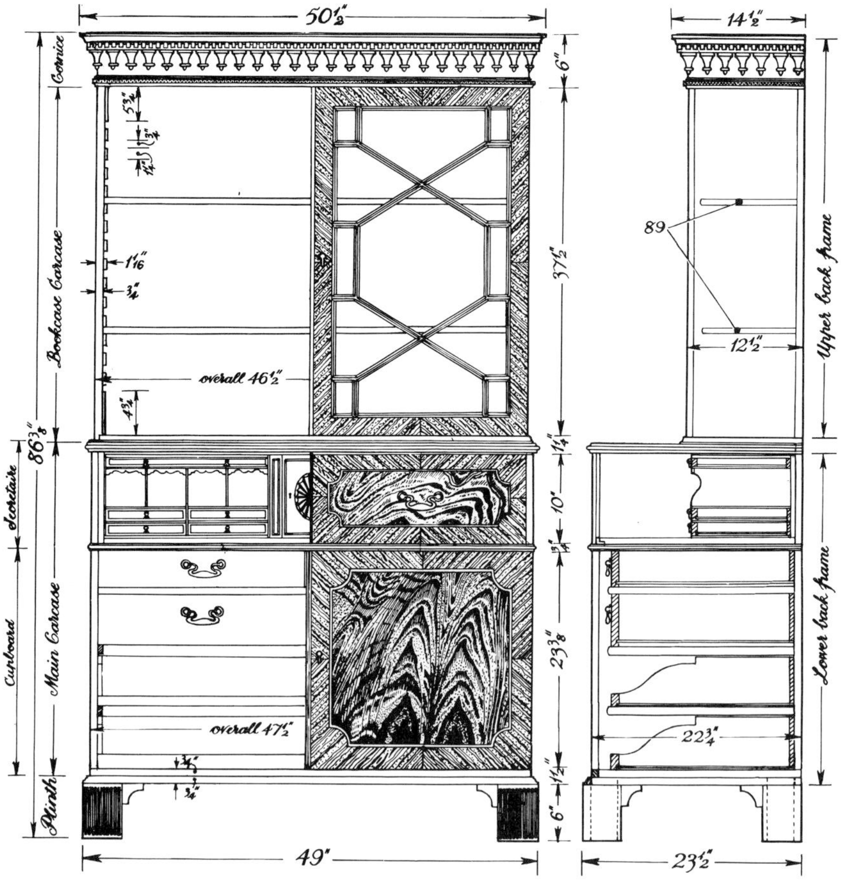

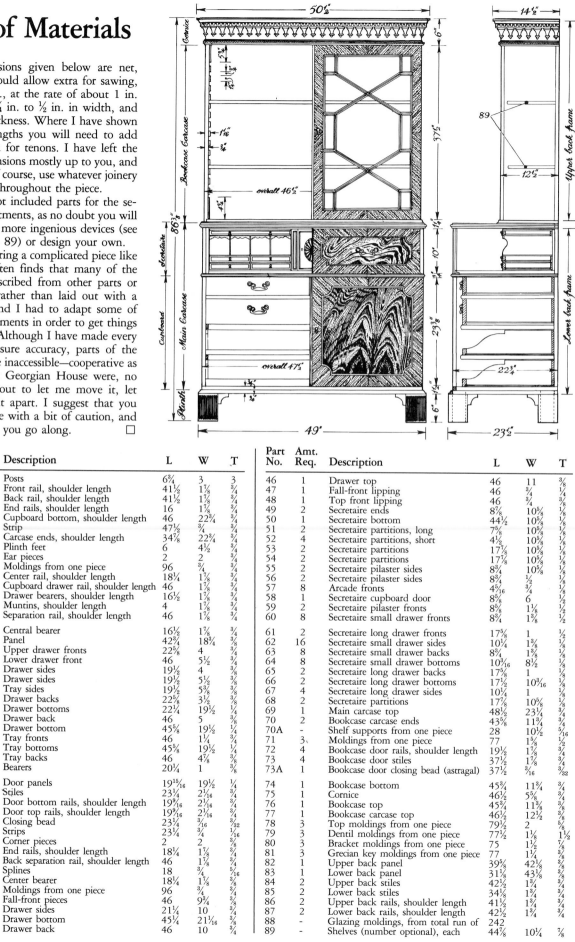

Part No.	Amt. Req.	Description	L	W	T
1	4	Posts	6¾	3	3
2	1	Front rail, shoulder length	41½	1⅞	¾
3	1	Back rail, shoulder length	41½	1⅞	¾
4	2	End rails, shoulder length	16	1⅞	¾
5	1	Cupboard bottom, shoulder length	46	22¾	¾
6	1	Strip	47½	¾	¾
7	2	Carcase ends, shoulder length	34⅞	22¾	¾
8	8	Plinth feet	6	4½	¾
9	8	Ear pieces	2	2	¾
10	3	Moldings from one piece	96	¾	¾
11	1	Center rail, shoulder length	18¼	1⅞	¾
12	1	Cupboard drawer rail, shoulder length	46	1⅞	¾
13	2	Drawer bearers, shoulder length	16½	1⅞	¾
14	2	Muntins, shoulder length	4	1⅞	¾
15	1	Separation rail, shoulder length	46	1⅞	¾
16	1	Central bearer	16½	1⅞	¾
17	1	Panel	42¾	18¾	⅜
18	2	Upper drawer fronts	22⅝	4	¾
19	1	Lower drawer front	46	5½	¾
20	4	Drawer sides	19½	4	⅜
21	2	Drawer sides	19½	5½	⅜
22	4	Tray sides	19½	5⅜	⅜
23	2	Drawer backs	22⅝	3½	⅜
24	2	Drawer bottoms	22¼	19½	¼
25	1	Drawer back	46	5	⅜
26	1	Drawer bottom	45⅝	19½	¼
27	2	Tray fronts	46	1¼	¾
28	2	Tray bottoms	45⅝	19½	¼
29	2	Tray backs	46	4⅞	⅜
30	4	Bearers	20¼	1	⅜
31	2	Door panels	19 15/16	19½	¼
32	4	Stiles	23¼	2 1/16	¾
33	2	Door bottom rails, shoulder length	19 9/16	2 1/16	¾
34	2	Door top rails, shoulder length	19 9/16	2 1/16	¾
35	1	Closing bead	23¼	3/16	3/32
35A	2	Strips	23¼	¾	1/16
36	8	Corner pieces	2	2	⅜
37	2	End rails, shoulder length	18¼	1⅞	¾
38	1	Back separation rail, shoulder length	46	1⅞	¾
39	2	Splines	18	¾	5/16
40	1	Center bearer	18¼	1⅞	⅜
41	3	Moldings from one piece	96	¾	¾
42	2	Fall-front pieces	46	9¾	⅜
43	2	Drawer sides	21¼	10	¾
44	1	Drawer bottom	45¼	21 1/16	⅜
45	1	Drawer back	46	10	¾

Part No.	Amt. Req.	Description	L	W	T
46	1	Drawer top	46	11	⅜
47	1	Fall-front lipping	46	¾	¼
48	1	Top front lipping	46	¾	⅜
49	2	Secretaire ends	8⅞	10⅝	⅛
50	1	Secretaire bottom	44½	10⅝	⅛
51	2	Secretaire partitions, long	7⅝	10⅝	⅛
52	4	Secretaire partitions, short	4½	10⅝	⅛
53	2	Secretaire partitions	17⅞	10⅝	⅛
54	2	Secretaire partitions	17⅞	10⅝	⅛
55	2	Secretaire pilaster sides	8¾	10⅝	⅛
56	2	Secretaire pilaster sides	8¾	½	⅛
57	8	Arcade fronts	4 5/16	¾	⅛
58	1	Secretaire cupboard door	8⅝	6	½
59	2	Secretaire pilaster fronts	8⅝	1⅛	½
60	8	Secretaire small drawer fronts	8¾	1⅜	½
61	2	Secretaire long drawer fronts	17⅝	1	½
62	16	Secretaire small drawer sides	10¼	1⅜	⅛
63	8	Secretaire small drawer backs	8¾	1⅜	⅛
64	8	Secretaire small drawer bottoms	10 3/16	8½	⅛
65	2	Secretaire long drawer backs	17⅝	1	⅛
66	2	Secretaire long drawer bottoms	17½	10 3/16	⅛
67	4	Secretaire long drawer sides	10¼	1	⅛
68	2	Secretaire partitions	17⅞	10⅝	⅛
69	1	Main carcase top	48½	23¼	¾
70	2	Bookcase carcase ends	43⅝	11¾	¾
70A	-	Shelf supports from one piece	28	10½	5/16
71	3	Moldings from one piece	77	1⅝	½
72	4	Bookcase door rails, shoulder length	19½	1⅞	¾
73	4	Bookcase door stiles	37½	1⅞	¾
73A	1	Bookcase door closing bead (astragal)	37½	3/16	3/32
74	1	Bookcase bottom	45¾	11¾	¾
75	1	Cornice	46½	5⅝	¾
76	1	Bookcase top	45¾	11⅜	⅜
77	1	Bookcase carcase top	46½	12½	⅜
78	3	Top moldings from one piece	79½	2	⅝
79	3	Dentil moldings from one piece	77½	1⅛	1½
80	3	Bracket moldings from one piece	75	1½	⅞
81	3	Grecian key moldings from one piece	77	1¼	⅜
82	1	Upper back panel	39⅝	42⅛	⅜
83	1	Lower back panel	31⅛	43⅛	⅜
84	2	Upper back stiles	42½	1¾	¾
85	2	Lower back stiles	34⅛	1¾	¾
86	2	Upper back rails, shoulder length	41½	1¾	¾
87	2	Lower back rails, shoulder length	42½	1¾	¾
88	-	Glazing moldings, from total run of	242		
89	-	Shelves (number optional), each	44⅞	10¼	⅞

Hidden Drawers

Some eighteenth-century examples

by Alastair A. Stair

In the George II bureau bookcase above, the columns on either side of small cupboard just above the writing surface push out by spring action to reveal drawers. In the George I box below, the side raises to reveal drawer.

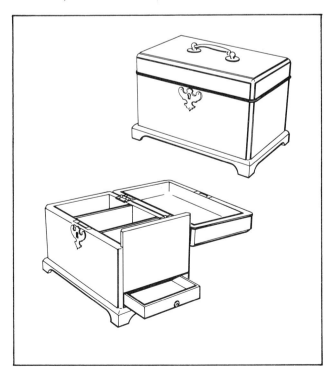

Before the invention of the burglar-alarm system and the combination safe, ladies and gentlemen of means concealed their valuables in all manner of locked boxes and containers. Furniture often contained secret drawers and compartments cleverly hidden by the cabinetmaker. The need for such concealment afforded many opportunities for the English craftsman to exercise his highly developed sense of invention and surprise and his fondness for devices, to the delight of his clients.

Many items that are readily available today were difficult to obtain in the 17th and 18th centuries due to the slowness of trade, and were therefore very expensive. Tea, sugar and spices were precious enough to be kept under lock and key. Small tea chests, today called "caddies," became popular for carrying tea to the table. They are partitioned or fitted with canisters and often contain hidden compartments. Tea chests and various other boxes and caskets designed as receptacles for coins, jewels and documents were made with locks and sometimes carrying handles, themselves often hidden from view. Some boxes, fitted with padlocks, were used for the dispatch of confidential communications; one key was kept by each correspondent. Boxes of all types were so much in demand that an independent trade guild of box-makers was incorporated in the 17th century.

One of the most fascinating pieces I have seen is a small George I rectangular box, inlaid and veneered with walnut. The interior is divided into triple compartments. To the eye, the container is all of a piece. However, when open, one short side cleverly slides up to reveal a shallow drawer which runs the length of the box and can be pulled by a tiny ivory knob.

Slope-front desks and secretaire bookcases will almost always reward the seeker of the secret drawer. These are fitted inside the flap with a series of pigeonholes for ledgers, documents and letters and very often a small central cupboard. The pigeonholes often hold one or more secret compartments most cunningly contrived in what appears to be part of the fixed construction. The cupboard often contains a secret compartment hidden under a sliding panel, sometimes operated by a wooden or steel spring.

A walnut slope-front desk (c. 1725), shown at Stair and Company, illustrates several ingeniously arranged hiding places. The central cupboard appears to be fixed, but is actually a box in itself which pulls out entirely and when reversed reveals two high, narrow drawers located behind the half columns. In addition, the decorative carving on top of the pigeonholes appears to be one-dimensional. In fact, four of the sections are, but the last pigeonhole at either end has a carved molding which is in reality the end of a very shallow

Desks

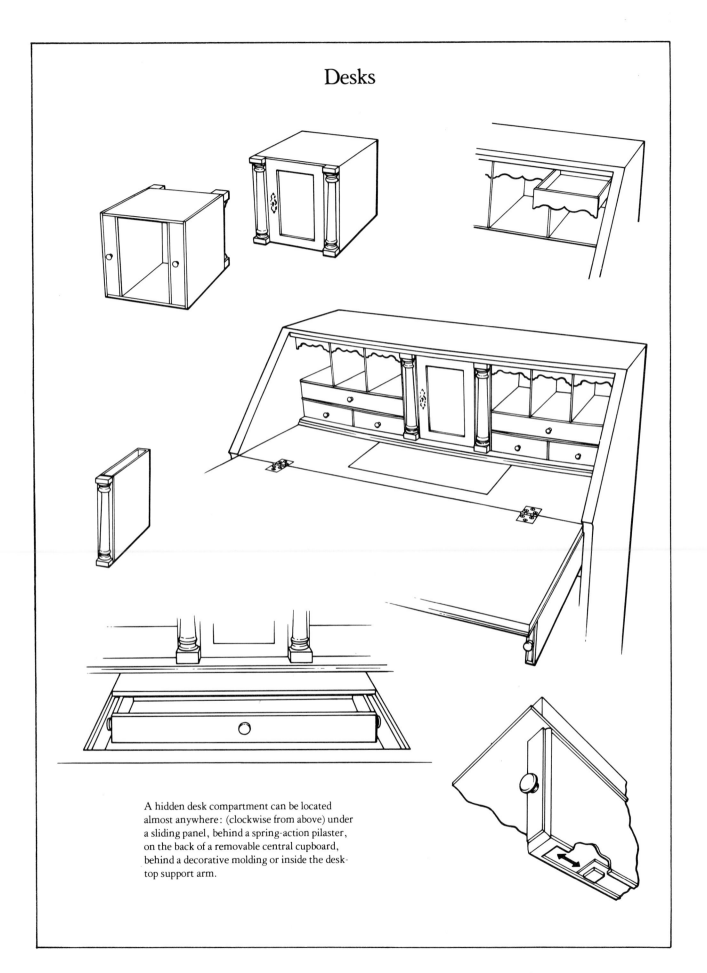

A hidden desk compartment can be located almost anywhere: (clockwise from above) under a sliding panel, behind a spring-action pilaster, on the back of a removable central cupboard, behind a decorative molding or inside the desk-top support arm.

drawer which pulls out by hand. This is a very common device.

There is also a George I walnut bureau bookcase that has a central cupboard flanked by half columns. When one takes hold of the capitals, these columns reveal the fact that they are the short sides of rather deep sections, perfect for the secreting of important papers and currency. And here once again we find the common practice of using a decorative molding on a pigeonhole to hide a shallow drawer. Sometimes the entire pigeonhole or series of pigeonholes will pull out to show smaller, concealed sections behind. I recently sold a George II mahogany bureau bookcase (c. 1740) in which the skilled cabinetmaker had hidden a pair of drawers, the ends of which are disguised as two inlaid pilasters which flank the central cupboard. When slight pressure is applied to them, they pop forward by spring action. Such bureau bookcases sometimes contain wells revealed by panels which slide back or lift up on hinges to show one or more secret drawers.

Probably one of the rarest and most ingenious hiding places contrived by the 18th-century English cabinetmaker is located within the sliding supports that hold the slant top of a bureau open. When purchasing a case piece of this type, I always move my fingers along the underside of these supports in search of a sliding panel. Old guineas will often drop out.

Hidden drawers are found less often in tables than in case pieces. When present, they are rather skillfully camouflaged as in a small Sheraton kidney-shaped writing table (c. 1780). Here a central drawer, marked by a keyhole, is obvious to the eye. But two more drawers are disguised in the frieze, in the shape of wedges which swing out from each side of the table when hand pressure is applied to the underside.

Another very interesting example of a drawer concealed in the frieze of a table is found on a George II mahogany card table. Almost the entire frieze is in fact a rather large drawer, extending for 23 inches. Because it lacks both escutcheon and brass pull, its existence completely eludes the eye.

A Chinese Chippendale card table (c. 1760) contains a secret drawer which defies detection due to the screen of open fretwork around three sides. The small drawer is under the table directly behind the gate leg which swings out to support the table when open. It is invisible when the table is closed.

Many secret drawers and hidden compartments are awaiting discovery by the diligent collector of antiques. Even today it might be a wise idea to remove one's valuables from the burglar's eye by tucking them away into devices created two hundred years ago. Or some craftsmen may wish to incorporate hiding places into new pieces. □

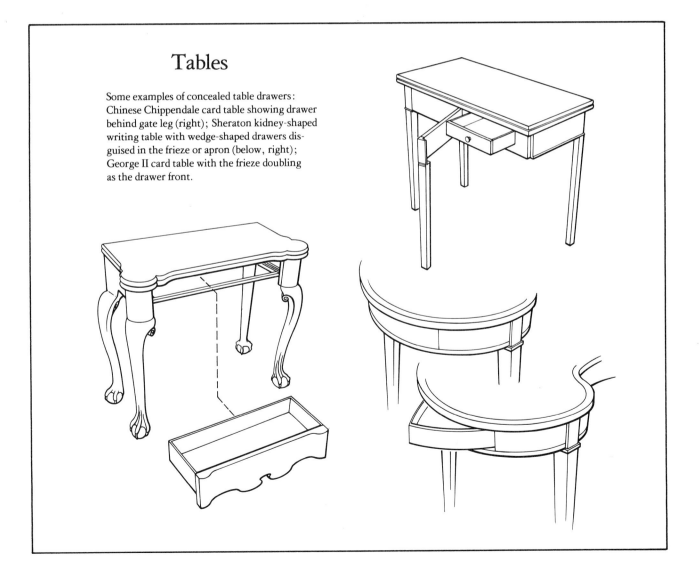

Tables

Some examples of concealed table drawers: Chinese Chippendale card table showing drawer behind gate leg (right); Sheraton kidney-shaped writing table with wedge-shaped drawers disguised in the frieze or apron (below, right); George II card table with the frieze doubling as the drawer front.

Straightening Up an Old Secretary
What Winterthur conservators do about 200 years of sag

by Gregory J. Landrey

You need only glance at the asking prices in antiques shops to realize that many people believe that the furniture made in the mid to late 18th century is the epitome of quality. We don't lack for 200-year-old examples proving this point, and some furniture of the day has survived virtually intact. Yet the craftsmen of the "golden age" were far from infallible, and sometimes were guilty of significant oversights in the way they built the furniture we so highly revere.

A case in point is the Chippendale secretary pictured here, a 1951 acquisition of the Henry Francis du Pont Winterthur Museum, which I was recently assigned to prepare for a traveling exhibit. An impressive piece standing 103 in. tall, 45 in. wide and 23 in. deep, it's typical of the work done by Pennsylvania German cabinetmakers around the time of the American Revolution. Except for the usual dings, nicks and areas of deteriorated finish, it looked to be in good shape. A close inspection showed otherwise.

The arched rails of both doors were cracked, because the joints didn't allow for seasonal wood movement. The desk's rear feet were fastened by joints too weak to support its weight, a condition made worse by years of abuse and a couple of inept repair attempts. The most serious and difficult-to-repair deterioration was in the desk carcase itself. The sides bulged noticeably under the weight of the upper bookcase, because the joints which lent lateral support to the case were too weak and had failed.

The secretary had been on view at Winterthur, but before it could travel to exhibitions outside the museum, these structural flaws and some finish problems had to be corrected. We had no intention of restoring the piece to like-new condition. The task of conservators at museums like Winterthur is to examine old furniture methodically, to record their findings objectively, and to make repairs to retard further deterioration. When possible, we try to make the piece visually appropriate to its period. In this way, we often discover unknown aspects of historic craft, while preserving valuable specimens for the enjoyment of future generations.

Saving the desk—Our survey of the secretary eventually included many pages of notes and more than 300 photographs. Research showed that the piece was built for Michael Withers in Lancaster, Pa., between 1785 and 1800, possibly by a cabinetmaker named Michael Lind, though the elaborate pediment molding and carving may have been the work of an itinerant carver. Both upper and lower carcases are basically simple boxes, made of cherry boards joined by dovetails that still fit flawlessly. The bottom of the lower case is poplar. The wide dovetail pins, along with the use of pegs and wedges in construction, are in the tradition of northern European craftsmen. While far from crude, the carving, construction, and the choice of cherry rather than walnut or mahogany indicate that the secretary came from a shop out of the Boston-Philadel-

Though hardly a paradigm of the 18th-century furnituremakers' art, this Chippendale secretary is a good example of the work done by Pennsylvania German cabinetmakers of the late 1700s, reason enough for Winterthur conservators to repair damage done to it during two centuries of use.

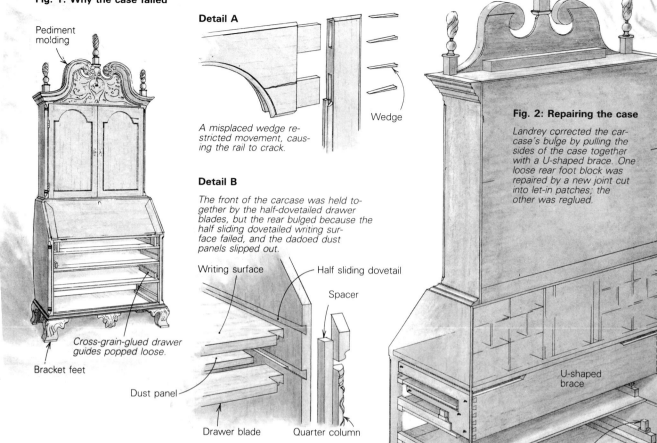

Fig. 1: Why the case failed

Pediment molding

Cross-grain-glued drawer guides popped loose.

Bracket feet

Detail A

A misplaced wedge restricted movement, causing the rail to crack.

Wedge

Detail B

The front of the carcase was held together by the half-dovetailed drawer blades, but the rear bulged because the half sliding dovetailed writing surface failed, and the dadoed dust panels slipped out.

Writing surface

Half sliding dovetail

Spacer

Dust panel

Drawer blade

Quarter column

Fig. 2: Repairing the case

Landrey corrected the carcase's bulge by pulling the sides of the case together with a U-shaped brace. One loose rear foot block was repaired by a new joint cut into let-in patches; the other was reglued.

U-shaped brace

Drawer-guide retainer

Right-angle braces strengthen the repaired foot blocks.

Drawer-guide detail

To hold the guides at the back, Landrey glued a retainer to the case. Mylar acts as a lubricant, allowing the case sides to move without cracking

Mylar

The drawer guides were spot-glued only at the front of the case.

phia mainstream. It's a sophisticated attempt to imitate English high-style design.

Once I had completed my survey, I discussed the project with Winterthur senior furniture conservator John Melody and museum curator Nancy Richards. We all agreed that the weakened desk carcase and loose rear feet should be repaired first, leaving lesser problems until later.

The desk carcase repair illustrates how conservation ethics can be at odds with sound woodworking practice—you can't always make the best repair. The case sides were joined by the dovetailed top and bottom and by the two-piece writing surface, which was let into sliding dovetails running the full width of the sides. The three dust panels that separate the drawers, however, were only dadoed into the sides and thus they offered no help in keeping the carcase sides from bulging out under the weight of the 90-lb. bookcase, which may have weighed 200 lb. when filled with books. The carcase was braced at the front by drawer blades half-dovetailed into the case, but because these blades are only 3 in. wide, they provided no support at the back. The case back—three tongue-and-grooved poplar boards nailed into a rabbet—added little because the nails had pulled out of the short-grain ends of the poplar or had split the rabbet. As a result, the carcase sides curved out ⅜ in. at the back, and the entire piece swayed precariously if pushed from the side.

Rebuilding the dust panels and joining them with sliding dovetails the full width of the sides would have been the soundest repair, but such a drastic alteration would have changed the piece's character permanently, and was therefore ethically unacceptable. A cardinal rule of conservation is to

make repairs as reversible as possible and to supplement rather than alter existing constructions. Several of the ideas we considered, including dovetailing braces into the sides of the case, screwing on a plywood back or attaching an X-brace for diagonal support, entailed too much alteration. I finally decided to build a U-shaped brace (figure 2) that could be slipped into the top two drawer compartments from behind and screwed in place. The idea of sinking screws into 200-year-old wood might raise the eyebrows of some conservators, but I considered this solution acceptable because the sides

Sliding dovetails join the foot blocks to the bottom of the secretary, a seemingly sound alternative to the usual practice of blocks glued to the inside of the bracket feet. But this joint proved too weak, and the right rear block (photo, left) failed.

To repair the right rear foot block, Landrey recut the joint after replacing damaged wood with poplar patches, as shown at right. He reglued, then reinforced both blocks with poplar right-angle braces. The end grain of this particular bracket foot shows circular sawmarks, indicating a previous restoration.

were solid and because it involved the least removal of material. Moreover, the brace can easily be taken out.

I made the brace out of cherry because that's what the piece itself is made of and because this wood is strong, light and stable. Fortunately, there is ⅞ in. between the drawer sides and the inside wall of the carcase—just enough room to fit the brace in. The sides of the brace are slotted to clear the drawer guides. To allow for wood movement (this is a cross-grain construction), I attached the brace to the carcase with ten round-head screws run through slotted holes. I put two steel washers under each screw head to minimize the chance of their binding in the slots. A piece of 1.5 mil Mylar placed between the brace and the carcase acts as a moisture barrier and a lubricant, further reducing binding. Mylar is a non-reactive plastic that finds many uses in the conservation lab.

Fixing the loose rear feet was next. The desk actually rests not on its bracket feet but on four 3-in. by 3-in. by 6½-in. poplar blocks joined to the bottom with tapered sliding dovetails. While this is quite an ingenious alternative to the usual practice of simply gluing blocks to the inside of the bracket feet, it caused trouble. First, the sliding dovetail just about cut off the outermost pins of the carcase dovetails, weakening both joints. Also, this construction left weak short-grain that crumbled under years of stress. The secretary would have been better supported by glue blocks attached with the grain running in the same direction as that on the bracket feet. The front feet were sound, probably because they'd been supported by the bracket feet on two sides rather than just one. The right rear foot (photo, above) was the weakest. Insertion of wedges, shims, and excessive amounts of various adhesives, including epoxy, during previous repair attempts had aggravated the problem. We often see this sort of damage, which is difficult to treat for two reasons. First, it usually requires replacing the damaged original wood with new wood—a last resort in conservation. Second, it's hard to date old repairs. Recent ones may be unimportant, but those done a century ago may shed light on unknown techniques of the past and should therefore be preserved.

I chiseled out the weakened wood from the foot block and the case bottom, and glued in poplar patches with hide glue, which is reversible with warm water. So future conservators will know when the repair was made, I marked the date and my initials on both the glueline and the outside of the patch. I then recut the sliding dovetail and glued the leg back in. To keep the rear leg joints from failing again, I reinforced them with right-angle poplar braces, hide-glued in place.

Minor structural repairs—Once the carcase repairs were complete, I began work on the less serious flaws. The most troubling of these were the ugly cracks in the arched rails of the bookcase doors. At first, we couldn't determine why the rails had cracked. They were joined with double, through mortise and tenons, a good choice that should have accommodated the seasonal movement of the 6-in. wide rails.

An X-radiograph of the right door solved the mystery. One of the two wedges driven into each mortise had restricted the rail's movement, and when it shrank, a crack opened up in the weak short-grain near the base of the arch. The wedges blended into the end grain of the tenons so well that we couldn't see them without the X-radiograph. Extracting them to repair the rails would have altered the original construction and caused more damage. Since the joints were stable and tight, we left them alone. If the tenons had been wedged only on their outside edges, the rails might not have cracked.

We found many examples of cross-grain construction in the secretary, and while some had weathered seasonal movement well, others had not, particularly the battens glued to the ends of the desk's fall front. Since the battens hadn't shrunk with the top, their ends eventually stood about ¼ in. proud of the fall front's hinge edge. When the front was opened, the projecting end of the battens acted like a prybar on the hinges, splitting two chunks off the edge of the writing surface. Trimming the ends of the battens flush was more alteration than we could tolerate, so I simply reattached the hinges with new brass screws, left a little loose to allow some movement (figure 3, facing page). I glued the cracked pieces

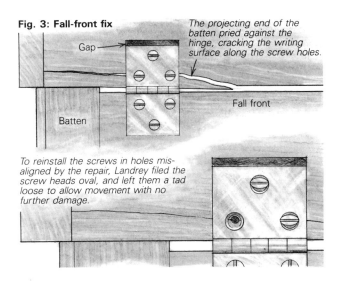

Fig. 3: Fall-front fix

The projecting end of the batten pried against the hinge, cracking the writing surface along the screw holes.

Gap

Batten

Fall front

To reinstall the screws in holes misaligned by the repair, Landrey filed the screw heads oval, and left them a tad loose to allow movement with no further damage.

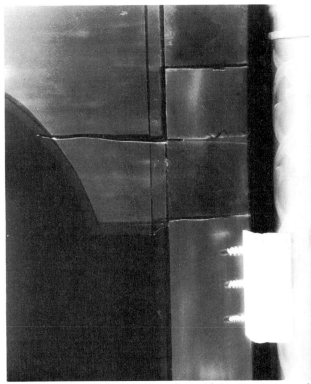

X-radiographs reveal much about how old furniture was made and why certain constructions fail. This one shows how a wedge next to the tenon cracked the arched rail of one of the bookcase doors. It also reveals evidence of previous repair work: The top hinge screw has coarse, hand-filed threads and is probably an original. But the finer, machine-cut threads of the bottom screw indicate that it was installed many years later.

back in place, filled with dowels the screw holes left by a previous repair attempt, then patched the surface with shellac stick. I saved the original hinge screws and they are kept in an envelope in the desk.

Restoring the desk's eight drawer guides was next. Originally, they had been hide-glued cross-grain to the inside wall of the carcase. They probably popped loose not too long after the piece was completed. If glued back in place with a modern, less forgiving adhesive, they could restrict wood movement enough to crack the carcase sides. To solve this problem, I hide-glued only the very front 1½ in. of the guides to the inside of the case, holding them in place at the back with the retainer shown in figure 2. Lubricated by a sheet of Mylar, this retainer allows the case sides to move independently of the drawer guides. Instead of replacing the bottom guides, which were badly worn, I made a positive mold of the missing wood out of modeling clay and used it as a guide to carve patches. When the drawer guides were back in place, I moved on to the final step: restoring the finish.

In conservation work, we try to preserve as much of the old finish as possible, making finish repair an arduous task that is further complicated by the arcane, often hard-to-identify finish recipes used by some cabinetmakers. Lab analysis of these finishes rarely helps, but we can sometimes identify a finish by the way it has cracked or crazed over time. The surface of spirit varnishes—solutions of shellac and other resins in alcohol—crazes into irregular-shaped islands. Oil varnishes form regular squares or rectangles. Lacquer, a relatively modern finish, crazes into elongated rectangles.

The craze pattern on the secretary suggested shellac; I confirmed this by dissolving a small patch with an alcohol-soaked swab. I suspected that the piece had been refinished, but except for the carcase sides, the finish was in reasonably good shape on the lower case. I was able to restore it to the appropriate sheen by rubbing it with pumice and rottenstone applied with a soft cloth soaked in mineral spirits.

The finish on the upper case, however, was more severely crazed and flaking, possibly because it had been exposed for many years to the warmer upper air of heated rooms. Because it was unrestorable, I removed the old shellac with alcohol, using a stiff brush to loosen stubborn patches. Then I brushed on six coats of 2-lb.-cut shellac rubbed with 0000 steel wool between coats. After I touched up minor losses on the rest of the piece, a final rubbing with a carnauba-based wax on all finished surfaces completed the conservation work.

This secretary was one of the most difficult conservation challenges I've ever undertaken, and from it I learned some valuable lessons. True, there were flaws in the design and construction of this piece, but, interestingly enough, some of the most sophisticated of the Philadelphia Chippendale pieces had more serious defects. Although Lancaster was the largest inland city in the United States at the time, its rural setting meant fewer resources than were available to the cabinetmakers of the major port cities. The fact that this piece has survived two centuries is a notable tribute to the 18th-century craftsman who built it. He did not have our advantage of hindsight to see how two hundred years of wear, abuse, seasonal changes and eventually central heating would affect his furniture. Through scientific conservation, we can record the successes and failures of our predecessors, and apply these lessons to improve our own work. □

Gregory J. Landrey is a conservator at the Henry Francis du Pont Winterthur Museum in Winterthur, Del. After a cross-country tour during 1983 and 1984 that included stops for exhibitions in Houston, San Francisco and Chicago, the secretary described in this article has been returned to its permanent home. It may be seen in the Port Royal Bedroom of the Winterthur Museum. *For another look at 18th-century secretaire-bookcases, see page 80.*

What To Do With a Walnut Beam
John Hallam's blockfront treasure

When John Hallam of Livermore, Calif., finished building a secretary with 12 secret compartments, he figured he could take a bit of a rest. But then two passing strangers offered him a bargain he couldn't refuse—two 8x8 walnut beams 8 ft. long. His wife, Jo Ann, noting that the hallway ceiling was 8 ft. high, asked for a china cabinet to fit.

Hallam proceeded to draw up the plans. He augmented his basic machine tools (a Shopsmith and a router) by buying and tuning-up a Sears table saw. He enrolled in the local high school's adult education woodworking class so he could use their planer on weekends. For making the cabinet's wide curved moldings, he devised a way to use his Shopsmith as an overarm router, as shown in the photos on the facing page.

Hallam took his time making the cabinet, enjoying every phase of the project. He spent a couple of months researching the design for the shells on the drawerfront, then took a year to finish the drawer. "I worked 12 hours a week on the average, though 12 hours a day, sometimes. I really enjoyed carving that drawer."

He said the most fun in the three-year project came from steam-bending the trim and the mullions for the doors, a tricky operation he had never before attempted. He used copper pipe, a packstove, and faith, bending the steamy pieces around a 27-in. bicycle wheel. He figures he did pretty well, since he cracked only three strips.

Hallam admits to having done "a lot of carving," but still he picked up new skills and tricks, including regrinding router bits, before he was through with this job. Through? He still has the other walnut beam.... —*Jim Cummins*

Top drawerfront is carved from a solid block of walnut.

China cabinet, designed and built by John Hallam. Hallam's shop is half-a-garage; his basic machine tools are a Shopsmith, a Sears table saw, and a router.

Routing wide moldings

by John Hallam

The Shopsmith runs at a peak speed of 5500 RPM, slow for routing, but a shop-made jig serves as a guide that lets you go slowly enough to get a clean cut. Make the jig from a piece of plywood with ½-in. dowels screwed on from the bottom (photo below). The shaper collars on the dowels must turn freely so the work doesn't bind.

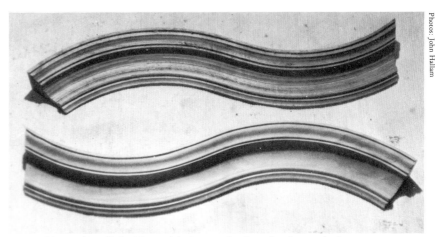

Top molding is hot off the Shopsmith; its mate has been hand-smoothed.

Design the molding with enough flat surface to bear against the collars, and with about an inch extra on the ends as a bearing surface for starting and finishing the cuts. Remove excess wood on the bandsaw. Attach the dowels to the board so they're slightly wider than the work. If the screw holes in the dowels are a little off center, you can make fine adjustments by rotating the dowels on the resulting eccentric axis. Feed the work against the back collar. The front collar prevents the work from moving forward and ruining the contour.

Start each cut by pushing one end of the work against the back collar, and rotating it into the cutter. Take a series of overlapping light cuts. Draw a line through the shaper-collar centers, and use this line as a guide on the radius of the curves as you feed the work. Feed straight moldings straight through. Below, a 1-in. straight router bit performs the initial shaping, wasting the wood rather than shaping the profile.

Draw the molding outline on the end of the stock. Then with a ½-in. corebox (round-nose) bit, start removing wood, repositioning the jig as necessary. Work down close to the penciled outline. You'll find that slight wandering between the dowels doesn't affect the shape much.

With an assortment of ⅛-in. and ¼-in. fluted straight and core-box bits, define the small coves and beads. You could also use specially ground cutters to achieve almost any molding shape.

The process leaves a slightly ridged surface (photo, top), which can then be smoothed with carving tools, scrapers and sandpaper. It takes me about two hours to cut a pair of curved and return moldings, and another three to four hours for the final smoothing. □

Scratch Beader

Simple tool makes intricate moldings

by Henry T. Kramer

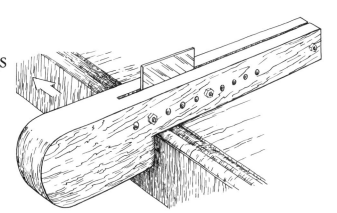

The scratch beader is a tool of many virtues. It is quickly and easily made. With practice, it is a substitute for a router (table or hand) and for molding planes. It can do things those tools cannot, depending on the particular job. It can cut any molding (or groove or rabbet) you are willing to make a cutter for, including intricate shapes.

The beader consists of hardwood stock with a projecting arm, which has a vertical saw kerf along its length. The tools are held in the saw kerf by bolts. The shoulder between the stock and the arm guides the tool as it is drawn along the edge of the work.

Making a cutter for the beader is easy. File or grind a piece of any scrap steel—old saw blades or cabinet scrapers are ideal, but in a pinch one can use almost anything. The steel should be wide enough to accommodate the desired shape plus another ¼ in. or ⅜ in. to recess behind the shoulder. Recessing the tool stiffens it during each stroke. It should be long enough to accommodate the design and stick out the top, and no thicker than the kerf in which it will be placed.

The cutter is formed by cutting and filing the desired shape, as a negative cross section, in one end of the blank. The cutting edge is filed straight across the edge of the tool. With steel no thicker than an old saw blade, a mere awareness that the trailing edge should not extend below the cutting face will allow sufficient clearance. With heavier steel, a more deliberate relief will be required, as on the sides of a tool that is to follow a curve. But do not leave any more relief than necessary. The tool cuts like a scraper, not a chisel, and it should not want to cut the wood under vertical or horizontal pressure.

If you wish to harden and temper the tool, fine. It is not ordinarily worth the effort for one-of-a-kind applications. If the shape is complex and not easily sharpened without destroying the design, hardening may be desirable. Usually one is not obliged to harden unless the molding to be cut involves a lot of wood. This is not a production tool. It is for small or non-repetitive jobs, and it permits a flexibility of shapes that production tools cannot match.

It is used by placing the beader at right angles, vertically and horizontally, to the shape or groove to be cut. With cuts of any depth, say ⅛ in. or 3/16 in. or more, the tool is first placed part way below the arm and secured tightly on both sides by two or more small machine bolts of any convenient size. The beader is then drawn along the surface to be cut, holding its shoulder against the nearest edge or surface, and at a right angle to the surface to be cut. The beader should be held upright at all times, but at the very start some slight tilt in the direction of the stroke may be useful. One or two trials will show that the leading edge of the cutter will then have the effect of providing a quite shallow cut. But as soon as the cutter has got into the wood, the beader should be used upright. As the work progresses, the cutter may have to be reset

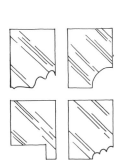

Scratch beader is easily made from hardwood and steel scraps; cutter can be bolted in saw kerf at various positions along projecting arm. Left, cutter profiles are negative cross sections of desired shapes. Drawing below shows tool's rounded shoulder, which allows the beader to follow curved edges.

deeper until the final design has been cut.

A beader will be used most often to shape an edge, but may also be used to cut a groove (for inlay, for example) or molding in the surface of a plank following a straight or curved edge. In this case the shoulder of the tool, which locates and maintains the distance between the groove (or inner edge of the molding) and the outer edge, may be rounded to about the smallest arc of the curved edge being followed. This makes it easier to hold the tool steady as you follow a curve, it keeps the distance of the cut more constant, and it permits you to keep the long axis of the tool normal, or perpendicular, to the curved edge as you follow it.

The beader is best used on hardwood and with care it will cut across the grain—even in situations where a plane or router would tear. It will not cut cleanly to the very end of a blind groove, nor, in the case of sharp angles, can it be worked right to the intersection. Work up to about a half-inch away and finish with a knife or chisel. Take care always to keep the shoulder bearing on the work as you scrape. And put a bolt through the hole nearest the end of the arm, so the saw kerf won't pinch your hand as you work.

Beaders may be made in a variety of sizes, although they are difficult to use for large moldings. Some beaders, for delicate work, are quite small. Start with simple designs; later, all sorts of applications will invite your interest. Whatever size you try, keep to the general proportions shown in the drawing. Too long a beader encourages twisting as you scrape, which is not good. Beaders don't last forever, because the cutter tends to enlarge the kerf in which it is held during use. When this happens, you'll have to make a new beader. Make one and practice on some scrap and you'll soon appreciate the versatility of this inexpensive device. □

Henry Kramer, of Somerville, N.J., is in the reinsurance business. He'd rather make and fix tools and furniture.

Moldings
Applying geometry with style

by Victor J. Taylor

Moldings dramatically affect the look of any piece of furniture. Their main purpose has always been to visually connect elements and to add richness, subtly controlling the viewer's appreciation of a design. They have several other functions, too. They frequently serve as placeholding keyways for separable parts of a piece of furniture. They may mask joints that would otherwise show, or conceal screw and nail heads, or cover end grain. And their style and proportions set the style for particular furniture periods.

Our knowledge of classical moldings comes from edge treatments used in ancient architecture. In the surviving examples that have come down to us, these were already a highly evolved form. Perhaps the first moldings were merely an effort to smooth off the arris (the edge) where two surfaces meet at an angle. It is possible to round off an arris in several ways, affecting the relationship between the planes. In figure 1, **A, B, C** and **D** represent cross sections through various tabletops. The equally distributed radius of **A** is neutral. The flattened curve of **B** makes the tabletop appear thinner, diminishing its bulk. Conversely, the curve shown in **C** accentuates the thickness of the tabletop. The bevel in **D** tends to reduce the bulk of the tabletop even more.

Fillets can be cut in to define the extent of each curve, adding to the emphasis. The bevel, as applied to panel or carcase rails, can add a decorative element in the way that it stops near a corner or where two rails meet. It is easy to imagine how attached moldings evolved from these edge treatments, and one very good reason was that the grain of moldings could be chosen so that they could be worked easily, whereas all too often the grain of a solid top, particularly the end grain, was difficult.

Weight and transition—In figure 2, **E, F** and **G** represent a bookcase/cupboard, a chest of drawers on a stand, and a long-case clock, respectively. In the first column, each has been reduced to its basic elements. As functional furniture, all three pieces could be constructed as I have drawn them, without embellishment, and, more significantly, without any visual transitions between the components.

Yet in **E,** the uppermost unit looks insignificant compared with the others, and the whole piece looks unfinished. The same can be said of the chest-on-stand shown at **F.** The long-case clock at **G** is more complicated. It comprises four disparate units—the plinth, surbase, trunk and hood. All three pieces of furniture will benefit from more visual weight at the top. In **E** and **F** a cornice immediately makes each piece look just a bit more imposing. In **G** a pediment counterbalances the bulky surbase and plinth.

But still the appearance of each piece is stark and unfinished until moldings are added to relate one unit to another. At this juncture we have two choices. We can employ a convex molding, which will accent the units, or we can use a concave molding, which will smooth the transition between the units.

It is obvious that the profile of the molding affects the outline of a piece of furniture. A subtler factor to be considered is how the molding surface reflects light and how its elements create shadow. Moldings above eye level, as for instance on a cornice, should be mounted so that the decorative elements face downward. The reverse applies to the moldings on a plinth or a base. In this way the interplay of light and shadow adds vitality and interest to what could otherwise be a lusterless object. Sharp curves generate brighter highlights than do gentle ones. A sprightly piece of furniture therefore calls for vigorous moldings. Conversely, a sedate piece is enhanced by broad, gentle curves.

The particular molding design we

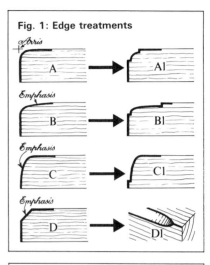

Fig. 1: Edge treatments

Arris
A → A1
Emphasis
B → B1
Emphasis
C → C1
Emphasis
D → D1

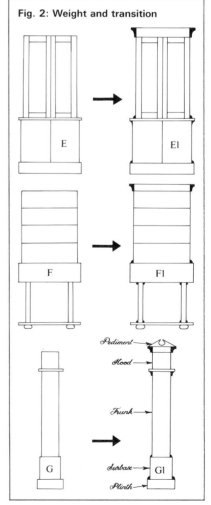

Fig. 2: Weight and transition

E → E1
F → F1

Pediment
Hood
Trunk
Surbase
Plinth
G → G1

Fig. 3: Typical period moldings

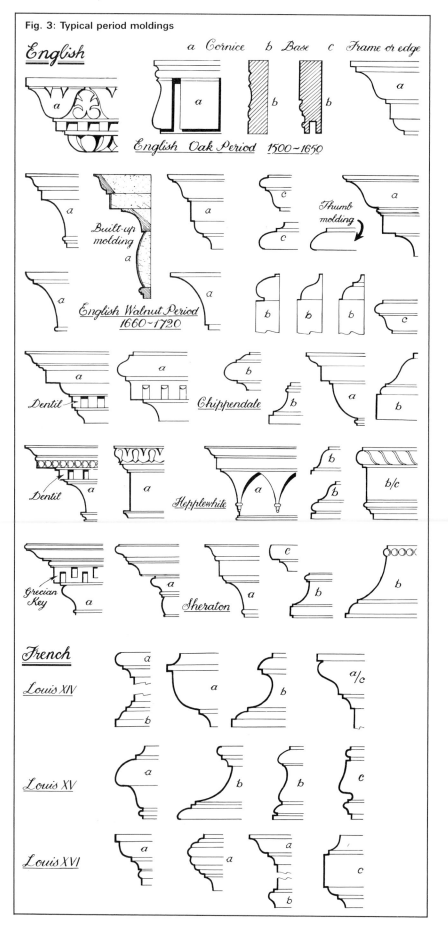

English

a Cornice   b Base   c Frame or edge

a

English Oak Period 1500~1650

Built-up molding

English Walnut Period 1660~1720

Thumb molding

Dentil

Chippendale

Dentil

Hepplewhite

Grecian Key

Sheraton

French

Louis XIV

Louis XV

Louis XVI

apply depends on the nature of the furniture, on whether an individual unit needs to be given prominence because of the craftsmanship lavished upon it, or because the design is of a period which must carry the moldings appropriate to its age. Figure 3 shows a few typical moldings found on English and French furniture of various periods.

Geometry—The Greeks and the Romans had different approaches for designing moldings. Roman designs were based on segments of a circle; the Greeks began with conical sections—ellipse, hyperbola, parabola.

Some basic curves can be combined into any of hundreds of complex moldings. Starting with the Roman style, figure 4 shows how to draw the cyma recta (ogee), the cyma reversa (reverse ogee), the ovolo, the cavetto and the scotia. All of them use a square grid as the starting pattern.

To lay out the Greek equivalents, draw the size of the stock and divide each side into the same number of parts. The greater the number of divisions, the more accurate the profile. Then draw the radiating lines to the grid points, as shown. In the case of the Greek scotia and cavetto profiles, one of the centers for the plotting lines is found by extending the sides of the section.

Making moldings—Figure 5 shows how to make a backed cornice, based on the instructions given by Thomas Sheraton in his classic *Cabinet Maker and Upholsterer's Drawing Book*. You remove the bulk of the wood with rabbet planes, then shape the curves using the appropriate molding planes. The first step (detail 1) is to draw out the section full-size, and then draw in the rectangle *abcd* to indicate the size of the mahogany show wood. Draw the size of the rabbets that can be planed square, and mark points *e, f, g, h* and *i.*

Now prepare a piece of mahogany to the size *abcd,* and glue a piece of pine to the back of it, as shown in 2. Turn the assembly over (3), and scribe *e, f, g, h* and *i* along the full length of the molding. Next, set your gauge from *a* to *y,* and again from *c* to *z,* and mark them off along the full length.

Proceeding to **4,** mark and plane off the corners to match the profile.

In **5,** the rabbet plane has completed its work and the stock is ready for final shaping with the molding plane.

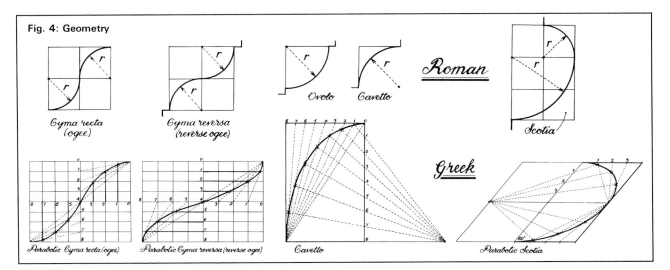

Fig. 4: Geometry

Cyma recta (ogee)

Cyma reversa (reverse ogee)

Ovolo   Cavetto

Roman

Scotia

Parabolic Cyma recta (ogee)

Parabolic Cyma reversa (reverse ogee)

Cavetto

Greek

Parabolic Scotia

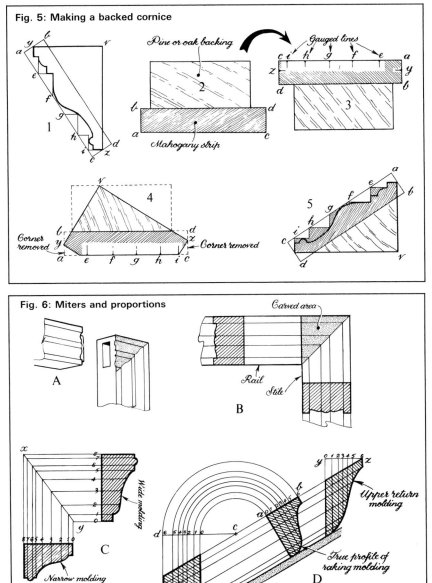

Fig. 5: Making a backed cornice

Pine or oak backing

Gauged lines

Mahogany strip

Corner removed

Corner removed

Fig. 6: Miters and proportions

Carved area

Rail

Stile

A

B

Wide molding

Narrow molding

C

Upper return molding

True profile of raking molding

Lower return molding

Cornice

D

Moldings and miters—One of the most common ways of joining moldings in medieval times was to use the "masons' miter," which looks like a miter, but is actually a disguised mortise-and-tenon joint. In figure 6, **A** and **B** show how it was carved.

True miters are not always 45°, even though the pieces meet at 90°. At **C**, two moldings of different widths need to be mitered. Drawing the outer lines of the moldings on paper indicates the miter angle—line **xy**. Extending the profile points of either molding to the line will indicate the necessary proportions for the other.

The example at **D**, in which the "raking" molding of a cornice is pitched at an angle, requires three different profiles. To calculate them, draw the raking molding at its correct angle, and superimpose a drawing of its true profile. Draw reference lines parallel to each other along the molding and then mark off the profile points on the line **ab**. With a compass at center **c,** describe arcs from each reference point on the line **ab** to cut the horizontal line **cd**. Drop perpendiculars, and the intersections will provide plotting points for the lower return molding's profile.

Similarly, you can find the profile of the upper return molding by drawing line **yz** and transferring the dimensions.

You don't, of course, need to begin with the profile of the raking molding, as this procedure works with any of the profiles as a starting point.   □

Victor J. Taylor, of Bath, England, spent years in the furniture business. The author of several books, he was editor of the magazine Woodworker.

Curved Moldings on the Radial-Arm Saw
Shaper setup can cut a swan-neck

by Wallace M. Kunkel

My particular interest is copying 18th-century furniture, and nothing delights me more than bonnet-tops for highboys and tall clocks. Many woodworkers are capable of all the necessary joinery for such pieces yet are stymied by the swan-neck or sweeping ogee moldings. I make many joints by hand, but my moldings are a product of my DeWalt 10-in. radial-arm saw.

The swan-neck molding is a series of parallel profiles describing an ogee curve. On clocks and highboys, it is returned with a straight molding of the same profile along the sides of the case. This type of shaping is often done on the spindle shaper, but the radial-arm saw can make the series of cuts with a molding head, guided by a template screwed to the board being molded.

I usually make all four pieces of the molding—the right-hand swan-neck and the mirror-image left-hand swan-neck, each with its accompanying straight section—at the same time, on opposite edges of a single board. You can also use two shorter boards, as in figure 1. If you do, just flip the template for the mirror-image molding. Start by laying out the innermost curve of the molding on one edge of each board. You can enlarge the curve from figure 1, which is taken from Lester Margon's *Construction of Early American Furniture Treasures,* or you can design your own profile. For the molding shown here, I started with a straight-grained cherry board 26 in. long, 8 in. wide, and 1⅛ in. thick. The molding stock should be screwed, down the center, to a piece of ¾-in. particleboard that is the same width as the molding stock but 6 in. longer on each end. The particleboard will serve as a template and it will elevate the molding stock to give the arbor nut room under the molding head. The particleboard's extra length makes entering and exiting the shaping operation

safer. With the molding stock attached to the particleboard template, transfer the curve to this assembly and bandsaw the shape. Hand-sand or use a drum sander to smooth the curve, particularly on the template since it determines the smoothness of the final cut.

I use a Rockwell 4-in. molding head with interchangeable knives. This 3-knife head describes a 5½-in. diameter circle with knives in place. If you are making moldings requiring a tighter inside radius, Rockwell sells a smaller head that works inside a 2¾-in. diameter, using the same knives.

To set up, make a new back table for your saw. Since you won't be using the fence for this operation, make the new table ¾ in. wider than the old one. Use a flat piece of particleboard or plywood, and make sure the joint between the front and back table surfaces is flush. With the new back table temporarily locked in place, remove the sawblade,

Swan-neck moldings are a dramatic element of 18th-century furniture that can readily be made on the radial-arm saw. The sweeping ogees and returns of this clock were made with a molding head and guide jigs. Rosettes were laid in after shaping.

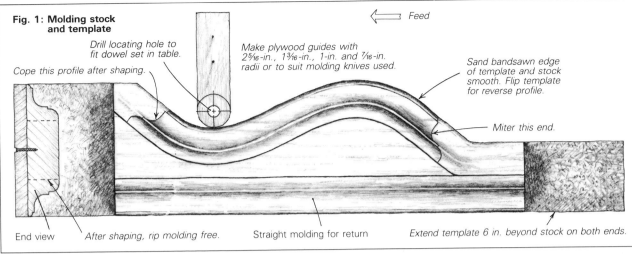

Fig. 1: Molding stock and template

Drill locating hole to fit dowel set in table.

Cope this profile after shaping.

Make plywood guides with 2⁵⁄₁₆-in., 1³⁄₁₆-in., 1-in. and ⁷⁄₁₆-in. radii or to suit molding knives used.

⟵ *Feed*

Sand bandsawn edge of template and stock smooth. Flip template for reverse profile.

Miter this end.

End view

After shaping, rip molding free.

Straight molding for return

Extend template 6 in. beyond stock on both ends.

collar and guard, and swing the arbor to the vertical position. Then move the arbor about 3 in. behind the table joint and mark the arbor center on the back table. Remove the back table and drill an arbor-size blind hole (usually ⅝ in.) in the tabletop, almost but not quite through the thickness of the table. Put the back table in position, and move it and the motor until the arbor drops into the hole as you lower the arm. Lock the back table in this position. Then lock the roller head in the arm and leave it locked throughout the entire shaping operation. To add extra rigidity, I next adjust the roller-head bearings so they bind in their track—that way the roller head won't wobble. Keeping the motor rigid is important, otherwise the cutter may chatter during shaping. Elevate the arbor out of the hole. The arbor-size hole you drilled will be filled with a dowel that sticks ¼ in. above the table surface. This dowel serves as a positioner for the guides.

Next make the guides—various-size ¼-in. plywood jigs tacked to the saw table that control the distance the template is held from the center of the arbor, and hence the depth of the cut. Making them is no problem if you understand the relationship between molding head diameters and the cuts they make. The Rockwell cutterhead with knives installed describes a 2¾-in. radius at the outermost portion of the knife. The simplest profile, that made by the Rockwell #104 straight knives, will have a radius of 2¾ in. at all points. If the knife describes a 2¾-in. radius and you wish to make a cut 1 in. into the material, for example, you need to make a guide that has a radius of 1¾ in.

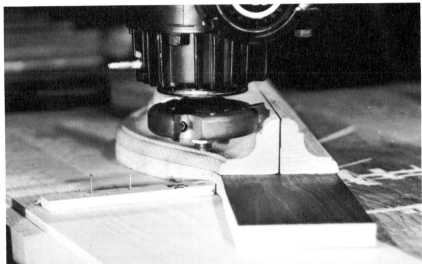

A radial-arm saw won't cut all the moldings that a spindle shaper will, but it works well for swan-necks. The stock to be molded, here ripped into two pieces for clarity, is screwed to a particleboard template. The saw's fence is then removed and replaced by a radiused-end plywood guide that bears against the template as the stock is fed into the cutter. Make the template 6 in. longer on each end so you'll have a bearing surface to start and finish the cut.

Any kind of molding head can be used, but make sure you check its radius before making the guides.

The sizes I use are shown in figure 1, but you can vary them to suit the radius of your molding head and knives. The length of the guide should be at least 6 in. The locating hole in the guide must be the same diameter as the dowel pin set in the table. Touch up the edges of the radius with sandpaper.

For my molding head, four guides are needed—from ⁷⁄₁₆-in. to 2⁵⁄₁₆-in. radius, as shown in figure 2 on the next page. Each guide is placed over the dowel, squared with the table and secured with two brads at the back. Changing knives and guides can be tricky. Without unlocking the motor in the arm, you can raise the arm and pivot

the motor to the crosscut position to make it easier. Also, you can swing the arm to the side to give yourself room to hammer brads to attach guides.

On deep cuts, the nut on the bottom of the arbor might rub against the wood, marring it. To prevent this, the first cut is made with the straight knives and it removes enough wood to allow the second cut to be made without the arbor nut rubbing. This "relief" cut won't be part of the finished profile, but it must follow the edge of the template.

With the setting up done, the actual shaping is a matter of feel. Running the first or relief cut is good practice since the results are not critical. With the 2⁵⁄₁₆-in. guide, make the relief cut with the straight cutters ¼ in. into the stock and to a depth of 1¼ in. To start the

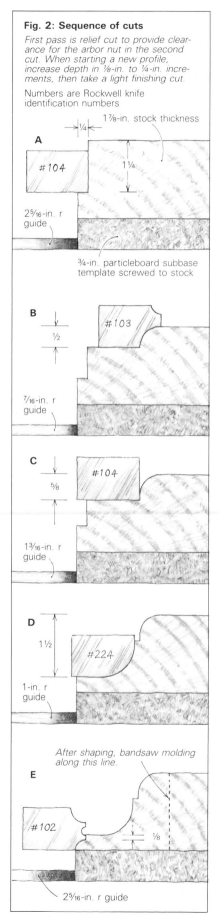

Fig. 2: Sequence of cuts

First pass is relief cut to provide clearance for the arbor nut in the second cut. When starting a new profile, increase depth in ⅛-in. to ¼-in. increments, then take a light finishing cut.

Numbers are Rockwell knife identification numbers

¼ → 1⅞-in. stock thickness

A #104 1¼

2⁵⁄₁₆-in. r guide

¾-in. particleboard subbase template screwed to stock

B #103

½

⁷⁄₁₆-in. r guide

C #104

⅝

1³⁄₁₆-in. r guide

D 1½ #224

1-in. r guide

After shaping, bandsaw molding along this line.

E #102

⅛

2⁵⁄₁₆-in. r guide

cut, lower the cutters with the motor off until they touch the top of your material. Move the stock away from the cutters and lower the arm exactly three turns—⅜ in. Turn the motor on, and with the extended portion of the particleboard template held against the guide, feed the stock slowly into the cutters. Despite the curves, feed the work as nearly parallel to the fence line as possible. The subbase template will guide you into and out of the cut easily, and the stock sort of wraps around the molding head as the radius of the curve nears the radius of the head. Continue with the first cut in increments of two or three turns of depth until you reach the full depth of 1¼ in. Continue shaping using incremental depth settings and the sequence of knives shown in figure 2.

As you begin each new profile, you can take cuts as deep as ¼ in. But after that, stay with ⅛ in. until you get the feel of the cut. Total depth measurements are shown for each profile, but you can vary them to suit your own needs. Remember that each turn of your elevating handle equals ⅛ in. in depth. Each pass must be made on both edges of your stock—the curved edge and the straight edge. Be patient, and as you approach the final depth of each profile, leave a quarter turn of the handle for a clean-up cut. Fine sandpaper will smooth any remaining irregularities.

For a clean, safe cut the molding knives require hand-honing. Work the flat face (bevel up) on a fine slip stone until the entire profile shows the result of the honing. The bottom edge of the knives is relieved (slightly beveled), so you also hone that bevel because most of these cuts reach deep into the material, and the bottom of the knives must do some planing. The knives described here are among the most useful. Whether you purchase them specifically for this molding or not, you'll eventually need them if you do much shaping. They cost about $15 per profile plus $40 for the head (1982 prices). After you have made this molding, one of the most difficult, you'll be able to apply the same method to other radial-arm shaping jobs with ease. The key is understanding how the guides work and getting the feel of moving the stock into the cutters. □

Wallace M. Kunkel operates the Mr. Sawdust School of Professional Woodworking in Chester, N.J. Photos by Jeff Kunkel.

Clock tops and planing on the radial-arm saw

by Raymond H. Haserodt

I often hear people insist that a radial-arm saw is just too inaccurate to do really fine work, but I've found that with patience and a little thought, I'm able to use it to perform all the operations I need to do in my shop—from planing rough boards to shaping fancy, radiused moldings. A radial-arm saw's settings need more attention than a tablesaw's, but the reward is greater versatility. I've improved the performance of my saw—a Sears 10-in.—with these jigs, which you can make or have made inexpensively by a machine shop.

Locking the roller head: Getting the roller head to stay put is always a chore on a radial-arm saw, particularly when you want to nudge the saw this way or that to make fine adjustments for ripping. I made a pair of aluminum clamps that fit in the arm track, bearing firmly against both sides of the roller head (figure 1, at top of facing page). Adjusting screws allow me to move the roller head in increments of as little as a few

This is the radiused molding on one of the twelve clocks Haserodt made for his grandchildren. The molding is returned along the sides of the case.

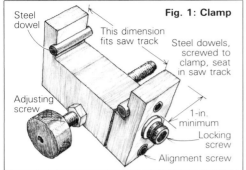

Christopher Clapp

Fig. 1: Clamp

Steel dowel

This dimension fits saw track

Steel dowels, screwed to clamp, seat in saw track

Adjusting screw

1-in. minimum

Locking screw

Alignment screw

To set up his radial-arm saw for planing, below, Haserodt rotates it to the rip position with the blade closest to the extra-high fence. With the aluminum blade-stiffening disc installed (visible behind blade), he feeds the stock on edge between the blade and fence. A spring attachment, right, is clamped to the table to hold the stock against the fence on the out-feed side. Note the aluminum clamps (figure 1, left) holding the roller head in place. The clamp's adjusting screws must bear firmly on the roller-head frame.

thousandths of an inch—that's certainly more than accurate enough for woodworking applications.

The dimensions aren't critical, but the throat opening of the clamps must match the track of the saw on which the clamps will be used. On my radial-arm saw, the roller head rides in a cove-shaped track, so I screwed small steel dowels to the clamp. The dowels fit tightly into the cove, so the clamps seat snugly when tightened down.

Radial-arm planing: Since I don't have a planer, I've developed a method that lets me do the job on my saw. I rotate the roller head to the rip position, as in the photo at right, and run the stock vertically against the fence. I turned an aluminum disc (figure 2) which stiffens a 12-tooth raker blade I use for planing. The surface produced is surprisingly smooth and accurate. I've found that finer blades don't produce a better surface and do take more power to turn. Since I can't plane boards wider than 4 in., I rip boards in the rough, plane them and glue them up to the width I need.

Curved moldings: I use a molding head and the jig shown (photo, bottom right) for making radiused moldings for the clocks I build. I don't have a bandsaw, so I glue up the stock in bricklay fashion in roughly the shape of the radius. Then I attach it to the jig from below with screws and mount the assembly on the saw table. Jig and molding stock pivot on a dowel located so that the molding-head cutter arc passes through the stock at the proper point. I cut the inside radius first, then I move the roller head and cut the outside radius. You can use any combination of knives to get the profile you want. □

Raymond H. Haserodt is a retired tool-and-die maker. He lives in Lyndhurst, Ohio.

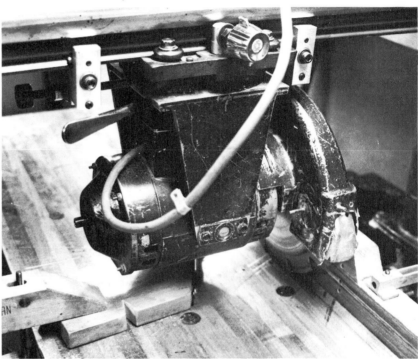

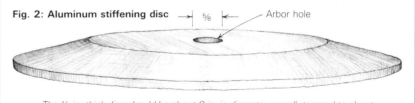

Fig. 2: Aluminum stiffening disc — ⅝ ← — Arbor hole

The ½-in. thick disc should be about 8 in. in diameter overall, tapered to about 5 in. in diameter on the side facing the motor.

Haserodt cuts radiused moldings for his clocks by attaching the stock to this jig with screws. The jig itself pivots on a dowel screwed into the saw table, at right. An arm is attached to the jig to swivel it. Several passes, moving both roller head and depth controls, produce the desired profile.

Antiqued Pine Furniture

Distressing won't hide sloppy work

by B. D. Bittinger

Antiqued pine furniture has become increasingly popular in recent years. This style of furniture is characterized by thick (1-in. to 1-1/2-inch) table and case tops, and correspondingly sturdy carcase construction. It is constructed from knotty white pine. The antiqued and distressed finish is medium dark brown, with lighter brown highlights.

The line of commercial antiqued pine furniture marketed under the Ethan Allen trademark is a good example of this furniture style. I view the style as a romanticized version of the pine furniture built by skilled joiners in rural America during the last half of the 18th century—not rustic or common, but well-made country pine furniture.

Antiqued pine furniture designs for use in present-day homes are necessarily adaptations, not authentic reproductions. After all, rural colonial families did not have king-size beds with "sleep sets" or stereo and TV cabinets. Free-standing desks were rare and all-drawer chests with large, plate-glass mirrors were unknown. They had as much use for coffee tables and bookcases as we have for dough boxes and flax wheels. Antiqued pine furniture designs are based more on feeling than on fact.

Eastern white pine was used by early cabinetmakers and knotty eastern white pine can still be found. Western white pine serves as well and is available at most lumberyards. There

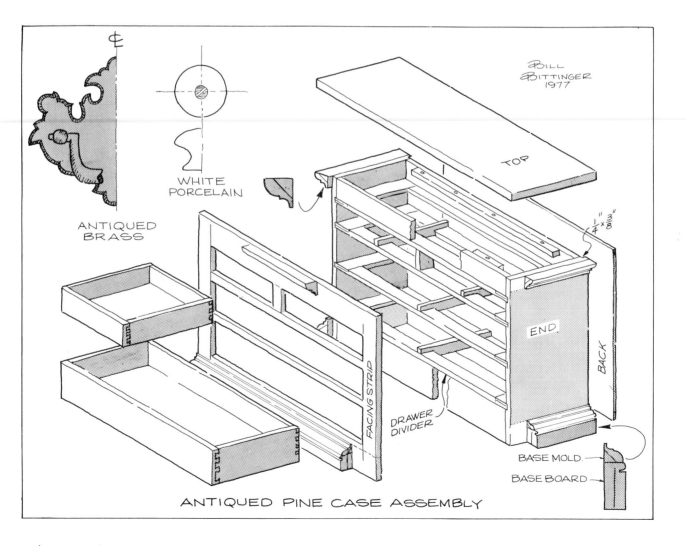

ANTIQUED BRASS

WHITE PORCELAIN

TOP

FACING STRIP

DRAWER DIVIDER

END

BACK

BASE MOLD.

BASE BOARD

ANTIQUED PINE CASE ASSEMBLY

are several varieties of western pine, ranging in color from almost white to tan to pink. Kiln-dried knotty white pine is generally available as #3 common 1x12 shelving in lengths of up to 16 ft. Sugar pine is my choice when I can get it. It is usually tan in color with rust grain lines. Some boards also have a distinctive brown fleck marking. The knots are generally small and red-brown in color.

Most furniture parts are less than 4 ft. long and 5 in. wide. In selecting material, I look at a 1x12 shelving board in terms of the number of good pieces it may contain, not its overall appearance. Some white pine boards are full of sap, heavy and sticky, and are useless for making furniture. Thick (4/4, 6/4, 8/4) knotty white pine is not available at most lumberyards so I usually order from a dealer such as Educational Lumber Co. in Asheville, N.C.

White pine is weak compared to most cabinet woods and this must be considered when designing joints. Tenons in pine, for example, should be as large as possible and somewhat longer than they would be in hardwood. Chair turnings should be hardwood, but heavy pine seats and arms may be used in combination with the hardwood. Pine turnings for table legs should be heavy with simple, bold patterns. I prefer to glue up turning blocks from 3/4-in. stock. Small, firm knots in a turning block will usually cut and finish well.

Tools must be extremely sharp for cutting pine because it is so soft that the fibers tend to tear. I use a plywood-tooth saw blade on the radial arm saw and always crosscut with the good side up. Even with a sharp, small-tooth blade the fibers may break out on the bottom and leave a rough surface. Carving chisels must also be extra sharp.

Let me emphasize that workmanship must be of the highest quality. Antiquing and distressing will not cover or hide sloppy or careless work. Quite the opposite, antiquing will emphasize poor joints, hammer marks, clamp marks, and other evidence of careless workmanship.

Carcase construction

A carcase for a large chest of drawers includes most of the particular problems of working with white pine. The large drawing shows the basic construction of such a case. What follows are the working methods and finishing techniques I have developed for achieving the style I like.

Carcase end pieces (using 3/4-in. stock) may be solid edge-glued pine or frame-and-panel assemblies. Doweling or shaper-edge joining is not necessary with Titebond glue. It is important, however, to align the boards in the clamps, thus minimizing planing and sanding the finished panel. Wide shelving (12 in. or more) should be ripped into at least two strips and the grain alternated before gluing, to reduce cupping. Excess glue squeezed out of the joints should be removed at once with a wet cloth. Glue will seal the wood and cause light spots when the stain is applied.

If solid ends are used, special consideration must be given in assembly to avoid restraining the boards across their width, else the case will be damaged by shrinkage or expansion.

Raised-panel case ends are visually pleasing and solve the problems of expansion and contraction. Although a frame

Bill Bittinger has been a woodworker for more than two decades. Trained as an engineer, he is production superintendent at a tire cord factory. He lives in Shelbyville, Tenn.

made from 3/4-in. stock with a 1/2-in. thick panel is light in weight and relatively weak, it is satisfactory for this application because it will be amply reinforced by the back drawer dividers and facings. The frame is assembled with mortise and tenon joints and the panel is retained in grooves in the stiles and muntins. The front edge stile should be 3/4 in. narrower than the back stile so that after the facing is applied the stiles will be the same width.

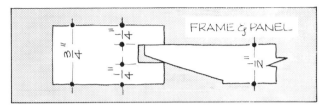

After the end panels (frame-and-panel or solid) are cut to size, a series of 3/4-in. wide by 1/4-in. deep dadoes is laid out and cut to house the drawer dividers. Remember to cut a rabbet 3/8 in. wide by 1/4 in. deep on the back edges of the carcase sides to accommodate the back panel of the case.

Drawer divider units are made from 3/4-in. pine joined with mortise and tenon or half-lap joints. The width of the divider strips will vary according to the overall dimensions of the case. The strips at the ends of the divider frames, which run from front to back, should be about 1-1/2 in. wider than the vertical facing strips of the front frame, so that they can support and act as a bearing surface for the drawer sides.

The carcase is assembled with glue—on the front edge only of solid end pieces—and plug-covered, flat-head wood screws through the end panels. Plugs may be surface-cut round plugs, end-grain round plugs or square patch plugs. Finishing nails, set below the surface, may also be used for case assembly. After setting the nail I use a modified nail set with a square tip (about 1/8 in. by 1/8 in.) to make a square set hole. The small round or square holes will blend with the overall distressed appearance. The facings and back panel will be glued and fastened to the edges of the end panels and to the drawer dividers, to provide adequate strength whether the case is assembled with nails or screws.

The front facing frames may be assembled as a unit with dowels, mortise and tenon joints or half-lap dovetails and then fastened to the carcase; or each strip may be individually attached with butt joints. I prefer the latter. In either case, the facing is fastened with glue and plug-covered screws or finishing nails. If nails are used, they should be located at random on the facing boards to avoid a regular pattern. Plugged screws, however, should be placed in a symmetrical pattern. Whether or not the facings were preassembled with mortise and tenon joints, 1/4-in. dowels may be set into the surface to simulate draw-bore locking pins.

I usually make the base boards about 1-1/2 in. thick to balance the thick top overhang. They may be scroll cut or left full width. The base is assembled with mitered corners and is glued and fastened to the carcase. On some pieces, such as dower chests, the base boards may look better if they are joined with through dovetails. The base mold is a modified stock molding.

The bottom dust panel and back (lauan plywood) should not be attached until the drawer slides are installed and each drawer is accurately fitted to its opening.

Case tops vary in thickness from 7/8 in. to 1-1/2 in.,

depending on the scale of the piece and the width of the carcase facing strips. Tops are made from solid edge-glued pine. I use dowels on edge-glued thick pine to help level the pieces in the clamps. If bread-board strips are not used, the end grain of the top should be carefully sanded or it will soak up extra stain. Case tops are attached with screws from underside in oversize holes in the top mounting strips.

Bread-board strips across each end of the top add to the appearance and strength of projects such as coffee tables and heavy trestle tables. Before joining the strips, I run either a 1/8-in. by 1/8-in. rabbet across the ends of the top or a quirk mold on the joining edge of the strip. Narrow strips may be attached with screws through oversize holes, to allow for expansion. The counterbored screw holes are covered with round or square plugs. The edging strip should be glued only at the center on a tabletop, or at the front edge on a case top. To attach unsupported strips to tabletops that are subjected to heavy loads, I use 2-in. wide stopped splines made of 1/2-in. plywood and two or more concealed tie bolts cut from 1/4-in. threaded rod. The spline is glued only at the center, to equalize misalignment caused by shrinkage or expansion of the top.

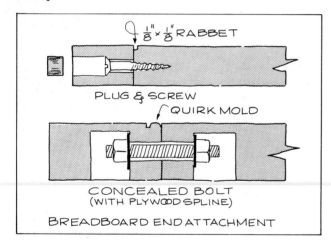

BREADBOARD END ATTACHMENT

Drawers

I don't think pine drawers should be lipped because a thin lip is fragile and a heavy lip is clumsy. I install drawers and doors with 1/8 in. of the edge exposed. When they are rounded by sanding, the chest has a soft—not flat—appearance.

Cut the 3/4-in. drawer fronts for a snug press fit in the openings, and index-mark each front to its corresponding

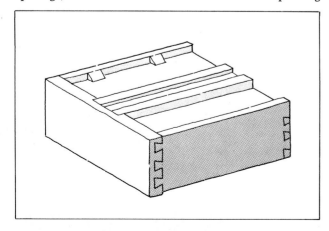

opening. Knots should be at least 1 in. from each end.

Cut the sides about 1/8 in. narrower than the front and about 2 in. shorter than the case depth. Drawer sides should be about 5/8 in. thick. Cut 1/4-in. by 3/8-in. bottom retaining grooves in the sides and front, and cut a mortise on the bottom edge of the back side of the front for the drawer slide part.

Dovetail joints should be cut by hand. It is difficult to obtain sharp clear lines in soft pine with an ordinary marking gauge. I use a sharp 3H pencil with a shop-made marking gauge to lay out the dovetails. Dimension A is usually about

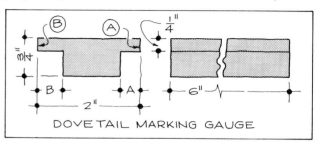

DOVETAIL MARKING GAUGE

two-thirds the thickness of the drawer front and dimension B is 1/32 in. greater than the thickness of the side pieces. Side A is used as a marking gauge on the end of the front and on the matching side piece, to provide cutting lines for the length of the dovetails. Side B is used to mark the dovetail depth line (side thickness plus 1/32 in.) on the inside end of the front piece.

I use another shop-made marking jig to lay out the half-blind dovetail on each drawer front end. The marker is used to draw the pins and the vertical-cut guide lines on the inside of the front.

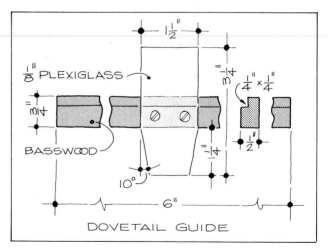

DOVETAIL GUIDE

I start marking with a half-pin on each end, so that a tail will cover the bottom retaining groove in the side, and then fill in between by eye. Each end of the drawer front has the same number of pins and sockets but they are not all identical in size or spacing. Pins in pine should be only slightly smaller than the dovetail sockets. After sawing on the waste side of each pin line, I clamp the front to the bench to remove the waste with a very sharp chisel to within 1/16 in. of the guide lines. I trim the pins and the sockets to exact size with the front held vertically in a vise. Then I lay the side piece on the table saw and stand the front piece on top of it, using the saw fence to hold the front piece vertical. With the ends of the two pieces exactly aligned, I can use a sharp pencil to trace the pin outlines onto the side piece. I cut the tails to size on the band saw. There should be enough interference in the joint to require moderate pressure to assemble. I do not dry-fit dovetail joints because this compresses the pine and causes a weaker joint. The dovetails are assembled with glue.

The back piece is joined to the drawer sides with through dovetails. The bottom (lauan or pine plywood) is nailed to the lower edge of the back part with coated box nails. The drawer slide is attached with brads and glue. Beveled glue blocks keep the bottom from rattling.

When the glue in the assembled drawer joints has set, I sand the protruding ends of the front with a belt sander. This sanding, if carefully done, will leave about 1/32-in. clearance at both sides when the drawer is installed.

Install slides in the case and adjust them to center the drawer fronts in their openings. Sand to round off the top edge of the drawer front, to provide about 1/32-in clearance. A gap of up to 1/16 in. around the drawer is acceptable. Attach the 1/4-in. plywood back panel with glue and small coated box nails to the drawer frame edges and all around the case edges for maximum strength.

Doors

Raised panel doors are included in some case designs such as a hutch base. Doors may be made from 1-in. or 3/4-in. pine stock. But conventional frame construction for a raised panel door of 3/4-in. pine is structurally weak, and the door does not feel comfortably heavy. To avoid weakness and add weight, I set the panel in a rabbet instead of a groove and add a back plate of plywood. First, I assemble the frames (rails, stiles and muntins) with dowels and glue. Then I rout a rabbet 3/8 in. deep by 1/2 in. wide on the inside back edges of the frame, squaring up the rabbet corners with a chisel. Then I cut the panels from 3/4-in. solid pine, allowing 1/8 in. for clearance on all four sides. I ''raise'' the panels by cutting a bevel all around the front face, so that when the panel is laid into the frame it will protrude by the merest 1/64 in. at the back. Finally I glue a piece of 3/16-in., 1/4-in. or 5/16-in. pine or lauan plywood to the back of the frame only, thereby pressing the panel into the rabbet and completely covering the door.

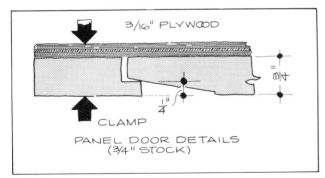

PANEL DOOR DETAILS
(3/4" STOCK)

Moldings

One of the advantages of working with pine lumber is the wide range of commercial moldings. Before mitering and applying commercial flat molding, I glue a pine backing strip to the molding and then resaw to provide a larger glue surface. This is particularly important when attaching large cornice molding around the top of a cabinet. Resawing to 45° also helps in cutting miters on large moldings.

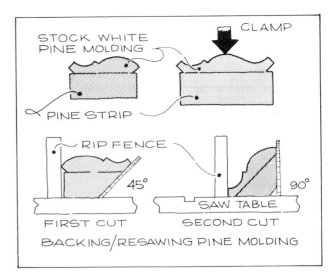

BACKING/RESAWING PINE MOLDING

Large crown molding may be assembled from several parts. The three-part composite molding shown below is made up from: 1) shop-made dentil backup piece, 2) modified commercial flat-crown molding, and 3) a nose-molded pine strip. The dentil backup piece is machined to leave a 1/4-in. to 3/16-in. raised strip. The dentil is laid out and cut after the backup strip is beveled to fit the cabinet. The ''teeth'' should be laid out from the center to ensure symmetry, taking care to locate one full tooth on each side of the bevel joint. The pieces of crown molding and the pine strips are mitered and installed in turn over the backup strip.

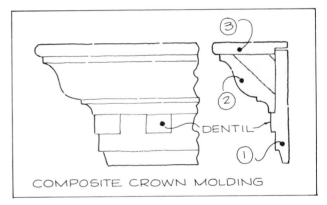

COMPOSITE CROWN MOLDING

Some projects are enhanced by a closed dentil molding (a row of square depressions) along the top horizontal facing strip. This decoration is particularly effective in bedroom sets where it can be incorporated in chests, mirror frames, bedside tables, headboards and footboards.

To make the closed dentil facing strip, cut the facing about 1/2 in. wider and longer than finished size. Rip out a strip from the facing board where the molding is to be located. Start the dado layout in the center of the strip to ensure symmetry, and plan the cuts so that a raised tooth, at least full width, will remain on the end of the strip at the facing joint. Cut and sand the dados, joint the glue edges and edge-glue the strip back in place.

Distressing

The piece should not be distressed until after complete assembly and coarse sanding. Experimentation is the only way to determine the amount of distressing that will suit your taste. The procedure includes surface marking and removal of

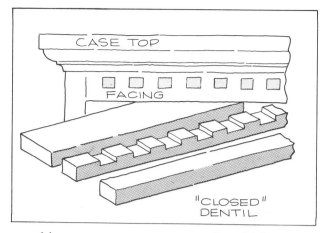

CASE TOP

FACING

"CLOSED" DENTIL

material to create a worn appearance, and special finishing to make the marks look authentic.

I do not like excessive surface marking. I usually make a few dents with the corner of a hammer claw and a few randomly spaced holes with an awl. The claw indentations are triangular and the awl holes appear as small black dots when the finishing glaze is applied. Distress marks are always randomly spaced and are more numerous around the bottom and on the top of a piece than on vertical surfaces. A tall bookcase, for example, would have very few indented distress marks above the height of 4 ft.

Wear distressing should correspond to the imagined, as well as the actual, use of the piece. Stretchers and legs that are rubbed with shoe soles should be much more severely worn than areas touched by other parts of the body. Wear distressing may be done with planes, coarse sandpaper or even rasps and files. In any case, the worn surfaces should be carefully sanded so that no tool marks remain.

After the piece is distressed, I sand with a high-speed orbital sander using 100-grit, 120-grit and 150-grit garnet paper. I complete the sanding by hand with 180-grit garnet paper wrapped around a felt pad. If scratches or other unplanned surface defects show up at this stage, they should be removed by going back to a coarser grit paper. Distressing does not camouflage sloppy and clumsy work or incomplete finish sanding.

Finishing

I use Minwax Early American oil stain to antique pine furniture. Apply the first stain coat to all surfaces, inside and outside, following the manufacturer's directions. After 24 hours, apply a second coat to the outside surfaces. This leaves drawer and case interiors lighter in color than the exposed surfaces. At this point in the finishing schedule your beautiful piece of furniture will look very disappointing—dull and splotchy—but do not despair.

I spray McCloskey Eggshell or semigloss Heirloom Finish for the seal coat and the final varnish coat. Glaze solvents do not soften it and it has good rubbing (sanding) qualities. It can also be brushed on.

After the seal coat is dry (depending on the climate, this may take up to a week) sand all surfaces with wet/dry #320 paper. When the varnish is properly dry, sanding will form a white powder on the surface.

There are a number of antiquing glazes on the market and James M. O'Neill, in his book *Early American Furniture,* gives a formula for mixing an antiquing glaze. I use Tone 'n

Tall chest: Designs are based on feeling more than on fact.

Tique deeptone antiquing glaze, made by C.H. Tripp Co. But I suggest you make up sample blocks to determine your preference. Rub or brush the glaze on the outside surfaces of the project and take care to fill all the distress marks with glaze. Wipe off when the glaze begins to appear dull. The glaze changes the color of the finish even though most of it is wiped off. Leave a film but not streaks. Wipe in the corners and at surface intersections with a wadded cloth so that some of the glaze remains. If too much glaze is wiped off, you can recoat and start over. At this point the finish on your project will look very good and it will improve with the final steps.

After the glaze has dried for 24 hours apply the second coat of varnish. Allow several days for drying and rub again with used #320 emery cloth and 2-0 steel wool. The final step is to coat the entire piece with a good grade of paste wax. The wax should fill any nail set holes. Rub and polish.

If you want an antiqued painted finish, substitute the paint of your choice for the stain and first coat of varnish and proceed as described above. I like the clean, bright appearance of painted interiors on pieces such as hutch bases and dry sinks. Light blue paint goes well with the antiqued finish.

I usually use antiqued brass drop bail or white porcelain pulls and mortised antiqued brass hinges. Black-finished H or L hinges and hardware are also suitable for some pieces.

These comments on design, construction and finishing also apply to small decorative pine projects such as spice cabinets, letter boxes, spoon racks, stools and picture frames. □

Tall-Case Clock
The typical 18th-century design

by Eugene Landon

During the 18th and early 19th century, tall-case clocks were made in infinite varieties, yet their basic construction is the same. They consist of a base, a waist section enclosing the weights and pendulum, and a hood, which houses the clockworks. The feet could be ball, straight-bracket, ogee-bracket, French or simply straight-turned. The base might have a plain board front, a raised panel and fluted quarter-columns, or a scalloped panel front. The waist could have a flat, rectangular door with a "bull's-eye" (a window to see the pendulum), a "tombstone" door or a carved arched door flanked by fluted quarter-columns. The top could be flat, stepped, broken-arched or bell-shaped. The combina-tions seem to be inexhaustible. By detailing the construction of one particular clock, Philadelphia style c. 1770 by James Gillingham (my reproduction of which appears at right), I will present the basic elements necessary in the construction of any typical tall-case clock of this period. Note that this particular clock is exceptionally tall, approximately 109 in. to the top of its carved cartouche. If the room in which this clock is to be used cannot accommodate such a height, obviously this piece must be scaled proportionately.

It is best to construct the hood first because dial size and shape determine all other dimensions. The dial size for the drawings that follow is the most frequently used size during the 18th cen-

Reproduction of tall-case clock (original by James Gillingham) follows typical 18th-century construction, as shown in the drawings on the following pages. The cartouche in place of the center finial and the applied carvings on the scrollboard are ambitious, optional embellishments.

tury, 12 in. by 12 in. with a 5-in.-radius moon dial atop. Dials are available from James A. Zerfing, 123 Linden St., South Williamsport, Pa. 17701; high-quality reproduction clockworks are carried by Merritt's Antiques, Inc., RD 2, Douglasville, Pa. 19518. Begin with the base frame of the hood, which is mortised-and-tenoned together and mortised through its upper face to

Carving the gooseneck molding

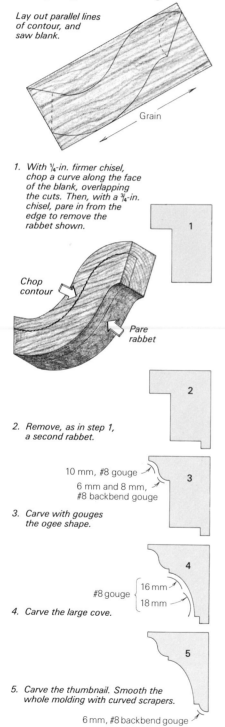

Lay out parallel lines of contour, and saw blank.

Grain

1. With ¼-in. firmer chisel, chop a curve along the face of the blank, overlapping the cuts. Then, with a ¾-in. chisel, pare in from the edge to remove the rabbet shown.

Chop contour

Pare rabbet

1

2. Remove, as in step 1, a second rabbet.

2

10 mm, #8 gouge
6 mm and 8 mm, #8 backbend gouge

3

3. Carve with gouges the ogee shape.

4

#8 gouge
16 mm
18 mm

4. Carve the large cove.

5

5. Carve the thumbnail. Smooth the whole molding with curved scrapers.

6 mm, #8 backbend gouge

receive the hood sides (be sure to make a right and left side). Glue the hood sides to the base frame, set it aside and begin to construct the pediment box. The front of this box is called the scrollboard, and to it attach the moldings, rosettes and center cartouche. Note that the arch is cut in the scrollboard and its backing board before they are assembled as part of the pediment box. After gluing up the half-blind dovetails that join the pediment box together, you can apply the moldings. Over the years I have taken to making my moldings using the old wooden planes; however, one can use a shaper or other tools to make them. I carve the gooseneck molding of the broken pediment by hand, as shown in the drawing at left.

To attach the moldings I rough the glue surfaces with a toothing plane, glue them in place, and then brad them after the glue is dry. This is the way the old clocks were done, and reproduction brads are available from Tremont Nail Co., 21 Elm St., Wareham, Mass. 02571. To ensure that the miter will look tight, I relieve the surface behind the visible corner.

Next make the corner plinths and caps. Drill a ½-in. hole in each plinth top to receive the finials, which will be carved later. The plinth in the center of the broken pediment has the same molding as the scrollboard. Glue on all these pieces; later, when the pediment box is capped, you will mount a block behind the center plinth and bore it to receive the cartouche.

Now make the dial frame so that it will overlap the dial no more than ⅛ in. on all sides. The inside edge is molded with a thumbnail to match the front of the hood sides, and the corners are coped. Half-lap the frame together and cut the arch for the moon dial, also ⅛ in. smaller than the radius of the moon dial itself. Then carve the thumbnail molding into this arch. Slide the completed dial frame into the ⁵⁄₁₆-in. channels in the hood sides; it will be secured in a moment.

Mount the pediment box on the hood sides. The front and rear of the hood sides are cut away, and the pediment box should fit snugly enough over the wide tongues of the sides that it must be tapped into place with a hammer and block. Secure the hood sides to the pediment box with glue and/or nails and screws from the inside. Also secure the dial frame to the

backing of the scrollboard with small brads. It is not necessary to glue the sides or bottom of the dial frame because a good fit in the channels will secure it indefinitely—I've seen it so on many a tall-clock hood. Last, nail the top (use a secondary wood, such as pine) to the pediment-box sides.

The door is the next element of the hood to be made. Don't cut the arch until after gluing up; otherwise short grain in the top member makes clamping dangerous. Use a paper pattern to transfer the hood arch to the door-frame blank, allowing about ¹⁄₁₆ in. for clearance. Lay out the arch, the inside with a radius 2 in. shorter than the outside. Cut the thumbnail and the rabbet for the glass on the inside arch before cutting the outer arch; again, once the outer arch is cut, the piece is fragile. Now cut the outer arch with a bevel to correspond with the hood-arch bevel and fit the door. Its outer edge should line up with the shoulder of the dial-frame thumbnail. Brass hinges hold the door at the top and bottom so it swings from the right. I don't know why, but almost all tall-case clocks have hinges mounted to swing this way. I made my own clock-case hinges, but you can order them from Merritts.

Next the columns can be turned and fastened to the hood. Four free-standing columns can be used, or, as shown in the drawing, two free-standing front columns and two half-columns mounted on backboards applied to the side. I like to flute the columns with a 2-mm #9 gouge, though a scratch beader can also be used.

The rosettes can be carved and applied next. They start as turnings. Since I made two of these clocks concurrently, I varied some of their elements, the rosettes being among them. Two options are given in the drawing. Flame finials in the 18th century were usually made in three parts—the plinth, the urn and the flame, which makes the last easier to carve. The cartouche in place of a center finial and the applied carving of the scrollboard are ambitious embellishments that could be omitted.

Now that you have the hood finished, set it aside and begin construction of the base unit. Cut a rabbet in each of the side pieces to receive the back before dovetailing the two sides to the pine bottom. The bottom is to be flush with this rabbet and extend ¼ in. in front; the reason will be clear when

Tall-clock-case hood

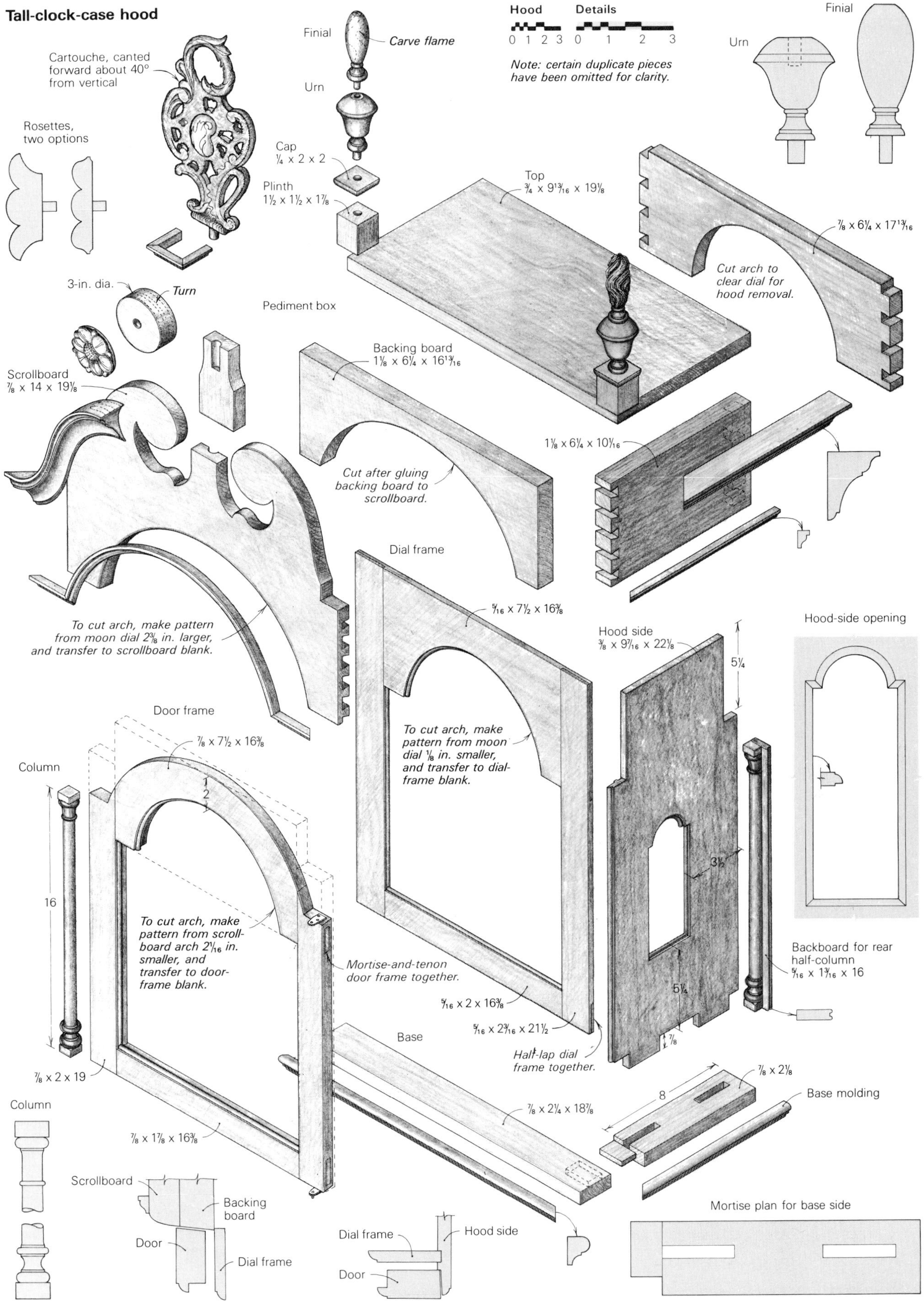

Hood Details
0 1 2 3 0 1 2 3
Note: certain duplicate pieces have been omitted for clarity.
Cartouche, canted forward about 40° from vertical
Finial
Carve flame
Urn
Cap
¼ x 2 x 2
Plinth
1½ x 1½ x 1⅞
Rosettes, two options
Top
¾ x 9 13/16 x 19⅛
Urn
Finial
⅞ x 6¼ x 17 13/16
Cut arch to clear dial for hood removal.
3-in. dia.
Turn
Pediment box
Backing board
1⅛ x 6¼ x 16 13/16
Scrollboard
⅞ x 14 x 19⅛
Cut after gluing backing board to scrollboard.
1⅛ x 6¼ x 10 1/16
Dial frame
5/16 x 7½ x 16⅜
To cut arch, make pattern from moon dial 2⅜ in. larger, and transfer to scrollboard blank.
Hood side
⅜ x 9 7/16 x 22⅛
5¼
Hood-side opening
Door frame
⅞ x 7½ x 16⅜
2
Column
To cut arch, make pattern from moon dial ⅛ in. smaller, and transfer to dial-frame blank.
3½
16
To cut arch, make pattern from scrollboard arch 2 1/16 in. smaller, and transfer to door-frame blank.
Mortise-and-tenon door frame together.
5/16 x 2 x 16⅜
5/16 x 2 3/16 x 21½
Backboard for rear half-column
5/16 x 1 3/16 x 16
5¼
Base
Half-lap dial frame together.
⅞
⅞ x 2 x 19
⅞ x 2⅛
8
Base molding
Column
⅞ x 2¼ x 18⅞
⅞ x 1⅞ x 16⅜
Scrollboard
Backing board
Door
Dial frame
Dial frame
Hood side
Door
Mortise plan for base side

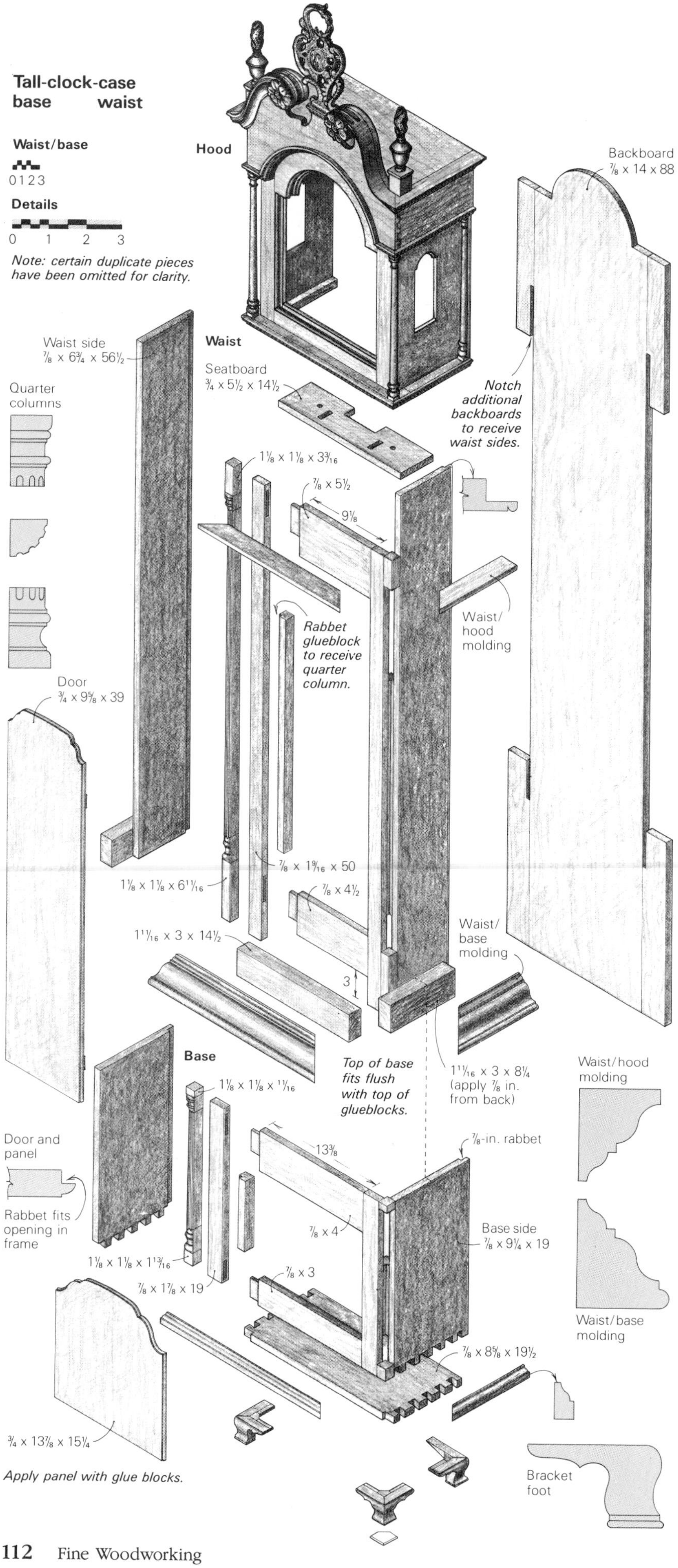

Tall-clock-case
base waist
Waist/base
0123
Details
0 1 2 3
Note: certain duplicate pieces have been omitted for clarity.
Hood
Backboard ⅞ x 14 x 88
Waist side ⅞ x 6¾ x 56½
Waist
Seatboard ¾ x 5½ x 14½
Quarter columns
Notch additional backboards to receive waist sides.
1⅛ x 1⅛ x 3 3/16
⅞ x 5½
9⅛
Rabbet glueblock to receive quarter column.
Waist/hood molding
Door ¾ x 9⅝ x 39
⅞ x 1 9/16 x 50
1⅛ x 1⅛ x 6 11/16
⅞ x 4½
1 11/16 x 3 x 14½
Waist/base molding
3
Base
1⅛ x 1⅛ x 11/16
Top of base fits flush with top of glueblocks.
1 11/16 x 3 x 8¼ (apply ⅞ in. from back)
Waist/hood molding
13⅜
⅞-in. rabbet
Door and panel
Rabbet fits opening in frame
⅞ x 4
Base side ⅞ x 9¼ x 19
1⅛ x 1⅛ x 1 13/16
⅞ x 3
⅞ x 1⅞ x 19
Waist/base molding
⅞ x 8⅝ x 19½
¾ x 13⅞ x 15¼
Apply panel with glue blocks.
Bracket foot

the quarter-columns and front are attached. Mortise-and-tenon the front frame together, as in the drawing, and to it glue 1⅛-in. by 1⅛-in. blocks that will become the tops and bottoms of the quarter-columns. Then glue the frame to the sides and base using glueblocks with a rabbet cut along one corner to receive the quarter-column. The quarter-columns I turn from oversize stock, about 2¼ in. square (turn to 2⅛ in.), leaving an unturned square section at each end to support the stock while I flute and slice it, first in half, then in quarters, on the band saw. I then plane the two sawn surfaces until I have quarter-columns with 1-in. radii. Turn the quarter-rings that form the capital and base of each quarter-column from separate stock, 2½ in. square, then glue these to the 1⅛-in. blocks and mount the quarter-column between.

Apply the base molding around the bottom of the sides, covering the exposed dovetails, and then apply the bracket feet to this molding. Since the clock will be heavy, be sure to reinforce all four feet with glueblocks. The front panel can now be attached to the base unit with glueblocks from behind. Choose attractively figured wood—bookmatching is common here. A thickness of no more than ⅜ in. should extend beyond the face of the frame; however, the panel can be made thicker with a rabbet around the sides. Now set the base aside and construct the waist portion of the clock.

First prepare the back and sides. The backboard is made of pine or some other secondary wood. Begin with a piece 88 in. long—the excess will be trimmed to fit under the dial arch later when the hood is slipped on from the front. Rabbet and bead the two walnut sides along their back edges and attach them to the backboard, 16 in. up from the bottom. Be sure the sides are square across from each other (scribe a line across the back of the backboard) as this will determine if the waist sits straight in the base. Along the lower edge of each side, on the outside face, apply a glueblock of pine ⅞ in. from the back to allow for the thickness of the backboard. To these blocks will be attached the base. Now make a front frame, which is joined with mortise and tenon like the frame used for the base. Again, attach 1⅛-in. by 1⅛-in. blocks to the corners for the top and bottom of the quarter-columns and apply this frame to the back/side assembly, keeping the frame and side bottoms flush. Make and apply the quarter-columns with quarter-ring capitals and bases, all the same in section as for the base. Cut the mortise for the lock, and mount the door using butt hinges, again on the right.

After completing the waist unit, the waist is slipped into the base, and the blocks previously glued to the bottom of the waist sides are now glued and clamped to the inside of the base sides. The backboard will extend to the bottom of the base, where it is nailed, but because it is only as wide as the waist, additional backboards must be fit to cover the extra width of the back of the base. Make and apply the waist moldings, upper and lower.

If you have bought an authentic reproduction clockworks, you will have to mount it on a seatboard, slotted for the cables and pendulum. Then you can fit the hood to the top of the waist. The base molding of the hood slightly overlaps the upper waist molding; if necessary, shave the edges of the waist molding, so the hood will slide over and rest on this molding. Note that the hood will not slide all the way on because the backboard and the back of the pediment box have yet to be cut. Remove the hood and place the seatboard, with the movement attached, atop the waist sides, which are over-long. Replace the hood, measuring the distance that the dial sits high in the dial frame. Remove the hood and the seatboard, and cut down the waist sides the distance the dial sat high plus ⅛ in. When you replace the movement and the hood, the dial should be properly framed in the dial frame. All that remains is to cut an arch in the pediment-box back and in the backboard, as shown in the drawing, so the hood will pass over both the dial and the backboard when being slid on and off. With the hood finally in place, glue additional backing boards to the backboard to cover the extra width of the hood.

After you have done all of the above, apply your favorite finish, and you should have something that resembles the clock for which James Gillingham was paid in 1770 the princely sum of 15½ lb. of veal. □

Gene Landon makes and restores period furniture in Moutoursville, Pa.

Photos: Gene Landon

Tall-case clocks are adorned in various ways. Hood of a Philadelphia clock (left) from the same period as the Gillingham example has basket of ferns for central finial and diminishing spirals in place of rosettes. Tobacco-leaf finials top country clock (right) from Reading, Pa., c. 1770.

Philadelphia clock (1725), left, with step top and fretwork bell-speaker is high-style compared with Lancaster County clock, above, whose arched pediment is probably a country cabinetmaker's rendition of various elements he'd seen.

Period Furniture Hardware
How it's made and where to get it

by Simon Watts

Everyone who makes or restores period furniture is bound to face the problem of choosing the appropriate hardware. The choice is complicated by the wide range of hardware available from many different periods, as well as by several distinct levels of authenticity and quality. This question of authenticity often troubles people most. What is the "correct" hardware for a particular piece of period furniture? All reproduction hardware is copied and there is no such thing as a genuine copy. The copy may be so close to the original that it can be spotted only by an expert, or it may depart to the point of caricature. If your furniture is a faithful copy of an historical original, then you should use only the best hardware. This means accurate copies taken from the right period and, when possible, made in the same way. On the other hand, if your furniture is "in the style of"—similar in appearance but using materials and methods inconsistent with the period—then the choice of hardware is broader. Recognizing this, a number of reputable firms now offer a choice between expensive and historically correct hardware, and a cheaper alternative made at least in part by machine. Modern versions of old hardware are not necessarily inferior, and sometimes the opposite is true. Drawn brass hinges, for example, are stronger and work more smoothly than do the original cast versions.

How hardware was made—To choose period hardware intelligently, you must know the materials and the manufacturing processes in use at the time the furniture was made. This is not as difficult as it seems. Prior to 1750, hardware makers really had limited choices of materials and techniques. They could cast hardware by melting metal and pouring it into molds to cool and harden, or they could forge parts by heating the metal and beating it into the desired shape with hammers. After 1750 the development of the brass rolling mill opened up new design possibilities, and for the first time hardware could be produced on a large scale. Further improvements in technology eventually brought about stamped and die-cast hardware—and with it the excesses of ornament—that enjoyed great popularity in the Victorian era.

Practically all furniture hardware made in America during colonial times was forged by hand by local blacksmiths. Iron was the favored material because it was available and easily worked. Colonial blacksmiths forged a huge variety of hard-

If you make period furniture, chances are you'll be using reproduction hardware. Original brasses like this pull-with-escutcheon from a Newport bureau, c. 1780, are rare.

ware—from the most delicate thumb-latches to massive hinges suitable for the heaviest doors. When heated sufficiently, iron becomes semi-plastic. In this state it can be hammered out in thin sections, bent, cut, folded back on itself and even welded. It is this hammering that gives wrought or forged iron its distinctive look. No two forged pieces look exactly alike—there is a pleasing variation and asymmetry. Hand-wrought iron still has many applications on accurate period reproduction furniture and in the restoration of colonial-period architecture. In trying to meet the current demand for this hardware, modern manufacturers often use machines to speed production of forged parts. The basic shape is stamped out by a press and then hammered only to add detail. If you suspect you are looking at hardware made this way, just put two pieces side by side. Although the surface detailing will vary, their profiles will be identical.

Hand-forging is still done with hammer, anvil and coal fire, but its modern version (machine or drop-forging) uses dies and huge power forges. A red-hot bar of metal is placed on a massive iron table on a die in the shape of the hardware to be made. An upper die mounted in a heavy, power-driven hammer is then slammed onto the metal to forge the part. Some metal is squeezed out between the dies, and the eventual trimming of this waste leaves a faint trace that often remains visible after finishing. Machine forgings are identical and lack the surface variations of hand-forged hardware. The forging process toughens materials, so forgings tend to be stronger than castings in the same metal. They also have a distinct "grain" caused by the flowing of the hot metal. This is conspicuous if the surface erodes; an old forged anchor looks like weathered wood.

Historically, casting was used only for brass furniture hardware, particularly that made before 1750. Colonial furniture makers in America did use brass hardware, but by law it had to be imported from England. This fact causes confusion even today. Some good reproductions made in brass are patterned after originals that were made only in wrought iron. The familiar rat-tail hinges and H-L hinges are examples of this; however accurate they may be in form, brass versions cannot be considered authentic.

Brass was commonly used to make a type of hardware known as the pull-and-escutcheon. These "brasses," typically

The basic tools of the blacksmith—fire, hammer and anvil—have remained unchanged for hundreds of years, and the smith's products are similar to those made by his colonial forebears. Wrought thumb-latches and H-hinge by Woodbury Blacksmith and Forge Co., right, show the distinctively varied profiles left by the process—no two are identical, and the marks left by the smith's hammer and anvil are evident.

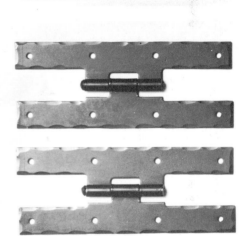

Courtesy Renovators Supply, Inc.

H-hinges, above, show a mass-production attempt to mimic a wrought look. Profiles of the hinges are identical, but edges have been hammered to add surface detail.

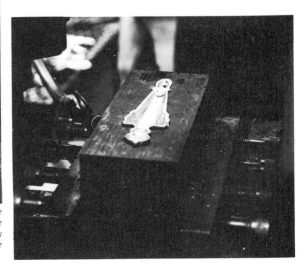

Baldwin Hardware Manufacturing Corp. uses four of these English-made power forges, above. At right is a lower die into which a hot brass rod will be placed. When the upper die slams down, a new piece of hardware is instantly formed, needing only edge-trimming and a shine. Forged parts can be made with fair detail, but each one is identical to the next.

Sand-casting is slow, highly skilled work. Above, foundry-man Joe Bossio of Franklin Alloys tamps sand around a pattern which will then be removed to form a cavity shaped like the hardware to be made. At the Horton Brasses foundry, right, co-owner Jim Horton and an assistant pour brass into a gate, an opening in the mold. Too much moisture in the mold can cause the hot brass to geyser back out of the gate, an occupational hazard of foundry work.

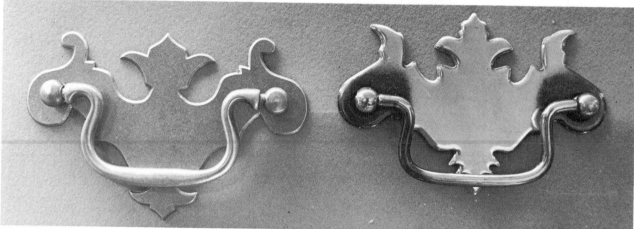

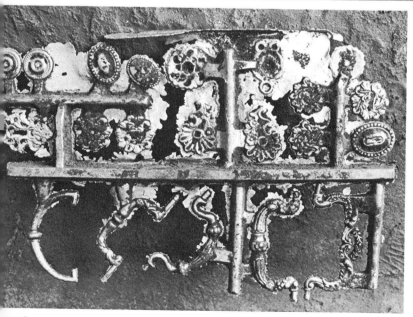

A close look will reveal the difference between cast and stamped parts. The Chippendale pull, above left, is all cast — backplate, bail and loose posts. The pull, above right, is a thin stamping with its edges bent down to create the illusion of thickness. The bail is of bent brass wire, and instead of loose posts the pull is attached to the drawer with studs fastened to the backplate. The assortment of knobs, bails and escutcheons, left, has just come from the sand mold. Even after polishing, you can recognize them as castings by the slight irregularities and traces of the flash lines where the two parts of the mold met. Below, backplate cast in a sand mold is recognizable by the pitting and unevenness on the back side. The front will be polished smooth. This plate has an identification number cast into it at lower right.

consisting of a floral-shaped backplate (escutcheon), and a bail mounted between a couple of posts, were a feature of Chippendale and Queen Anne style furniture. Brass, a copper/zinc alloy, was difficult to forge and weld in the 1700s. But its low melting point makes it ideal for small sections of furniture hardware because it can be poured hot enough to run easily into all the crevices of a mold before it hardens. Thus, brass casting was a good way to make the thin escutcheon, the slender bail, and the threaded posts and nuts that attach the pull to the drawer front. Compacted sand molds (sand-casting) and later metal molds (die-casting) were used in brass hardware manufacture. Sand molds must be made in two halves so they can be separated and the pattern extracted before pouring. This leaves a distinct joint or flash line on the casting that remains visible after finishing. A sure way to tell a sand casting is by the slight pitting in the surface of the metal caused by the sand. Although mostly removed in polishing, pitting can be seen in hard to reach corners of a part. Since a sand mold is destroyed when extracting the casting, no two castings are ever quite the same. They may have slight irregularities or be slightly heavier on one side. Die-castings are smoother and any two in a thousand will be identical.

After the 1750s, the advent of the rolling mill made quantity production of brass sheet possible. Until then, sheet had been used sparingly because it was cast and hand-hammered to thickness. The rolling mill inspired an entirely new design in brass—the Hepplewhite. Instead of being cast, the escutcheon is a thin brass sheet struck between two steel dies often engraved with exquisite designs. Hepplewhite bails were cast but the cast posts were soon replaced by ones machined from newly available brass rod.

Later, the powered blanking press could untiringly stamp out brass sheet to any profile required. This machine could be adapted to cut slots and holes, and to bend and fold the metal. The invention of the screw lathe made possible the replication of accurately machined parts by the thousands.

The unleashing of all this technology did not at first result in any new style of hardware but in the debasement of the old. Copies of earlier hardware continued to be made, but most of the subtle irregularities of sand casting, hand-filing and polishing were lost. It took a while for designers to make the most of the blanking press's potential for new approaches to hardware design. Much of the later, machine-made Victorian hardware has a directness and vigor that is still appealing.

Up to the 19th century, cast iron was little used for hardware. Its melting point is too high to be easily poured in thin sections and it is brittle. But with the new coke furnaces, cast iron came into wide use. Hinges, rim locks, cabinet catches and window hardware were made cheaply and in huge quantity. Cast-iron hardware soon replaced forged for most applications. Later still, a process called extrusion produced hardware that was stronger. Extruded parts are made from metal that is passed through a heated die and then cut into lengths. Extruded stock, also called "drawn," is easily identified by the fine, parallel lines that run along its surface, in the direction of extrusion.

Brass remains a popular metal for period hardware. Polished brass is usually given a coating of clear lacquer to prevent surface discoloration. Some firms lacquer all of their products while others do so only if the customer insists. Brass can be darkened or antiqued, by chemicals that duplicate the effects of time. Cheaper hardware is darkened and then

The invention of the rolling mill made possible large quantities of sheet brass and a new style of hardware. At top are the various steps in the making of a Hepplewhite oval pull, starting with a brass blank. The soft metal is struck once, softened by annealing and then struck again for the fine detail. Above is the lower die of the blanking press.

buffed on a satin wheel to create highlights and to simulate wear. Brass can be finished to look like other metals and sometimes other metals are made to look like brass. A small file will uncover the deception. The most frequent substitutes for brass are anodized aluminum and brass-plated steel or zinc alloys. Aluminum is too light to fool anyone; steel will reveal itself to the magnet.

Buying period hardware—The largest period hardware manufacturer is Ball and Ball of Exton, Pa. With a staff of only 42, the firm uses an adroit mixture of skilled handwork and clever machinery to meet the demand for 900 individual items spanning several periods. With its own foundry and blacksmith shops, Ball and Ball makes iron and brass hardware and has recently added Victorian items to its line. Much of the hardware, iron strap hinges for example, is offered handmade or semi-handmade. The former are made in the traditional way, while the latter are cut out of rolled sheet with a nibbling machine—a compromise for sure but a far cry from the manufacturers who stamp their hinges from a coil of pre-textured sheet. "They think they are duplicating a hand-

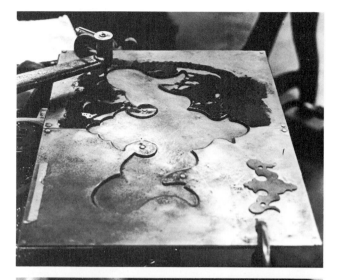

At Ball and Ball in Exton, Pa., backplates for pulls are made not only by the traditional sand-casting method, but by a metal-cutting pantograph. An overlarge template, top, guides the machine's cutter, center. The pantograph-cut plates are then filed by hand to sharpen the detail of the edge, above

forged finish," says Whitman Ball, "but they are just making modern junk. Unfortunately a lot of people buy it because the price is right."

For some of its brasses, Ball and Ball casts its backplates thick and then sands down the front. The result is practically indistinguishable from an original, thin casting. For those not needing this museum-level authenticity, the firm cuts backplates out of sheet brass on a metal-cutting pantograph. These look like castings until you turn one over and see the diagonal sanding scratches instead of the pitted unevenness of a sand casting. They will also sand-cast posts and even nuts to match, but most are made on automatic screw machines.

The firm even uses cast bails. When asked, Whitman Ball admitted being tempted to substitute a stamping. "But every one of them would be absolutely identical. It just wouldn't look right," he maintains. Ball and Ball sell direct only, from the Exton showroom as well as by mail. If a catalog item can't be filled from stock, there may be a lengthy delay. The firm's catalog can be purchased by mail; write to the company at 463 West Lincoln Highway, Exton, Pa. 19341.

Horton Brasses of Cromwell, Conn., makes fewer items, but the service is speedier than Ball and Ball's. Both firms will copy from a customer's patterns. Horton sells brass and iron hardware and has its own foundry. It's a family-run business and Jim Horton specializes in the decorative "chasing" of brasses, done entirely by hand. A backplate, drilled and finished, is set on a thick iron block and the design is transferred with a single hammer blow to a small, steel stamp. Some dies are elaborate, others are plain circles, dots, crescents or lines. Horton casts its own bails, but they use a blanking press for most of the backplates. Horton's prices are retail and there is a quantity discount. To purchase the catalog, write them at P.O. Box 95, Cromwell, Conn. 06416.

Period Furniture Hardware Co. is a small. merchandise-jammed shop at the foot of historic Beacon Hill in Boston. One wall is small drawers, a sample of their contents screwed to the fronts. This company makes less than half of the brass, iron and other items they sell. Instead, they buy from other manufacturers such as Baldwin Hardware Manufacturing Corp. They too try to offer their customers a choice—but within limits. When I visited the shop recently, the manager was explaining to a customer why three apparently similar door knockers were priced differently. "This is imported from England," he said, pointing to one knocker, "this is a machine forging, and this we make ourselves." The English import, $65, is marred by conspicuous sand pits. The manager snorts. "They think these pock marks make it more authentic, but that's rubbish. The old ones were perfect." We both examine the $45 machine forging. "Notice there are no sand pits, the surface is perfect but there's no detail either." Period Hardware jobs out its casting work—its own version of the knocker at $160 is perfect. The company has a large variety of architectural and household hardware, and I found its selection of weathervanes unique. Period Hardware sells wholesale and retail and its current catalog can be purchased by writing to 123 Charles St., Boston, Mass. 02114.

Baldwin Hardware Manufacturing Corp. is best known for door hardware, but the firm also has two lines of colonial brassware that include cabinet knobs, candleholders and a range of household hardware. Baldwin sells no iron hardware nor do they do casting—most of their products are made on four massive forging machines. Adjacent to each is a gas-fired furnace. One man continuously feeds pre-cut brass rod into the furnace at one end while another swiftly places the hot metal between two steel dies that strike the finished part. The process takes less than a minute. Employing 600 people, Baldwin is a factory and there is no attempt to add authenticity by using archaic methods. They choose original patterns carefully and then make close copies in the most efficient way. Baldwin uses forging where another manufacturer might cast the part. Locks need the strength of forging, but other items like candleholders seem a trifle over-engineered. Baldwin hardware is handsome, durable and reasonably priced but it has a uniformity that may not suit everyone. No sales are made from the factory and all of Baldwin's products are sold by retailers and wholesalers throughout the country. Write Baldwin for a catalog at Box 82, Reading, Pa. 19603.

The Renovators Supply was born out of the frustrations a young couple encountered when searching for hardware to restore their old farmhouse. A combination of large volume and foreign labor allows Renovators to sell period hardware very competitively. Renovators buys some of its hardware outright for resale and has some of it manufactured to order—much of it abroad. "We produce handmade components at low labor rates and then do the final assembling and finishing here," says Claude Jeanloz, Renovators' co-owner. They offer a considerable selection of hardware including house fixtures, iron, brass and Victorian reproductions. There are no pretensions to making exact copies, and traditional designs are freely adapted to modern needs. Much of their wrought iron has been stamped out by machine and then hammered by hand for detail. This results not in an inferior product but an excellent value for the money. Renovators sells mail-order only and offers quantity discounts. The firm's 35-page catalog can be had by writing to Millers Falls, Mass. 01349.

Frequently, a search through all the period hardware catalogs won't reveal the hardware needed for a particular job. If iron work is wanted, you might find a local blacksmith who can make it for you. This is not as fanciful as it sounds. Handworking of iron has made a remarkable comeback and the Artist-Blacksmith Association of North America has some 1,500 members. You can contact them by writing ABANA, P.O. Box 1191, Gainesville, Fla. 32602.

Tony Millham of Westport, Mass, is a member of the blacksmith association, an accomplished smith and one of a number of craftsmen who publish a catalog featuring hand-wrought hinges, door hardware, latches and bolts. "I let people order whatever they want. I may tell them it's wrong for their period or a wrong combination of materials, but I'll make it for them anyway," says Millham. He works mostly with the traditional tools of the trade—forge, hammer and anvil. But he also has an electric trip hammer, a bandsaw and welding equipment. To many, blacksmithing has the charm and nostalgic appeal of an earlier era, but as Millham points out, turning out quality reproduction hardware day after day is a struggle. He's firmly committed to his trade yet he sees some irrationality in the quest for authenticity. "People get neurotic about it. They all want it to be 'right,' but right is just what some expert tells you. I wish people would have more fun and simply choose what pleases them. After all, they are the ones who have to live with it." ☐

Simon Watts is a contributing editor to Fine Woodworking *magazine. Photos by the author, except where noted.*

Jim Horton of Horton Brasses, is an expert in the hand-chasing of brass pulls. A drilled backplate is placed on a steel surface, top, and detail is stamped in the surface with a single hammer blow to a steel die. Horton uses dozens of stamps with various designs, as above. Below is a close-up of a flower-motif stamp.

Index

FINE WOODWORKING
Editorial Staff, 1975-1984:

Paul Bertorelli
Mary Blaylock
Dick Burrows
Jim Cummins
Katie de Koster
Ruth Dobsevage
Tage Frid
Roger Holmes
John Kelsey
Linda Kirk
John Lively
Rick Mastelli
Ann E. Michael
Nina Perry
Jim Richey
Paul Roman
David Sloan
Nancy Stabile
Laura Tringali
Linda D. Whipkey

FINE WOODWORKING
Art Staff, 1975-1984

Roger Barnes
Deborah Fillion
Lee Hov
Betsy Levine
Lisa Long
E. Marino III
Karen Pease
Roland Wolf

FINE WOODWORKING
Production Staff, 1975-1984

Claudia Applegate
Barbara Bahr
Pat Byers
Deborah Cooper
Michelle Fryman
Mary Galpin
Barbara Hannah
Annette Hilty
Nancy Knapp
Johnette Luxeder
Gary Mancini
Laura Martin
Mary Eileen McCarthy
JoAnn Muir
Cynthia Nyitray
Kathryn Olsen

If you enjoyed this book, you're going to love our magazine.

A year's subscription to *Fine Woodworking* brings you the kind of practical, hands-on information you found in this book and much more. In issue after issue, you'll find projects that teach new skills, demonstrations of tools and techniques, new design ideas, old-world traditions, shop tests, coverage of current woodworking events, and breathtaking examples of the woodworker's art for inspiration.

To try an issue, just fill out one of the attached subscription cards, or call us toll free at 1-800-888-8286. As always, we guarantee your satisfaction.

Subscribe Today!

6 issues for just $29

Taunton
MAGAZINES
for fellow enthusiasts

The Taunton Press
63 South Main Street
P.O. Box 5506
Newtown, CT 06470-5506

B2BT

Fine WoodWorking®

1 year (6 issues) for just $29.00

— over 18% off the newsstand price

Outside the U.S. $38/year (U.S. funds, please).

☐ Payment enclosed
☐ Please bill me

☐ Please send me a *Fine Woodworking* books and videos catalog. (BBBP)

Use this card to subscribe or to request a *Fine Woodworking* books and videos catalog.

NAME

ADDRESS

CITY

STATE

ZIP

PHONE

I am a
1. ☐ novice
2. ☐ intermediate
3. ☐ advanced
4. ☐ professional woodworker.

B2BT

Fine WoodWorking®

1 year (6 issues) for just $29.00

— over 18% off the newsstand price

Outside the U.S. $38/year (U.S. funds, please).

☐ Payment enclosed
☐ Please bill me

☐ Please send me a *Fine Woodworking* books and videos catalog. (BBBP)

Use this card to subscribe or to request a *Fine Woodworking* books and videos catalog.

NAME

ADDRESS

CITY

STATE

ZIP

PHONE

I am a
1. ☐ novice
2. ☐ intermediate
3. ☐ advanced
4. ☐ professional woodworker.

B2BT

Fine WoodWorking®

1 year (6 issues) for just $29.00

— over 18% off the newsstand price

Outside the U.S. $38/year (U.S. funds, please).

☐ Payment enclosed
☐ Please bill me

☐ Please send me a *Fine Woodworking* books and videos catalog. (BBBP)

Use this card to subscribe or to request a *Fine Woodworking* books and videos catalog.

NAME

ADDRESS

CITY

STATE

ZIP

PHONE

I am a
1. ☐ novice
2. ☐ intermediate
3. ☐ advanced
4. ☐ professional woodworker.

Taunton
MAGAZINES
for fellow enthusiasts

NO POSTAGE
NECESSARY
IF MAILED
IN THE
UNITED STATES

BUSINESS REPLY MAIL
FIRST CLASS MAIL   PERMIT NO.19   NEWTOWN, CT

POSTAGE WILL BE PAID BY ADDRESSEE

**Fine
WoodWorking**

63 SOUTH MAIN STREET
PO BOX 5506
NEWTOWN CT 06470-9971

Taunton
MAGAZINES
for fellow enthusiasts

NO POSTAGE
NECESSARY
IF MAILED
IN THE
UNITED STATES

BUSINESS REPLY MAIL
FIRST CLASS MAIL   PERMIT NO.19   NEWTOWN, CT

POSTAGE WILL BE PAID BY ADDRESSEE

**Fine
WoodWorking**

63 SOUTH MAIN STREET
PO BOX 5506
NEWTOWN CT 06470-9971

---

for fellow enthusiasts

NO POSTAGE
NECESSARY
IF MAILED
IN THE
UNITED STATES

BUSINESS REPLY MAIL
FIRST CLASS MAIL   PERMIT NO.19   NEWTOWN, CT

POSTAGE WILL BE PAID BY ADDRESSEE

**Fine
WoodWorking**

63 SOUTH MAIN STREET
PO BOX 5506
NEWTOWN CT 06470-9971